CAPTIVE
W·O·M·E·N

Cultural Studies of the Americas
Edited by George Yúdice, Jean Franco, and Juan Flores

CAPTIVE
W·O·M·E·N

Oblivion and Memory
in Argentina

SUSANA ROTKER

Translated by Jennifer French
Foreword by Jean Franco

Cultural Studies of the Americas
Volume 10

University of Minnesota Press
Minneapolis
London

Originally published as *Cautivas: Olvidos y memoria en la Argentina,* copyright 1999 Ariel, Buenos Aires, Argentina.

Published by the University of Minnesota Press
111 Third Avenue South, Suite 290
Minneapolis, MN 55401–2520
http://www.upress.umn.edu

Library of Congress Cataloging-in-Publication Data

Rotker, Susana, 1954-2000
   [Cautivas. English]
   Captive women : oblivion and memory in Argentina / Susana Rotker ;
translated by Jennifer French ; foreword by Jean Franco.
     p. cm. – (Cultural studies of the Americas ; v. 10)
   Translation of: Cautivas : olvidos y memoria en la Argentina.
   Includes bibliographical references and index.
   ISBN 0-8166-4029-7 (HC : alk. paper) – ISBN 0-8166-4030-0 (PB : alk. paper)
   1. Indian captivities – Argentina. 2. Argentina – Historiography. 3. Women –
Argentina – Social conditions – 19th century. 4. Disappeared persons – Argentina.
I. Title. II. Series.
F2822 .R67413 2002
982′.00498 – dc21

                                        2002013794

To Sol Ana, my daughter:
this book about Argentina,
where she grew up,
after the oblivion.

CONTENTS

FOREWORD
Jean Franco

"This atrocious solitude of rejection and oblivion obsesses me," writes Susana Rotker in the first chapter of this book. She is referring to the fate of women captured in Indian raids before the Argentine interior was finally "pacified" in the 1870s, but she is also referring to the solitudes and silences of her own time — the disappearance of men, women, and children during the Argentine military regime that was in power from 1976 to 1983, and the silence of the victims of the Holocaust. A child of Jewish refugees, she was born in Argentina but grew up in Venezuela, a country in which there were no family memories, no past to which she could lay claim. She returned to Argentina at a time when memory, amnesia, and state violence were hotly debated topics and there were daily revelations of torture, death, and disappearance in the dirty wars that had left an estimated thirty thousand dead. The civilian government that came into power in 1983 first put the military leaders on trial and then declared an amnesty when the trials proved too divisive.

The military government's devious tactic of "disappearing" those it deemed subversives veiled a regime of torture and death. By denying all knowledge of the disappeared, the military had absolved themselves of responsibility while creating a climate of uncertainty and fear. When President Alfonsín decreed a full stop to the trials of the military and declared an amnesty, he virtually guaranteed the slow burn that would consume Argentine politics down to the present. The Mothers of the Disappeared, who continued to circulate every Thursday carrying photographs of their children, and the Grandmothers of the Disappeared, who traced the children of the disappeared, became the bearers of memory. Already deeply aware of the disappearance of her own family's past in the Holocaust and the inevitable memory losses of exile, Susana Rotker was intensely affected by the struggle between individual memory and official history, and this eventually led her to inquire into other excisions from the historical record and eventually to all the disappearances and exclusions from Argentine national history.

Rotker's main area of research was the nineteenth century. On a visit to the Historical Museum of Buenos Aires, she came upon images of people who scarcely existed in the historical record. Drawings and paintings from the beginning of the nineteenth century depict the substantial black population of Buenos Aires and show white women being carried off captive by Indians. The black population simply disappeared in the course of the nineteenth century, probably through assimilation. The captive white women and their mestizo children were even more thoroughly forgotten.

During the colonial period what is now Argentina consisted of scattered settlements, cities, and missions that were linked precariously to the great viceregal capital of Lima by mule train. The unfenced pampa was the home of the nomadic Indian tribes and gaucho cattle herders. After the consolidation of independence in midcentury, Argentina's identity as a white nation was created by the urban intelligentsia whose Europeanized ideal excluded Indians, blacks, and mixed races. Domingo F. Sarmiento, the postindependence thinker whose book *Facundo: Civilization and Barbarism* is a classic of Argentine literature, wrote of "the vast emptiness of the country" as if the nomadic tribes did not count. He also believed that the introduction of Africans into the Americas had produced "fatal results." For the other great Argentine political thinker of the time, Juan Bautista Alberdi, "those of us who call ourselves American are nothing more than Europeans born in America" — a statement that clearly indicated that indigenous and blacks did not count as citizens. A series of nineteenth-century liberal thinkers and politicians vigorously supported a policy of immigration from Europe that was put into practice so effectively that it rapidly changed the ethnic composition of the nation.

Like the United States, Argentina expanded its frontiers in the nineteenth century at the expense of the native population, who fought against the invasion and seizure of the hitherto unfenced pampa. The Indian tribes — Pampas, Ranqueles, Puelches, Picunches, and Huiliches — attacked and raided army forts and captured women and children. But the fight against the invaders finally wore the Indians down. Decimated by a desert campaign, the nomadic Indians effectively ceased to exist as a threat, and they left few traces (place names, camping sites), although as Tununa Mercado points out in her autobiographical narrative, *La Madriguera,* remnants of the Indians' language and customs survive in certain spoken dialects and in the everyday lives (ways of drying meat, the type of food cooked) of the population of the interior. Mercado recalls these people of the interior cooking "immense omelets with ostrich eggs," roasting ostrich wings in the garden, and boiling the legs in great pots with parsley and green onions.

But uncovering traces of the women captives is even harder than unearthing these remnants of the Indians, and what Susana Rotker mostly found about the former were oblique references that only rarely suggest the ugly realities beneath. Unlike the United States, where there are written documents by captive women, the Argentine captives left no personal stories, although stories were told about them. One or two of these women even acquired mythic roles in national literature, although only because they chose martyrdom over life with the Indians. Such was the story of Lucía Miranda, who first makes an appearance in a chronicle by Ruy Díaz de Guzmán written between 1698 and 1712. Miranda was a Spanish woman who, when captured along with her husband, refused an Indian chief's offer of marriage, preferring loyalty to her husband and martyrdom to copulation with a savage. One paradox of Spanish colonialism was that while the male conquerors were encouraged to people (*poblar*) the conquered lands with their own offspring, which meant peopling it with the children born of the coupling of conquistadors and Indian women, the coupling of white women and Indian males was inadmissible.

One of the few stories to evoke the captive women's exclusion and suffering was "Marta Riquelme," written by the nineteenth-century naturalist William Henry Hudson and included in his collection *Far Away and Long Ago*. It tells the tragic tale of a beautiful woman, Marta Riquelme, who was captured by Indians when on her way to join her husband. She bears three children by an Indian chief, who treats her brutally. When he lets her go and she returns to her native village, her husband repudiates her and she becomes an outcast who is eventually transformed into a *kakue,* a bird of the pampa whose cry fills people with horror.

For Rotker, this story is exceptional because it includes what is ordinarily left out — the suffering and anguish of the captives — and because its ending evokes their silence, the wordlessness of their grief. But she is struck most of all by the fragility of lives that, in one moment, the moment of capture, can be turned upside down, irrevocably altered to such a point that they pass beyond the bounds of what is culturally intelligible.

Rotker's lapidary judgment that Argentina is "the only country in Latin America that has determinedly and successfully erased the mestizo, Indian, and black minorities from its history and its reality" is an index of her passionate outrage. In fact, "whitening" was by no means exclusive to

Argentina, and discrimination against the indigenous is widespread down to the present.

But white Argentina's suppression of Otherness expressed a fear not only of the dark races but also of the frontier, the nomadic, the unstable as opposed to the settled and the civilized. Like the English travelers to Latin America, the Argentine land-grabbers who helped found the nation-state liked to imagine the interior as empty, unpopulated, as if its nomadic inhabitants did not count or counted only as the barbarous enemy outside any possible definition of civilization. Clearly the women captured by Indians who became mothers of mixed-blood children did not fit into this building of the white nation.

Given the absence of documentation and the preference of the historical record for consoling fantasies, the pickings for illuminating these captive women are slender — a short letter from an ex-captive, brief mentions in narratives of the encounter with the Indians. This does not amount to much. Of the four hundred pages of Lucio Mansilla's well-known *Excursion among the Ranquel Indians,* which claimed to be the first literary testimonial of life on the frontier, only two and a half pages describe women captives. Mansilla, who wrote the book "to correct the errors of others," can describe an Indian banquet in luxurious detail without apparently seeing the women captives who served him food. "Anonymous slaves of the Indians, they occupy the most marginal of spaces in an Argentina that was already looking forward to the twentieth century; on the margins of civilization, they occupy the margin of the margin, servants of the Indian, tortured and scarred bodies, scorned by the Indian women who did not want them as rivals, mothers of mestizo children whom they were forced to abandon if ever they returned to civilization."

Captive Women is not so much a history as the record of absence, a fascinating account of the way that history is founded on erasures. Out of meager scraps, Susana Rotker composes the counterhistories of Mirandas who consort with Caliban and give birth to mestizo children. Though she cannot give these women a history, she can and does account for their disappearance from the historical record.

I know of few critics who have embarked on historical research out of such a passionate need "to try to understand the complexities of memory and [personal] experiences." For Rotker, it was impossible to disassociate the undocumented lives of nineteenth-century women from the more recently forgotten; from the grief of survivors; from children, like herself, deprived of family memory; from the sadness she felt on coming across a photograph of her mother, who had dyed her hair in order to look *less* Jewish. She writes eloquently of what it was like to grow up among people for whom the past was so terrible that it had become unmentionable.

Violence of another kind increasingly occupied her thoughts in the two years before her own violent death. This was the everyday violence of Caracas, where murder and kidnapping were endemic, where young people would kill for a pair of Nikes. This was not the fear of citizens oppressed by military dictatorships but fear of the streets where everyone can become a victim. Characteristically, the conference and book that she coordinated, *Ciudadanías del miedo* (*Citizenships of Fear*), convey a sense of outrage at the reduction of life to hazard. She describes the feeling of insecurity, the sensation that there has been a cataclysmic change in people's relationship to urban space and above all to the concept of citizenship. As in all her writing, *Citizenships of Fear* transcends the protocols of academic writing to include the writing subject.

On the day the book *Citizenships of Fear* went to press, Susana herself became a victim. On a dimly lit road, she was knocked down by a car not far from her home in New Jersey. Her death deprived the academic community of a passionately committed scholar.

ACKNOWLEDGMENTS

This book is the result of a chance encounter between personal obsessions. It began as the topic of a day's discussion during a graduate seminar on marginal figures of nineteenth-century literature: slaves, bastards, mestizos, pirates, country folk, Indians, and captive women. About that time I gave a casual presentation among my colleagues, and I left that conversation with the idea that the abundance of material I had already accumulated could become the basis of a book. For their faith and patience I thank my colleagues in the Department of Spanish and Portuguese of Rutgers University.

I am indebted to the Latin American program of the Woodrow Wilson International Center for Scholars in Washington, D.C. The center's research grant gave me access to invaluable documents in the Library of Congress, as well as several months of seclusion in which to write. I am also indebted to Pilar Spangenberg, who acquired for me a large quantity of materials in private libraries in Argentina, as well as to the staff of the Biblioteca del Congreso, the Biblioteca Nacional, and the Instituto Ravignani, all of Buenos Aires. For ideas generously given and confidence in the project I am indebted to Joseph Tulchin, Kate Tulchin, Sylvia Molloy, Doris Sommer, Ricardo Cicerchia, Jean Franco, Nicolas Shumway, Margo Persin, Aníbal González, Elzbieta Sklodowska, Isabel Vergara, Simcha Dinitz, Beatriz González, and Erna von der Walde. Without the life-help of Ana María Escallón, Graciela Penchaszadeh, Victor Penchaszadeh, Silvia Halperín, José Halperín, Beatriz Oropeza, and Javier Martínez, I would not have made it to the end. I thank Paula, Gonzalo, Ezequiel, Tomy, and Blas Martínez, with my brother George and my parents, for their help in difficult moments. I thank Tulio Halperín Donghi for his advice and for voicing his occasional dissension.

Javier Lasarte had such confidence in this project that he dared to organize a seminar on the subject at the Universidad Simón Bolívar in Caracas, an experience that was invaluable for many reasons. I am especially grateful to Mary Lee Bretz for her professional and personal enthusiasm, and to Francine Masiello for the indispensable materials she discovered and for her encouragement. I owe particular thanks to Cristina Iglesia, who opened the path and granted me the almost unattainable photocopied text that ultimately awoke me to the subject of *Captive Women*.

I am grateful to Joseph Tulchin, Mabel Moraña, Carlos Alonso, and Roberto Fernández Retamar for publishing fragments of this book in the form of articles in the Wilson Center's Latin American series, *Revista Iberoamericana, Latin American Literary Review,* and *Casa de las Américas*.

The greatest debt is to Tomás Eloy Martínez, who not only read and discussed every one of these lines, shared their fever, acquired materials, and endured me during the years of the book's completion, but also allowed me to share his obsessions and his Argentina. This book is also for him, of him.

Chapter 1

AGAINST OBLIVION

> *Beginning with this trial...we have the responsibility of founding a peace based not on oblivion but on memory, not on violence but on justice.*
>
> *A partir de este juicio...nos cabe la responsabilidad de fundar una paz basada no en el olvido sino en la memoria, no en la violencia sino en la justicia.*
>
> —Concluding words of Civil Attorney Strassera during the Trial of the Commandants, Buenos Aires, September 1985

> *Is it possible that the opposite of "oblivion" is not "memory," but justice?*
> —Y. H. Yerushalmi, "Reflections on Oblivion"

I have no memory of my childhood because no story was ever told of it. That fact for a time disturbed my Argentine psychoanalyst until we both discovered that the lack of memories didn't hide some unconfessable trauma. Unfortunate episodes from other eras surged forth during our sessions, but I could never fill the void in the long years of childhood, not even with the simple pleasure of an anecdote.

My forgetfulness was so stubborn that, out of archaeological enthusiasm or a natural skepticism about happy childhoods, I tried every available recourse to fill the void: conversations with relatives and former neighbors, careful examinations of photo albums, exhumations of intimate diaries, trips to the countries where my parents and grandparents were born or met their death, in hopes that by discovering their childhoods I would find as well my own missing lineaments. My effort was in vain: there was no way to recuperate what had been lost. With time, I realized that this absence of domestic tales was shared by a large part of my generation, all of us the children of Holocaust survivors. This absence of memory was our parents' way of sparing us the unbearable weight of their memories. Raised with the ancestral mandate to remember collective History ("remember, so that the atrocities are not repeated," we were frequently

1

instructed in my Jewish high school), we nonetheless lacked memories of our personal lives. Like good children of survivors, we had learned to speak only of the immediate present. If we had not forgotten childhood, it was because one cannot *forget* — in the strict sense of "losing the memory of something" — what was never in one's memory.

The past is not simply there, in memory, but must be articulated in order to be converted into memory. What is chosen to be represented in culture and in memory — since all memory is representation — says much about the identity of individuals, social groups, and nations. To forget and to remember are not opposites; they are the very weave of representation. When I speak of tales and of memory, it is in the sense that, in the realm of culture, imaginaries are constructed: as narratives constituted by sequences of actions with a beginning, middle, and end, with protagonists who act and others who recuperate, remake, repeat those narratives through songs, myths, jokes, bedtime stories, books, rituals, and monuments. I speak of the imaginary: that rosary of narrations threaded on a cord that is both fluid and ordering, emblematic and cohesive as the unconscious. More than ideology, the imaginary is the poetics of collective identity. And, like every representation or assemblage of representations formed through language, narrative, image, or recorded sound, the imaginary is based in memory.

Recollections are no more than representations. What and how we remember says a good deal about what we are. Memory, oblivion, repression, displacement: the links in the chain of who I am or believe I am, of who we are or believe we are. Memory is our frame of reference; it is the marrow of our identity, the central tool by which we emit judgments, the *telos* to guide our responses. Even our ability to make judgments is based in memory, as Cicero affirmed in *De inventione,* since memory permits us to discriminate between good and bad. To which La Rochefoucauld sarcastically added, "everyone complains about memory, but no one complains about his own judgment."[1]

My sessions of psychoanalysis took place in Buenos Aires. Could I expand my examination of the nature of memory and transfer it to a larger field? My curiosity and bewilderment about the rough terrain of personal memory, until now so clearly marked by wells of identity and moral knowledge and the furrows of stories that were never told: Could these be transferred and answers found in the collectivity of a city that was at the time profoundly shaken by the necessity of remembering? I should explain that the year was 1985, the historical moment of the exhumation of the testimonies of survivors of the torture camps of the military dictatorship of the 1970s; more than an exhumation, it was also an unveiling, the exposition of that which had never before been recounted publicly. My encounter with Buenos Aires coincided with the Trial of the Commandants, in which the stories of the disappeared sought a language capable of communicating the terror to those who had lived always within normality and were or claimed to be ignorant of the atrocities that had been committed. There was in that time and place a struggle not only for justice, for the punishment of the torturers of the recent past and for the restitution of human rights and the values of democratic society, but also to develop a tale, to tell a story that would "correct" the macro-tale of what had happened in Argentina between 1976 and 1983, during the reign of the so-called Process of National Reconstruction (Proceso de reconstrucción nacional).[2]

One after another the witnesses appeared in the Tribunal Building; one after another had to explain his or her vocabulary, find linguistic equivalences, invent words to "make tellable" the experience. The judges watched them, amazed, trying to re-form or re-construct an enormous zone of reality that had been made to vanish from society in general. The very concept of "disappeared" is still overwhelming: How can thousands of people disappear forever, without leaving a trace or any account of what has happened to them? The concept is so inadmissible that former Commandant Jorge Rafael Videla had the brazen cynicism to declare, as head of the military government, that he did not understand the uproar of those who presented themselves as relatives of something (someone) inexistent, since one who has disappeared "is not an entity . . . is neither dead nor alive" (No tiene entidad . . . ni está muerto ni vivo).[3] The facts demonstrated how many of those "nonentities" had already been brutally tortured and murdered when Videla made his remark.

Michel Foucault observed that memory is an essential factor in the battle for power. Whoever controls the memory of the people controls also the social dynamic.[4] I recall that during the Trial of the Commandants the TV cameras registered ceaselessly the survivors' confessions, in the spirit not only of making them known, but in particular of archiving the videos: keeping the proof, the document, the account for memory. It is not surprising that for years a rumor had circulated that the majority of the cassettes had been erased and recorded over.[5] That story is uncertain, but it is worth noting that at the time the decision was made not to broadcast the trial via television. The sentence was pronounced on the radio, and fragmented recordings of the trials have been televised only many years later. The suppression of the recordings can be largely explained by the regime's fear that the force of the image would elicit a collective reaction. The entire episode of the dictatorship — but especially the laws of "Due Obedience" (Obediencia Debida) and "the Last Word" (Punto Final) and the decree of amnesty for the military murderers — speaks of erased memories, suppressed tales and disappearances. It is the official will forcibly to "cure" the memory of the community, to erase that memory or shut it up by legal means whose efficacity is doubtful, since the scars cannot be erased by acts of power.[6]

THE STYLE OF NATIONS

Voids in memory: there are also stories that never become registered. There are many examples of individuals who spent years insisting that they knew nothing about the violence and the repression; some whose neighbors were imprisoned swear they had no idea of the abuses. Others, having faced the disappearance or exile of a relative, are surprised to read about the period decades later and claim that they were never aware of the danger. In reality, fear is so great that to believe it is forgotten is itself a miracle of survival. One can speak of "recurrent lapses" since, like certain nightmares, bad memories resurge implacably and one must quiet them in the light of day. Suppression and rejection of the disagreeable: sometimes for convenience, other times out of complicity, but in the majority of cases it is a way to preserve one's sanity. I think back to the terrible irony of the phrase I used to hear in Caracas, where I grew up. There had been no dictators for decades, but the indexes of poverty and corruption were alarming. Each time I became frustrated in my attempts to investigate recent history and found neither archives nor documents, I was told that happy countries, like happy women, have no history.

What is suppressed is part of the story of what we are, the other side of the same coin. Ernest Renan expressed it precisely: "the essence of a nation is that all its individuals have much in common and that they have all forgotten the same things." Forgetting and historical error, he adds, are essential factors in the creation of a nation, since every origin involves acts of violence. Or as Benedict Anderson has said, communities distinguish themselves not by how genuine or false they are, but by the style in which they are imagined.[7] Although this last is a generalization that abstracts the multiple differences among the peoples, regions, and social classes that make up a nation, the affirmations of both Renan and Anderson provoke the following reflection: if to forget and to remember are two sides of what we are as individuals and as nations, if our identity is also the style in which we are imagined, it becomes important to ask why what is remembered is remembered and why what is forgotten is forgotten.

Thus, just as one hears that Venezuela is a young and happy country, it is often said — for example — that the United States is the country of the new and of immigrants, while France is the place of tradition. Historical statistics, however, show how different is the reality of facts from the reality of the "style" in which nations like to imagine themselves. In the 1930s, France became the country with the largest quantity of immigrants in the world, with an index of 515 foreigners for every 100,000 inhabitants; meanwhile the U.S. index was 492. In the 1970s, resident aliens constituted 11 percent of the population of France and scarcely 6 percent in North America. Why this discrepancy in the accounts? Because France sees itself as a nation that has been ethnically and linguistically united since the Middle Ages, and since it was the most populous European nation at the time of the French Revolution, it only conceives of immigrants as temporary labor. The United States, in contrast, has maintained an image of vast territories to be populated by immigrants, the American model of the "new man" and the new, unfinished country.[8] In Argentina, the Constitution continues to promote immigration to populate its territories, but the key fact there is that even today Argentina discriminates very clearly and encourages only European immigration. The 1994 Constitution makes this preference clear in Article 25.[9]

ARGENTINA: THE IMAGINARY OF A WHITE/EUROPEAN NATION

During the first days of my life in Buenos Aires, as a provincial overwhelmed by the dimensions of that colossal city and uncertain of my ability to understand the networks of public transportation, I preferred to limit the anxieties of adaptation to other necessities and reposed with confidence as I was shuttled about by the local taxi drivers. Only a short time had passed since the War of the Falklands had produced an upsurge of Latin American solidarity toward Argentina. But that mattered little: memory is fragile. It was enough for me to indicate to the driver where I wanted to go, and he would turn his head at the sound of my tropical accent, saying, "You're not from *here,* are you. Where are you from? From *up there, from Latin America?*" (Usted no es de aquí, ¿verdad? ¿De dónde es? ¿De allá, de América Latina?). I was never quick enough to respond by asking if the taxi driver's *here* was located on some other continent. I sensed then what today I believe I know: to be or not be Latin American (or at least to identify oneself as such) not only is the product of a co-ordinated history and geography, but is also a question of will, at least at the level of the macrotale shared by the community. The fact that there are Argentines who deny their Latin Americanness does not erase the fact of the map or the real circumstances, but their self-identification with Europe functions in this context more or less like the beliefs of France and the United States with relation to immigrants and national identity. The mode of representing reality is usually much more important than reality itself.

The subjects of memory and oblivion, of memory and repression, continued to expand. Trying to reconcile what I had read in Argentine literature with the experience of living in that country, I dedicated a period to visiting museums, believing I would find some clue in the representations hung on the walls. I devoted myself to the nineteenth century as the foundational era: the Paraguayan War of 1864–70 found moving expression in the paintings of Cándido López; the horror the secret police known as La Mazorca must have inspired during Juan Manuel de Rosas's rule (1829–52) was registered in the red cloths with their motto of "Death to the Unitarian savages" (Mueran los salvajes unitarios) and in the valises emblazoned with the dictator's face that were exhibited in the Museo Histórico. All confirmed my Argentine reading. Nonetheless, two unexpected images were repeated in one painting after another in subsequent museums: the images of Buenos Aires's black residents of the early nineteenth century and the images of white women at the moment of their kidnapping by Indians. Registered on the canvases, blacks and white captive women had disappeared from society and from almost all forms of memory. Blacks in Argentina? Captive women? Not even of the Indians did there remain many vestiges that the simple passerby would notice today, but the presence of blacks and captive women at some historical moment suggested a mestizo genealogy of which scarcely a trace can be found in the streets, in textbooks, or in national narratives.[10] Other Latin American countries repeat — at least on the level of sermonizing — the *mestizo* pride of José Martí's "our America," but in Argentina, Eduardo Mallea's idea that Argentines are Europeans exiled in America would be much more popular.[11] A white country in the Americas? Or a *discursively* white country? What remains of pre-Hispanic America, the history of the Spanish colony, and the history of slavery? Where are the black societies, especially women's groups, that actively supported Juan Manuel de Rosas's dictatorship later in the century?[12]

The past must be articulated in order to exist as memory. Every articulation (every account) is related to identity (to what one believes or wants to believe about identity), and for that reason, already carried to the sociohistorical level, it is pinned together with discourses on race, ethnocentrism, authoritarianism, progress, modernity, liberalism. Correction: the past must be articulated for the present in order to exist as memory. Worse yet, every image from the past that is not recognized in the present risks being irreparably lost, as Walter Benjamin warned. For that reason, the present has the responsibility of studying the disappearances of groups of people, of historical episodes: suppressions have more to do with the identity of the present than with the culture of the past. "The past can only be explained through those who are most powerful in the present," wrote Friedrich Nietzsche. This is not the place to cite those who, like R. G. Collingwood or Hayden White, have studied the narrative role of the historian, but in this investigation of memory we will inevitably remember them in passing: History is written from the present, and for that reason the reiterated oblivion of the existence of black Argentines, for example, speaks of the desires of the present.

I draw upon the work of Sande Cohen and Matt Matsuda to affirm two central elements of this effort. First, we must ask why a given phenomenon enters or does not enter that system of writing that is called History. Second, to read the past with the spirit of doing justice to those who have been forgotten, it is necessary to start with the idea that all History is uncertain and conflictive.[13]

I think about the white women kidnapped from Argentina's internal frontier, of whom nothing else was ever known. Although they corresponded to the nation's project of declaring itself ethnically white, their fate in the archives was no better than that of the omitted racial minorities. The only explanation I find for this silence is that to recognize their existence would have necessitated the revision of the foundational myths of modern Argentina and the recognition of kinship with an enemy that had to be destroyed (the savage). In fact, if the traffic in women (Indian and white) reveals mechanisms of race and gender in mercantile and labor exchange, it implies, above all, an exchange of bodies that creates new kinship relations. This exchange among opposing racial groups varied the norms of sexual access, genealogical status, and location in the system of social rights of the era.[14] The Indian women who became part of the domestic labor force of the whites were "normalized" within that culture, but no one is surprised or even notices this discrimination: white women who worked on the Indian side are scarcely mentioned. The traffic in women has served since antiquity to establish kinship bonds among human groups;

on the Argentine frontier of the nineteenth century, two essential elements are added: the human market and procreation. This establishes a historical kinship totally undesirable for a society whose national project has been to achieve whiteness.

The subject of women forgotten in a hostile environment impresses me relentlessly. I remember John Ford's film *The Searchers,* in which John Wayne seeks vengeance against a tribe of Indians that has murdered his family and kidnapped his niece, played by the beautiful Natalie Wood. When John Wayne, in his cowboy clothing, sees his niece dressed like an Indian, he renounces her. She isn't one of us anymore, he says, now she's one of *them.* Of course *they* are in reality part of the true national *us,* historically speaking, although John Wayne's many admirers would never accept them. In reality, every construction of *them* implies their disappearance, by either assimilation or death, two extremes that are both forms of oblivion. In the film, Natalie Wood is saved in the end by the love of her adoptive brother who — moved by his not-so-brotherly love — manages to demonstrate that the woman who was kidnapped as a small child is still a person, that is to say, white and "family." This is not what has happened to the Argentine captives. Unlike Gabriel García Márquez's character Remedios the Beauty, waving good-bye as she flies up to heaven in her hundred years of solitude, the Argentine captives bid farewell in a few paintings from the nineteenth century, idealized in a martyrdom of kidnapping on horseback, disappearing forever into silence.

This atrocious solitude of rejection and oblivion obsesses me. The trouble is twofold: the captives left no known written testimonies (there is no recuperable account), and the culture has omitted them or, what amounts to the same thing, relegated them to a place as secondary as it is obscure. In fact, the Argentine captives did not live the cinematic happy ending of Natalie Wood (the recuperation from *them* into *us*) and for that reason could not be recovered. Captives, disappeared, survivors or victims of different acts of violence throughout human history: scraps of memory, pacts of silence, vast and unjust solitudes of history. Memory is not only the gesture of recovering accounts or representations; it is also an action with profound political and cultural implications. So intimate is the relationship among memory, politics, and culture that the silence that obscures or erases the Argentine captives does not take the form of a lack of information per se. Whoever sets out to find facts will find them, even if the task takes years: the bibliography that accompanies this book is palpable proof of that. But for me the existence of the facts does not negate the existence of this silence, since those facts have not been accepted into collective memory. The enormous majority of materials are very difficult to attain, and it is necessary to search for them in specialized libraries, in unclear photocopies passed from hand to hand; others are and always have been accessible, as in the case of the paintings that hang in the museums or the images that illustrate, for example, Esteban Echeverría's book-length poem *La cautiva*.[15] But, for some reason, they have always been in the very background of the scene, never up front like the gauchos, never feeding the national imagination as a form of identity, never part of the story of national origins. And they have never been examined like a mirror that reflects the tensions generated by the imposition of a national project of racial whiteness.

Henri Bergson maintained that memory is a purely subjective phenomenon, a state in which our body actuates the accumulated past in the present. The opposite view interests me more: it is that of Maurice Halbwachs, for whom memory is collective and depends upon social frames or *cadres sociaux*. Understood in this way, the act of remembering is always related to the imaginary or the macrotale, which he describes as an assemblage of images and ideals constituting the social relations we share.[16] Memory depends not exclusively on the brain itself, but on a shared consciousness that is molded by the social agendas of the present. Collective memory is a tool that reconfigures and colonizes the past, obligating it to conform to the configurations of the present; it resembles Benjamin's *énoncé*, except here the modifying activity of the present (that which "forces" the past to correspond to an image of the origin) predominates. This process is complex and ever-changing, like the patterns that permit us to discern what is the truth (or rather, what is believable) or what is ethical at a given moment.

This book examines the subject of captive women in Argentine culture through a reading of what could be called the *poetics of memory*. I pursue this poetics by eclectically selecting concepts from different theories and by penetrating the voids, the ellipses, the creases in the writing on this subject. The captives allow me (they invite me, not with a historical clamor I lack the stature to address, but rather as a vague projection of my own history) to review the mechanism of memory, or more modestly, to approach a few of the tricks of the written word. They allow me to revise accounts and the voids in accounts as sequences of identity, sequences based in turn on an individual and collective rationale that is sustained by a social macrotale based on the parameters of power, political affiliation, pacts, fears, enemies. The temporal span of this book is limited: after reviewing many historical documents, it begins with the writing of Esteban

Echeverría's *La cautiva* (1837), considered the first national poem, and his discursive combat against the official accounts of the Rosas regime. I continue with an examination of some letters written on the internal frontier and Argentina's only known first-person captivity narrative, *Memorias del ex cautivo Santiago Avendaño,* which was begun in 1850 and written over the course of a decade.[17] The diverse versions of the story of Argentina's most legendary captive, Lucía Miranda, follow. I conclude with an analysis of memory and modernity in Lucio V. Mansilla's *Una excursión a los indios ranqueles* (1870), because it is the text of the first writer who actually traveled to the internal frontier in order to write about it, before the elimination of the Indians and the consolidation of the modern state in Argentina. Along the way I will collect the very few extant representations of captives: military documents, memoirs, travelers' tales, a few lines of *gauchesca* poetry, paintings.

OF SARMIENTO, BORGES, AND THE IMAGINARY

The contest between civilization and barbarism is the ordering axis of today's macronarrative of the nineteenth century in Argentina and also, in due measure, in Latin America in general.[18] The essence of Latin American modernity resides in that peculiar epistemic logic that divides history and reality in an opposition as simple as it is arbitrary. Domingo F. Sarmiento, educator, president of his country, defender of civilization; Sarmiento the writer invoking the "terrible shadow" of caudillo Juan Facundo Quiroga to understand the reality of his country; Sarmiento dreaming of Europe, of white immigration, imagining the inhabitants of the pampa as if they were savage nomads of the Arabian desert.[19]

Every generation has its language, its mnemonic resources, its allegories. In her beautiful book *The Art of Memory,* Frances Yates demonstrates how each historical period also has its own locus or place of allegorical images constructed within mental architectures. The systems of memory of the Renaissance, for example, obey the order of an intellectual universe different from those of the classical or Gothic ages. The allegorical system of nineteenth-century Argentina is summarized in Sarmiento's *Facundo: Civilización y barbarie.* Written and published at midcentury, *Facundo* stands as a center of gravity whose influence extends both forward and backward. The knowledge of reality is organized in bipolar oppositions: savage/civilized, Unitarian/Federalist, Rosas/Sarmiento, country/city.

Within this simplification, how should we think of the captives of Argentina's reality, those who didn't share Natalie Wood's cinematic return to the family home in *The Searchers*? The possibility of contemplating the recuperation of a social group is an element inherent in the construction of such a memory; if such a recuperation is not *thinkable,* there will be no account of the memory of recovery. There was not, there is not, the will to recuperate: the captives remained among Indians and there was no one to tell their story. Instead the simple, useful myth demonizing the barbarians of the wilderness was re-created.

Marxist criticism has shown us the development of a new process of categorizing reality in the nineteenth century, a process that separates the value of production from the value of the function performed by objects. Modernity has produced rationalization, or more precisely, *reification:* the process of representation by which cultural practices appear as given, natural, and unmodifiable, excluding their origin and the ties that could show them to be the result of a theory or assumption.[20] As Theodor Adorno wrote to Benjamin, "all reification is forgetting."[21] History ceases to be a complex project of social negotiations and remains simplified in a binary mobilizer of political practices: civilization and barbarism.

Even in the twentieth century, the articulation of relations with *them* or the Other/Indian continued to occupy the realm of the irrecoverable. Jorge Luis Borges's two best-known stories about captives are, once again, stagings of the unsalvable dichotomy.

It is well known that Borges's work searches reality for its mythic essence; in "El cautivo," the protagonist is a "blue-eyed Indian" (indio de ojos azules) captured as a boy and recovered many years later by people who believe they are his parents. The text never affirms that the Indian is really their son; the only act of recognition he produces on being brought back to his birthplace is the recovery of a "little antler-handled knife" (cuchillito de mango de asta) hidden in the kitchen. He has forgotten the language and does not appear to communicate with anyone. Full of nostalgia, he escapes one day and returns to the wilderness. The narrator adds, "I would like to know what he felt in that moment of vertigo when the past and present were confused; I would like to know whether the lost son was reborn and died in that moment of ecstasy, and whether he was ever able to recognize, even as an infant or a dog might, his parents and the house" (Yo querría saber qué sintió en aquel instante de vértigo en que el pasado y el presente se confundieron; yo querría saber si el hijo perdido renació y murió en aquel éxtasis o si alcanzó a reconocer, siquiera como una criatura o un perro, los padres y la casa).[22]

I, too, would like to understand that vertigo and his life in the wilderness, his desire to return. Those are not, of course, the theme of this

Borges story: they never are. What happens on the other side of the frontier is never represented. "El cautivo" is the tale of a certainty: definitely, despite his blue eyes, the protagonist is no more than a savage and scarcely lucid, like a dog or a child. The time he spends with the white family makes no change in his irredeemably savage soul, already corrupted by years of living among the Indians. Perhaps the years spent living on the pampa would have been enough for such irredeemable abjection, especially if we consider the diagnosis of Ezequiel Martínez Estrada. In *Radiografía de la pampa,* Martínez Estrada recounts the horrors colonial viceroys ascribed to settlers who became lost in the vast territory: "It was the victory of the earth, the triumph of prehistory. . . . Under indiscernible influences, the populations returned to an inferior state. . . . They have renounced civilization, returning by infinite paths, which also lead to the plains, to the depths of bestiality" (Era la victoria de la tierra, el triunfo de la prehistoria. . . . Bajo influjos indiscernibles, las poblaciones regresaron a un estado inferior. . . . Se ha renunciado a la civilización, retornando por infinitos senderos, que también salen al paso en la llanura, al fondo de la animalidad). Martínez Estrada describes Darwin's voyage to the Argentine interior, repeating various leitmotivs: "He saw the saturnalias of the Argentine Huns, the delightful slitting of cattle's throats, the drunkenness from steaming blood" (Vió las saturnales de los hunos argentinos, el fruitivo degüello de las reses, la borrachera con sangre humeante). Following this logic, not even a domestic dog can be redeemed once it is abandoned on the pampa, since it quickly and insalvably recedes several steps in the evolution of the species.[23]

"Historia del guerrero y la cautiva" is similar: as in the previous story and many of Borges's extraordinary fictions, the plot is largely a pretext to allude to the mysteries of coincidence and repetition, the annulment of time as a category and of the singularity of the individual. Borges's conception of persons as part of the succession of human beings — dreamed, perhaps, by Someone — helps to explain the remote comparison in "Historia del guerrero y la cautiva" between "Droctulft, a Lombard warrior who during the siege of Ravenna deserted his own people and died defending the city he had been attacking," and the narrator's English grandmother, exiled "to that end of the world," Argentina ("Droctulft, un guerrero lombardo que en el asedio de Ravena abandonó a los suyos y murió defendiendo la ciudad que antes había atacado," y la abuela inglesa, "desterrada a ese fin del mundo").[24] The grandmother meets a barefoot Indian woman with blond braids: it is another Englishwoman, but one of those who live on the other side, or what we call a captive. "Set in her coppery face, painted with fierce colors, her eyes were that half-hearted blue the English call gray. Her body was as light as a deer's; her hands, strong and bony. She had come in from the wilderness, from 'the interior,' and everything seemed too small for her — the doors, the walls, the furniture" (En la cobriza cara, pintarrajeada de colores feroces, los ojos eran de ese azul desganado que los ingleses llaman gris. El cuerpo ligero, como de cierva; las manos fuertes y huesudas. Venía del desierto, de Tierra Adentro y todo parecía quedarle chico: las puertas, las paredes, los muebles). They converse awkwardly because the Indian was the victim of a raid fifteen years ago and no longer remembers her original language. She is the wife of a minor chieftain and the mother of his children. The text continues in Borges's notable prose:

> [B]ehind this tale one caught glimpses of a feral life: horsehide tents, dung fires, celebrations with singed meat or raw viscera, stealthy marches at dawn; raids on corrals, alarm, plunder, war, the flood of naked horsemen into ranches, polygamy, stench, and magic. To this barbarism an Englishwoman had been reduced. Moved by pity and shock, my grandmother exhorted her not to return: she swore she would help her, swore to rescue the children. The other woman answered that she was happy and returned, that same night, to the wilderness. Francisco Borges would die soon after, in the Revolution of '74; perhaps my grandmother was able then to perceive in the other woman, also torn from her kind and transformed by that implacable continent, a monstrous mirror of her destiny.

> [D]etrás del relato se vislumbraba una vida feral: los toldos de cuero de caballo, las hogueras de estiércol, los festines de carne chamuscada o de vísceras crudas, las sigilosas marchas al alba; el asalto de los corrales, el alarido, el saqueo, la guerra, el caudaloso arreo de las haciendas por jinetes desnudos, la poligamia, la hediondez y la magia. A esa barbarie se había rebajado una inglesa. Movida por la lástima y el escándalo, mi abuela la exhortó a no volver: juró ampararla, juró rescatar a sus hijos. La otra le contestó que era feliz y volvió, esa noche, al desierto. Francisco Borges moriría poco después, en la revolución del 74; quizá mi abuela, entonces, pudo percibir en la otra mujer, también arrebatada y transformada por este continente implacable, un espejo monstruoso de su destino.

When the grandmother meets the blond Indian again, the latter drinks the hot blood of a decapitated sheep. The narrator says, "I don't know if she did it because she could no longer do otherwise, or if as a challenge and a sign" (No sé si lo hizo porque ya no podía obrar de otro modo, o como un desafío y un signo).[25]

These stories are striking, particularly with relation to this analysis, in that "I don't know" is repeated in each. The idea of recovery from captivity becomes a signal of what is not understood: the out and back across the frontier that divides culture from barbarism. The frontier is crossed, we are told at the story's end, because of a "secret impulse, an impulse deeper than reason, and the two followed that impulse that they could not have known how to justify. Perhaps the stories I have told are a single story. The obverse and reverse of the same coin are, for God, the same" (ímpetu secreto, un ímpetu más hondo que la razón, y los dos acataron ese ímpetu que no hubieran sabido justificar. Acaso las historias que he referido son una sola historia. El anverso y el reverso de esta moneda son, para Dios, iguales).

When Domingo F. Sarmiento re-creates the time Facundo Quiroga spent trying to adapt to the urban manners of Buenos Aires, he reproduces an image of the caudillo that is deliberately pathetic. Sarmiento preached the benefits of education, but his lack of confidence in the barbarian is so profound that the protagonist of *Facundo,* despite his efforts to learn moderation in the capital, ends up getting lost (or re-encountering himself) because of his "habit of waiting for anything, from terror" (costumbre de esperarlo todo del terror).[26] The savage remains, hiding, watching. Borges, more than a century later, also feels drawn to the mystery of *the other side;* but Borges was less attracted than repulsed, disgusted. In those stories, *the other side* is a damned space, pernicious and unsalvable: the essence of the tale is the impossibility of returning. These two encounters, the meeting of the two women as much as the "reunion" of the blue-eyed captive with his supposed birth-family, represent an emblematic relationship to Argentine society and its way of looking at itself. In these images there is a cultural convergence not unlike Benjamin's cultural artifacts, the evocation of a world that reveals classes, hierarchies, modes of thought of or about a group. The fact that Borges continued to write on this theme many years after the elimination of Argentina's so-called Indian problem with no alteration at all in the sense of fear toward the "uncivilizable" demonstrates the presence of a Lacanian symptom, a fissure, an ambivalence, an unresolved asymmetry. The fact that almost no one speaks of the limits that problematize the existence of the white nation does not mean that those limits do not remain, troubling like all symptoms. I will return to this theme in the chapter dedicated to Lucía Miranda.

The imaginary, the system of allegories or macrotale, is remade, re-inforced, and displaced. Personal memory becomes dim with the passage of time; collective memory in contrast is enriched with nuances, adjust-ments, additions, displacements, changing emphases and repetitions. In this way, culture opposes itself to forgetting and oblivion; with its omis-sions and fictions, it assails "even the reactive forces of the unconscious, the most recondite digestive and intestinal forces (the alimentary regimen somewhat similar to what Freud would call the education of the sphinc-ters)." Memory, to quote Nietzsche, is not the memory of traces. "This original memory is no longer a function of the past, but rather a function of the future. It is not the memory of sensibility, but of will. It is not the memory of traces, but of words."[27] Memory and writing: the will to what we believe we are or wish to be. William Saroyan commented that an image is worth a thousand words only if the image makes one think more than a thousand words. Words are essential to this process, as Saroyan's phrase suggests: the mere image would not be enough.

PLACES IN MEMORY, VOIDS IN SOLIDARITY

Argentina is not different from other nations in the sense that all are founded, as Renan would say, in violence and oblivion. What is excep-tional is the conceptual (and material) invention of the *disappeared* and that passion for trying to evade what the taxi drivers of my early days in Buenos Aires might have called "the Latin American destiny." For that rea-son, this book: out of the necessity to try to understand the complexities of memory and of my own experiences, because of the disappearances of people in the beautiful streets of Buenos Aires, because of the forgotten ones that nobody wanted to remember, because of the pain of the sur-vivors and because of the children who remained without stories. All of this is the background to my recovery of the captives: go to the mirror and look into it, to try to find many other answers.

Captive Women: Oblivion and Memory in Argentina tries to understand the foundation of a discursively white nation by reviewing the macronarra-tive or assemblage of images/texts that constitute this foundation, at least in the area of culture, during the nineteenth century. It is a study of the poetics of memory, or of pacts of silence: how to construct a version of identity, while silencing Indians, blacks, and captive women. Why pursue the captives? Perhaps because they embody an obsessive terror that has al-ways pursued me: the solitude of the people who, prisoners of events they cannot control, suddenly see themselves *on the other side* and can no longer return, because their families or relations will not forgive them for where they have been. I associate images, almost unconsciously, that are always related to a woman: the protagonist of *Hiroshima Mon Amour,* atrociously humiliated, her hair shorn off for having been the lover of a German soldier. A woman I never met, who was burned in the night by a stranger in her Maracaibo home, none of her neighbors reacting to the terrifying nocturnal screams. The photograph of my mother during World War II, her hair dyed light blond and a distant expression on her face, as if she wished to adopt an unconcerned and certainly un-Jewish identity. I myself thirty years later, wearing my mother's clothes and touring Auschwitz, seized by the sudden terror that by some trickery of time I will remain trapped inside the concentration camp.

Sometimes I am pursued by the image of Marta Riquelme, the protagonist of William Henry Hudson's story who was captured by Indians, her hair cut short as in *Hiroshima Mon Amour.* Indians find Marta starving to death and mad with the loss of her son, who died during a raid; she is bought by an Indian who can afford a beautiful white captive. Her owner has no compassion for her and, until she gives him a son, whips her every day, naked and tied to a tree. "He also cut off her hair, and braiding it into a belt wore it always round his waist — a golden trophy which doubtless won him great honour and distinction among his fellow savages."[28] After five years she is the mother of three new sons and obtains consent to return to her people; while making her flight the only child she was permitted to take with her is cruelly drowned in the river.

I don't know which aspect of this Argentine story impresses me most, but the effect it has on me is beyond rational. I don't know if it is because Marta loses her children each time she makes the painful crossing from one world to another, or if it is because no one recognizes her when she finally returns to her village after so much anguish and desperation. In Hudson's story the narrator searches around the surrounding area and finally finds Marta "seated on the trunk of a fallen tree, which was sodden with the rain," and half-buried in masses of rotting leaves, "in a crouching attitude, her feet gathered under her garments, which were now torn to rags and fouled with clay, . . . her hair in tangled disorder." Approaching, he is "transfixed with amazement and horror . . . for [her eyes] were round and wild-looking, opened to thrice their ordinary size, and filled with a lurid yellow fire, giving them a resemblance to the eyes of some hunted savage animal" (201). The narrator shows her a crucifix, but this infuriates Marta so much that her eyes turn to "two burning balls," "her short hair rose up," and "suddenly bringing down her skeleton-like hands she thrust the crucifix violently from her, uttering at the same time a succession of moans and cries that pierced my heart with pain to hear" (202). Her agony is so profound that the narrator covers his face and falls to the ground. "El kakué! El kakué!" his companion exclaims. "Recalled to myself by these words I raised my eyes to discover that Marta was no longer before me. For even in that moment, when those terrible cries were ringing through my heart, waking the echoes of the mountain solitudes, the awful change had come, and she had looked her last with human eyes on earth and on man!" Marta Riquelme has fled, converted into the *kakué* bird of the terrifying song, to hide forever in the mountains, alone forever.

The (fictional) story of "Marta Riquelme" helps to fill the voids in History and in public documents; it contains the anguish of the kidnapping, death and desire, pain, adaptation, the loss of the children (white and mestizo), and the loss of being itself. It is an exceptional story in this sum of experiences and emotions showing at the edge of the discursive void, recovering a fringe of reality and leaving it for memory. The story is doubly exceptional: because it describes what other texts omit and because its ending announces the silence that covers over the captives. Because the captive is no longer *from* anywhere. No one recognizes her: she is no more than the legend of a horrible bird, a cry of madness and pain that is hidden forever.

A combination of reasons drive my interest in the captives. Perhaps the most personal of them, aside from the genuine need to understand the poetics of collective memory, is the question of the collective pact. Renan and Anderson term "pacts" the sets of codes and traditions that societies share, but I refer instead to the group that maintains its coherence and survives thanks to its *lack of solidarity*. I am terrified by the fragility of human destiny: in one stroke, in an instant, life is changed forever, the individual has neither a vote nor a voice: a kidnapping on horseback, a Gestapo official knocking at the door, a Ford Falcon in the streets of Buenos Aires, in the front seat someone is hooded, someone who will never be heard of again. But behind this fear comes a worse one, fear of society's silence: the silence of the people who won't leave their houses to stop the suffering of the woman burned in the night, the silence of those who stay away so they are not "contaminated" by the victims who have been *on the other side,* the silence of the nineteenth-century intellectuals who follow the traditions of the time, looking the other way and speaking only of their own concerns (like the struggle against Rosas) in order to build themselves a position of personal power, while the extermination of blacks and Indians goes on. The silence that surrounds the captive women — that pact against solidarity—is so well represented in the story of Marta Riquelme, her dementia and conversion into a horrible bird, that the whole theme of *Captive Women* may perhaps be summarized in her. Her story impresses me because she should not have gone unknown, unrecognized, as those who are different are unknown. The captive women were *ours,* each of them was one of *us.* Nonetheless, it is enough that they have left the domestic space of our civilization (that they were forced to do so makes no difference), it is enough that they have *crossed to the other side of our tranquillity* for culture to have closed ranks and forgotten them. There were, yes, attempted rescues and commercial traffic in the bodies of the captives, but the women were by that time little more than anonymous and insignificant ciphers. The *decent people* had closed their doors so that cries would not disturb their sleep.

I cannot explain this *lack of solidarity* other than through the fear that we all feel toward death, toward the unknown. Perhaps, as in Borges's stories, the captives were the bearers of a *mestizaje* we did not wish to see. They bore above all a knowledge they could no longer forget, a knowledge that prevented them from returning to their previous life. The lack of group solidarity maintains the coherence of the group. But there is also the problem of the mourners and their silence: all those who throughout history have no access to the public space in which to claim their dead and disappeared (as the Mothers of the Plaza de Mayo have, on the contrary, so admirably achieved). I am struck by the relatives who remained in mourning, in silence, without anyone opening their doors or offering them pages on which to make their voices heard and remembered.

I will allow myself to return once more to Frances Yates's work, this time to cite her explanation of the invention of memory. Yates paraphrases Cicero's telling of a story that would have been much to Borges's taste: at a banquet in Thessaly, the poet Simonides of Ceos sang the praises of the host and of the twin gods Castor and Pollux. When he finished, the host unkindly answered that he would only pay for half the poem and the poet would have to collect the rest from the gods. Simonides was interrupted by a messenger who ordered him to leave the banquet and attend to two young men who were waiting for him outside. While Simonides looked for the mysterious visitors, the roof of the house collapsed and the guests died. Their bodies were unrecognizable, but Simonides remembered where each one was seated, thanks to which the families were able to recover their dead. Perhaps Castor and Pollux had compensated the poet for his homage by saving his life with their "visit," but the greatest reward was the invention of mnemonics. Simonides inferred that to sharpen the memory one must select places, form mental images of the things to be remembered, and store these images in their places so that the order of the places preserves the order of the things and the images of the things denote the things themselves. "We employ places and images like a wax writing tablet and the letters written on it."[29]

The art of memory was invented as a way to recover the identity of the dead. For that reason, perhaps, collective memory erases so many places, faces, words, so many of the dead; for that reason only certain monuments are erected. I approach the texts carefully, respectfully, as sites of memory, as what Pierre Nora in his admirable edition of various volumes rethinking the French past has called *lieu de mémoire*. The place of memory is like a temple: although profane, it is a circle in which everything counts.[30] I approach the captives with the certainty that everything is symbolic and significant, even the silence that surrounds them.

Chapter 2

IN CONQUEST OF A WHITE NATION: THE ELITES

FERNANDO: This is a most majestic vision, and
Harmonious charmingly. May I be bold
To think these spirits?

PROSPERO: Spirits, which by mine art
I have from their confines call'd to enact
My present fancies.

FERNANDO: Let me live here ever;
So rare a wond'red father and a wise
Makes this place Paradise.

— William Shakespeare, *The Tempest*

Father, I send you here a little captive to sell for one hundred
fifty pesos and two lengths of fine wool. I hope for this favor from
you. Do for me because I am very poor.

Padre ai le mando bender una cautivita en siento sincuenta
pesos y dos corte de paño fino yo espero este fabor de U. Que me
aga por que etoy muy pobre.

— Letter from Manuel Baigorria,
Poitagué, March 4, 1878, to Father Marco Donati

Argentina is the only country in Latin America that has determinedly and successfully erased the mestizo, Indian, and black minorities from its history and its reality. They have been omitted from national narratives and, in the early twentieth century, were purposely made to disappear from even census figures. In contrast to the rest of the continent, Argentina's minorities have been erased from even collective memory: today no one seems to notice that in this white country there must always be a child in blackface in patriotic school plays or that the Indians are represented as some few nomads in the remote historical role of devouring the first Spanish conquistadors who dared approach their shores.

It is as if the racial minorities had never existed. Negation has been one of the strategies to make them disappear: a reality has been silenced or omitted, excluded from tradition and history. But to speak of "forgetting" in this case exposes the trick: one can only forget from the present; we only forget what we have known. In this case oblivion has two instances: the first, in the generation who possessed the past and did not transmit it to their successors; the second, in the subsequent generations who — voluntarily or passively, out of antipathy or indifference — refused to reconstruct and reproduce those same areas of the past. To "forget" has here the sense of practice, of activity, of use, of convenience, of damage.[1] Silence and negation are the active exercise of oblivion.

Silence has had overwhelming consequences for every form of heterogeneity in Argentina: to the exterminated Indians not even the myth of origins was conceded, and it is a rare Argentine history that begins much before the period of independence from Spain.[2] Blacks were eclipsed slowly and completely through a policy of "whitening" (*blanqueamiento*) that was even more successful than the wars of extermination. After the Conquista del Desierto[3] commanded by General Julio A. Roca, the national government instituted a policy for replacing the local population so vigorous that by 1914, 30 percent of the population had been born abroad.[4] Afro-Argentines were eliminated at an amazing rate: at the beginning of the nineteenth century one in three persons in Buenos Aires was black, and by the end of the 1880s the proportion had been reduced to less than 2 percent.

In his celebrated *Facundo: Civilización y barbarie,* Domingo F. Sarmiento distills the hatred that all his generation manifested toward the dictatorship of Juan Manuel de Rosas. He also offers an explanation of the disappearance of the blacks that is especially significant given Sarmiento's stature as one of the leaders most influential in shaping the nation's future:

> The adhesion of blacks gave to the power of Rosas an indestructible base. Happily, the continuous wars have already exterminated the masculine part of this population, which found an appropriate fatherland and form of government in the master it served.

> La adhesión de los negros dio al poder de Rosas, una base indestructible. Felizmente, las continuas guerras han exterminado ya la parte masculina de esta población, que encontraba su patria y su manera de gobernar, en el amo a quien servía.[5]

In reality, the black population was diminished by emigration toward neighboring countries and racial mixing or *mestizaje,* but its ultimate disappearance was due predominantly to the national wars (in which blacks served in disproportionate numbers), the indifference of a racist government, and a variety of illnesses, especially the yellow fever epidemic that scourged the poor neighborhoods where blacks lived in the 1870s. In *The Afro-Argentines of Buenos Aires,* George Reid Andrews argues that the disappearance was achieved through a process of silencing: blacks were removed from the census and other statistics, which subsequently denied them any official support, sanitary improvements, or public financing because it literally decreed their inexistence: by this process they were ultimately erased from Argentina's reality.[6] The thesis contains much truth, but it downplays the reality of racial mixing: blacks who survived the wars and epidemics and did not emigrate to neighboring countries tended to mix with the local white population and the new European immigrants. If Reid does not absolutely deny the historical reality of racial mixing, his emphasis on the erasure of blacks from official discourse runs counter to the evidence that shows that if there are no blacks in Argentina today it is because they mixed in to such a degree that *they are no longer noticed.*[7]

The extremity of this silencing is unique in the entire continent. Negation repeats itself throughout Argentina's history, and the contemporary refusal to struggle for the "disappeared" is only the latest example. I do not know the original cause of this persistent rejection of heterogeneity and the habit of negation, but I explore their manifestations in an attempt to understand the mechanisms that act upon the social formation with regard to race, sexuality, and history from the perspective of culture and therefore the construction of collective memory.

Instead of the negotiation among diverse racial groups that occurred elsewhere in Latin America after the wars of emancipation — be it through difficult accords of tolerance and coexistence or through racial mixing — a white and predominantly urban project began in Argentina.[8] This project may be considered the consolidation of a style, as Benedict Anderson said: communities are distinguished not by how genuine or false they are, but by the style in which they are imagined.

This style of consolidating national projects abounds with mechanisms of negation. In the case of Argentina, a part of reality — of History — is rejected, is denied in order to impose the metropolitan conditions of which the lettered elites dreamed.[9]

Every culture, it is true, provides its members with organizing fictions or ideologies that define their relationships, create practices or "sites" for the exercise of memory (texts, monuments, maps, songs), and give cultural meanings. This identity clearly depends upon establishing differences, even if the term "identity" suggests equality, similarity, and identification with others. The paradox lies in the fact that, just as occurs in the formation of citizenship, identity is defined with respect to Otherness: the marginal, the different, that which I am not.[10] But one contains the other; as Edward Said recognized in *Orientalism*, European culture has long defined itself in opposition to its own fabrication of what the Oriental "Other" must be like.[11] Thus, Buenos Aires, as the emanating center of the organizing and cultural forms that were consolidated around the end of the nineteenth century, is at the same time the *desierto,* the frontier, the Indian, the fugitive, and the woman who was not allowed to return.

In the nineteenth century a relative unity of style is established in relation to the white national identity, founding a history (and a literature) that takes shape as a macronarrative in which some episodes are selected and others silenced, but that is presented as the result of chance or the exercise of objectivity. But what Argentina denies about its origins is a constitutive part of its identity.[12]

This particularity not only invites us to reflect on silence and disappearance, but also enables us to reassess the dynamics of colonial power after independence from Spain. It may seem an error to speak of "colonial" power in that period; if the term "neocolonial" is preferable, however, it is important to distinguish this sense from the way the term is used in contemporary analysis of the cultural and political gaze that the Occident directs toward the Third World or its former colonies.[13] My concern here is to address the tensions generated between the different white elites who occupy power and the rest of the population, especially the portion of the population made up of other ethnic groups. If this cannot be called "neocolonialism," how else are we to understand territorial expansion, the imposition of an elite and its values, the extermination of the Indian, the disappearance of blacks, and the notion of white supremacy, all of which were presented as if they were natural rights? The prevailing incomprehension toward the Other as a human being with a culture of his or her own is transparent in a letter written with all good faith from one priest to another: "A few days ago I began teaching the Christian truths to some thirty little Indians of both sexes. They don't understand any Spanish, I know nothing of Indian, so I feel like I'm teaching peacocks" (Hace unos días que he empezado a enseñar las verdades cristianas a unos treinta indiecitos de ambos sexos. Ellos no entienden nada de español, yo no comprendo nada de indio, así que me parece que estoy enseñando a papagayos).[14]

When someone speaks of "civilization or barbarism," defending the blessings of (white, urban, Europhile) civilization and dismissing the culture of the other inhabitants of the country as mere barbarism, is this not a reproduction, in the active style of collective memory, of the logic of the conqueror? Is this not the logic of Shakespeare's classic character Prospero, who so "naturally" presents the subjection of the original inhabitants of the island to the power of his magic? In the Latin American historical framework, the Creole Prospero had as his lord and master the Spanish Empire, but the local Ariels and Calibans did not attain the rights of full citizens even after its representatives had been expelled.

THE TEMPEST

The characters of William Shakespeare's *The Tempest* have often been drawn on to explain Latin America. The gesture is always the same: eclectically appropriate elements of another culture interpret them and modify them into something completely personal. But the passage of time and the change in point of view varied not only the interpretation but the sense or meaning of one or another character as well. Today, for example, the apparently ingenuous dialogue between Prospero and Fernando cited in the first epigraph of this chapter is almost repugnant. The conqueror's paradise is all harmony thanks to a paternal and wise master who has been able to confine the native "spirits": it has become almost commonplace to recognize that the enchanting harmony in which the duke and the prince delight has been achieved at the terrible price of slavery and death.

In Shakespeare's play, Prospero and his daughter, Miranda, find refuge on an island. Prospero, once a fugitive, makes himself lord and master of the island, subjugating both the pleasant spirit Ariel and the monstrous Caliban with the magic of his wisdom. The Uruguayan José Enrique Rodó published his version of the story under the title of *Ariel* in 1900, while modernist aesthetics were in full bloom; his reading exalts the spiritualism of Ariel as an example for the youth of the hemisphere. Rodó presents Prospero as "the old and venerated master" adored by his young disciples, Ariel as "the noble and praised part of the spirit" and the "empire of reason," while the deformed slave Caliban is "a symbol of sensuality and awkwardness."[15] In its time, the significance of Rodó's essay was to establish a confrontation between the values of Ariel and Caliban: Ariel was the idealistic, art-loving youth who represented the spirit and culture of Latin America in counterpoint to what Rodó saw as the gross materialism of the United States. Later Roberto Fernández Retamar, fresh from the experience of the Cuban Revolution, countered that Ariel could but poorly embody the best of our civilization, since he is also a servant of Power (thus the association intellectuals/Ariel). Writing from Havana, Fernández Retamar refutes Rodó and the many who shared his Europeanizing gaze, affirming that Caliban (whose name reflects the etymology of "cannibal") is not a deformed monster. "It is a question of the typically degraded vision offered by the colonizer of the man he is colonizing."[16] His central thesis is that "Our symbol . . . is not Ariel, as Rodó thought, but rather Caliban. . . . Prospero invaded the islands, killed our ancestors, enslaved Caliban and taught him his language to make himself understood: what else can Caliban do but use that same language — today he has no other — to curse him?"

WHITE MOTHERS OF LITTLE CALIBANS

It is necessary to develop a neocolonial reading of *The Tempest* by tracing the tensions among Prospero, Miranda, and Caliban, accepting the association of Ariel with the intellectual mediators and Fernando's role as an extension of Prospero himself.[17] In doing so, I speak of the colonizer not from the traditional point of view (as the foreign powers), but as the white elite (Prospero) who (with the help of local Ariels) subjugates the Other, holding him in servitude as if by natural right. Or simply making him disappear. I shall also speak of the Mirandas of reality: those for whom no prince came ashore, those who did not manage to form a "good" family in the New World, but were captured and violated, subjected to servitude and made mothers of mestizos whom the magnificent Prospero would never recognize as his descendants.[18]

I borrow (and expand) Dominique O. Mannoni's concept of "the Prospero complex," among whose symptoms is a paternalism that lacks awareness of the world of the Other and is unable to imagine a world in which the Other must be respected. "This is the world from which the colonial has fled because he cannot accept men as they are. Rejection of that world is combined with an urge to dominate." The Prospero complex defines the sum of neurotic tendencies of the colonizer and describes him as a "racialist whose daughter has suffered an [imaginary] attempted rape at the hands of an inferior being."[19] Frantz Fanon,[20] like Fernández Retamar, has reconsidered Mannoni's proposal, but what none of the three takes into consideration is that the purpose of Miranda, Prospero's daughter, is not only to add a female to *The Tempest*'s cast of characters. Her presence demarcates the relationships among the others: with the exception of the ethereal Ariel, each of these others invests her with his desire.

Prospero has for years hidden Miranda's true identity from her. He dedicates the better part of his time to her education, and it is she who physically contains the future of his dynasty. Virginal and beautiful, desired by Caliban, she finally meets Fernando, the son of the king of Naples who will marry her and make her a queen. Shakespeare imports Fernando to the island almost as if he has fallen from the sky, as if to preclude the possibility that Miranda might in reality have inherited the island, sharing a bed and power with the horrendous Caliban: the foundational myth of national lineages would not accept it. To cohabit with the legitimate, native ruler would have implied considering him an equal and, in consequence, questioning not only the superiority of the whites, but also the very logic that allows some to dominate others. In *The Tempest* nothing seems more natural than slavery.

The text demonstrates Prospero's vengeance against his enemies; along the way he also assures the best possible future for Miranda and his lineage. In the text, Ariel and Caliban are no more than instruments by which their master Prospero achieves his revenge. Ariel is graceful, he has powers, and his freedom is imminent; Caliban, in contrast, is so unpleasant that neither Prospero nor Miranda wants to look at him. But neither can they do without him: "But as 'tis / We cannot miss him. He does make our fire, / fetch in our wood, and serves in offices / That profit us."[21] The slave represents — Hegelianly, *avant la lettre* — all those who, because they pertain to races considered inferior, should occupy the role of servant. Thus the master/slave dynamic appears, as well as an aspect of the Prospero complex that should more precisely be called "Prospero's gaze." Every conqueror defines the Other in terms of what he lacks in relation to the self: he is ugly because he does not look like the dominator, he is barbaric because he stammers the language of the master (he uses *barbarisms,* hence the qualifier), and so on.

Prospero subjugates Caliban. He also accuses the slave of ingratitude because, in return for education and lodging (in a cell of his own), *Caliban tried to violate the honor of his daughter.* In the slave's response is one of the central knots of the Prospero complex: he not only laughs, but assures Prospero that *if he hadn't been prevented, he would have populated the island with Calibans*.

The Prospero complex radiates the panic of every dominator toward his dominated: the terror of the day when the subjugated will take vengeance and the secret suspicion that the furious body of the inferior will rape his daughter. It is the stereotype of the sexual threat eternally attributed to those held down: in a given country it may be attributed to blacks, Indians, gaucho soldiers, or the popular classes. In transferring the drama of *The Tempest* into Latin American history, it becomes clear that in many latitudes Caliban has been whitened; in others he has been completely subordinated. But before his disappearance, in Argentina and elsewhere, Caliban went beyond that ominous laugh and did kidnap Miranda, transformed her into a captive, traded her like cattle, and made her his servant, lover, and the mother of little Calibanish mestizos. Miranda might be the "little captive" cited in our second epigraph, one of so many women traded back and forth on the frontier by Indians who, like Manuel Baigorria, were trying to alleviate their own misery. What is striking is that while so much has been written on Caliban, Ariel, and Prospero, Miranda remains outside the equation, as if women had not occupied the very center of the tragedies of colonization.

One of Miranda's problems is that she does not know very well who she is: she has but vague memories of her childhood, and her identity depends upon the words of Prospero. But the identity of the father also depends upon the daughter: he will fully realize his destiny only when she, obeying the Law of the Father, learns her "true" identity (as revealed by him) and marries a white prince, a man at least as prosperous as Prospero himself.

What to do, then, with the Mirandas of reality, those who after the kidnapping shared Caliban's bed? Not to speak of them, not to know of them, to exile them from the narrative and from all discourse on the cultural identity of peoples, is to deny the reality of racial mixing and to repeat the condemnation that threatens every woman who is raped: at bottom, she is guilty of her disgrace. We will return to this issue in subsequent chapters, especially those dedicated to Esteban Echeverría's *La cautiva* and the differing versions of the Lucía Miranda legend.

Chance, incidentally, has chosen "Miranda" as the name of the first captive woman to appear in the written history of Argentina.[22] The legend of Lucía Miranda predates even *The Tempest.*

When I say that Prospero's identity depends upon Miranda's, it is enough to imagine what Prospero would become if, instead of visiting his elegant grandchildren in Neapolitan castles, he were to ride on horseback to a corral where "a half-dozen dogs" went out to meet him, "barking with all their might, like a sampling of the twenty races that could have crossed ... [with] the snout of a fox, looks of a wolf, teeth of a mastiff, head of a greyhound, ears of a pointer, bent legs of a collie, enormous mouth of a Great Dane, sizes of lapdogs and Newfoundlands, hair of a sheepdog, hairless tails and hairy ones" (que se podrían haber cruzado... [con] hocicos de zorro, miradas de lobo, dientes de mastín, cabezas de galgo, orejas de pointer, piernas torcidas de restrero, boca enorme de danés, tamaños de faldero y de terranova, pelo de ovejero, colas peladas y otras peludas). Let us say that these dogs belong to his daughter, now the concubine or wife of Caliban and an inhabitant of the frontier with "some seven or eight little creatures, ranging from black to whitish" (unas siete u ocho criaturas, entre negras y blancuzcas). Miranda, already contaminated (it could also be her daughter, as the story repeats itself), is "a mulatta, with the characteristic nappy hair, the face so black that one could affirm, without being entirely an anthropologist, that such accentuated color could not come only from the sun" (mulata, con la mota característica, y de cara bastante negra para que se pudiera afirmar, sin ser todo un antropólogo, que ese color acentuado no podía proceder únicamente del sol). These last descriptions are not from Shakespeare, obviously; they are from Godofredo Daireaux's reminiscences of what he calls the *mestización* of Argentina's internal frontier.[23] His scorn is so genuine as to appear ingenuous and illuminates some of the reasons why these captive Mirandas were forgotten forever. As if the above were not enough, Daireaux adds:

> Everything, in this blessed country, must be mixed by force: the sheep in vast flocks and the cows in rodeos, and the people everywhere, and if it is true that the best bull is the one who comes from farthest away, it is certain that, with time, they will be no colored man, however black he may be, who does not have blond grandchildren.

> Todo, en este bendito país, se tiene que mestizar a la fuerza: las ovejas en las cabañas y las vacas en los rodeos, y la gente en todas partes, y si es cierto que el mejor toro es el que de más lejos viene, seguro que, con el tiempo, no habrá moreno por renegrido que sea, que no tenga nietos rubios.

"Mixed" seeds (las semillas "mestizadas") improve the soil, he says, but "qualities and defects, in the people, also intermarry and, as good spouses, quickly fight between themselves, but they produce some offspring with unanticipated qualities and defects" (las calidades y los defectos, en la gente, también se casan y, como buenos casados, pronto pelean entre sí, pero echan unas crías de calidades y defectos inesperados).[24] Daireaux's ideas on miscegenation are not very different from concepts that Sarmiento expresses in *Facundo,* as will be shown.

But to speak of the captive women, it is necessary to consider first the powerful gaze of the island's master.[25]

PROSPERO ON THE PAMPA

It may be said, from this perspective, that the new nations — in all of Latin America — incorporated neocolonial values into their own identities. The Fathers of the Nations would have acted as reproducers of the social pathology of the colonizer.[26] This meant maintaining terms of racial domination based on the rationalization of the superiority of the white race, its mission of civilizing the rest of the world, and the alleged incapacity of the "natives" to govern themselves. In fact, literary modes of representing the nonurban/noncultured world (the non-Europeanizing regions, that is) tend toward the Manichaean absolutism typical of colonial narrative. Only in relation to colonialism can affirmations such as Juan Bautista Alberdi's be understood: "Make the wastrel, the gaucho, the half-breed, the elemental unit of our popular masses pass through all the transformations of the system of instruction; in a hundred years you will not make an English laborer of him" (Haced pasar el roto, el gaucho, el cholo, unidad elemental de nuestras masas populares, por todas las transformaciones del sistema de instrucción; en cien años no haréis de él ni un obrero inglés).[27]

"That is the question: to be or not to be savage" (De eso se trata: ser o no ser salvaje). So writes Domingo F. Sarmiento, displaying his extraordinary power of synthesis in the introduction to *Facundo.*[28] It does not matter if in this case he is referring to an indigenous group or to his enemy, the dictator Juan Manuel de Rosas, given that the logic of the rejection will always be the same: the Indians are "the barbarism from outside" (la barbarie de afuera).[29]

The rejection of the Other (the Indian, the gaucho soldier) was not only racial; it also represented the self-protecting fear that the liberal, modernizing sectors felt toward nonurban space, the space of the frontier where everything was mobile, unstable, disordered. The frontier represented the opposite of the limits and stable confines that the new nation sought. Furthermore, if the civilizing project had as its object the conversion of the great American-Argentine family into an urban society in the European style, that other space had to be erased, and its inhabitants along with it.

It is well known that for Domingo F. Sarmiento as for many of the nineteenth century's outstanding men, the health of the republic depended upon the development of a project that was urban, white, and European. In *Facundo*, Sarmiento states that "the principal element of order and moralization on which the Argentine Republic counts today is European immigration" (el elemento principal de orden y moralización con que la República Argentina cuenta hoy, es la inmigración europea) (chapter 15). Juan Bautista Alberdi agreed in postulating that the American man

> is poor most often because he is vague and idle; and he is idle not from a lack of work but from an overabundance of food. Educated in scarcity and the privation of certain commodities, he does not suffer for it physically, thanks to the clemency of the climate. He has something to eat and naturally enjoys the *dolce far niente*.

> es pobre las más de las veces porque es vago y holgazán; y no es holgazán por falta de trabajo sino por sobra de alimentos. Educado en la desnudez y privación de ciertas comodidades, no sufre por ello físicamente, gracias a la clemencia del clima. Tiene qué comer y gusta naturalmente del *dolce far niente*.[30]

According to these theories, the physical environment determines psychology and, in turn, institutions. The ferment of immigration must have been the basic political measure to make the modification of political and economic reality possible. Alberdi himself adds in his *Bases:* "Europe will bring us its new spirit, its habits of industry, its practices of civilization, in the immigrations that it sends us" (la Europa nos traerá su espíritu nuevo, sus hábitos de industria, sus prácticas de civilización, en las inmigraciones que nos envíe).[31] To govern is to populate: but only with white Europeans. From this perspective, the coexistence of the Indian threatened the integrity of traditions and identity, in the sense that the Indian, like every enemy during the nineteenth century, represented precisely the nondomesticated.[32]

Pierre Chaunu says that founding experiences are completely different in empty spaces and in full spaces; the sense of self-consciousness one imagines in the midst of the desert is different from that imagined at the foot of the Himalayas.[33] Accordingly, the group or individual identity formulated in an empty space is much stronger than that developed in other regions. Perhaps the vastness of the pampas ("the ill that plagues the Argentine Republic is its extension" [el mal que aqueja la República Argentina es su extensión], wrote Sarmiento) has made more extreme the need to establish clear limits, more urgent the necessity of defining the *we* in contrast to the *Others,* more imperative the project of ordering space: as Alberdi said, it was necessary to grid the *desierto.*

The image of the void is more than convenient for the Prosperos of the pampa, and here the magician's name may be read as a pun on "the prosperous." To declare the nonurban space *empty* is to avoid having to adapt the official national culture and language so that they are capable of explaining and interpreting that space. What is there is denied, and for that reason it does not exist: the space is empty. This hole in turn allows for the expansion of the conqueror's imagination and carries his desire to appropriate the territory more easily into practice.[34] But perhaps this is another of the *emblems* that, by dint of repeating the diverse Prometheuses and Ariels that have so often appeared in literature, solidify one characterization of Argentine identity and conceal others. In reality, one of the mechanisms to limit identity among the irreducible plurality of nations is to affix to geographic space a meaning that creates in turn a sense of natural fatality.[35] And, within that fixity, to set very extreme poles: the savage versus the civilized.

In this way, so little did it matter if the Indian himself actually resembled the savage caricatured by literature (like Caliban, "not honour'd with / A human shape") that when Sarmiento speaks of

> immense masses of riders who roam the plain, offering combat against the disciplined forces of the cities . . . dissipating themselves like the clouds of Cossacks, in every direction . . . to fall spontaneously upon those who sleep, steal their horses, kill the slow ones and the advanced troops; always present, intangible for their lack of cohesion

> masas inmensas de jinetes que vagan por el desierto, ofreciendo el combate a las fuerzas disciplinadas de las ciudades . . . disipándose como las nubes de cosacos, en todas direcciones . . . [para] caer de improviso sobre los que duermen, arrebatarles los caballos, matar los rezagados y las partidas avanzadas; presentes siempre, intangibles por su falta de cohesión[36]

he is not referring to a raid. Although the description sounds like an excerpt from Esteban Echeverría's *La cautiva* and closely coincides with military narratives about indigenous attacks, the author of *Facundo* is describing here the caudillo Artigas's troops: the enemy is a semantic construction combining characteristics of the uncivilized. These were applied equally against the gauchos, members of the irregular calvaries or *montoneras,* and

Rosas's followers, and they appeared even in the cry of La Mazorca, the special army that Rosas himself maintained: "Death to the Unitarian savages" (Mueran los salvajes unitarios). In the last example, the insulting term is directed against those who considered themselves the defenders of civilization.

As the international dynamic of colonizer-colonized is reflected in race relations, the tradition has been to associate the figure of the monstrous Caliban with black Eros, and the Indian with violence and barbarism or, in the most peaceful cases, with a primitive child who must be saved. Unlike the Afro-Argentines who quickly became "a passing accident" (un accidente pasajero),[37] the Indian remained as an infectious menace ("the virus of anarchy" [el virus de la anarquía])[38] and an obstacle for the national project underway.

The indigenous frequently assaulted frontier settlements, murdering men, stealing women, children, and horses. Estanislao S. Zeballos[39] summarizes:

> To the profound uneasiness of the entire Province, which in various ways was made felt in the atmosphere of the Government, the heartrending cry of the families of the Frontier joined with a thousand masculine voices clamoring for peace with the savages, resolved to contribute with all that was necessary to the payment of the tributes. The frontier settlers preferred to sacrifice the fortune of the present and of the future to save even the virtue of the women.

> Al profundo malestar de toda la Provincia, que de variadas maneras se hacía sentir en la atmósfera del Gobierno, se asociaba el grito desgarrador de las familias de la Frontera y de mil voces varoniles, que clamaban por la paz con los salvajes, resueltas a contribuir con todo lo que fuera necesario al pago de los tributos. Preferían los pobladores fronterizos sacrificar la fortuna del presente y del futuro, para salvar siquiera el pudor de las mujeres.[40]

Colonel Manuel Olascoaga, Roca's secretary, confirms:

> Until 1878 . . . [w]e lived surrounded, in the middle of our territory, whose immediate frontiers were scourged by innumerable hordes of barbarians who took a wealth of livestock worth millions of hard pesos annually, and detained the development of the frontier populations by murder, robbery, and fire: they made the life of the frontier soldier an eternal martyrdom, almost useless for his continuous efforts and sacrifices made with no lasting results; and yet we still paid

a strong annual tribute of money and goods to various tribes, whose friendship we scarcely managed to purchase even temporarily.

Hasta 1878 ... [v]ivíamos encerrados en la mitad de nuestro territorio, cuyas inmediatas fronteras azotaban innumerables hordas de bárbaros que absorbían por valor de millones de pesos fuertes anuales la riqueza ganadera, detenían el desarrollo de las poblaciones fronterizas por el asesinato, el robo y el incendio: hacían de la vida del soldado de frontera un martirio eterno, casi inútil por los continuos esfuerzos y sacrificios sin resultado durable; y todavía pagábamos un fuerte tributo anual de dinero y especies a varias tribus, cuya amistad apenas conseguíamos comprar temporariamente.[41]

The Indian inhabited vast territories that the white desired to occupy, the Indian was a threat to the stability of the frontier populations, the Indian embodied all the evils that the lettered elites repudiated. The problem was not only cultural, and it would not have been enough to impose a paternalistic regime to control violence and adapt the natives to civilized customs. Because there was also a problem of land.

This means that the "pacification" incursions into indigenous territory represented rich benefits for ranchers. A few examples will suffice: between 1822 and 1830, 538 individuals occupied 7,800,000 hectares on the pampa; during the same period the Anchorenas — cousins of Juan Manuel de Rosas, one of the most successful leaders of the so-called Desert Campaigns — accumulated 352,000 hectares and Rosas's brother Prudencio Rosas, 73,000.[42] The Conquista del Desierto commanded by Roca in 1878 and 1879 added some 54,000,000 hectares to the "national patrimony." As was customary, the territory was largely divided among speculators and landholders. The Rural Society, an important advocate in the search for solutions to the problem of the frontier, distributed the fertile new lands to its members.[43]

This combination of circumstances leaves no place for the image of the noble savage or the childlike Indian (Ariel?) to be educated and protected by the State. It necessitates instead an image of violence that must be avenged: the atrocities of the frontier (which did in fact exist) are emphasized, and the theme of the raid (Caliban) is repeated over and over. Since its apparent objective was to overpower women and children, the raid was represented as an attack against the foundations of the bourgeois family and the future of civilized society. Thus the whites attacked back in the name of self-defense.

Richard Slatta observes that residents of Buenos Aires, comfortably distant from the frontier, could satirize the horror of the raid: in October of 1876, the newspaper *El Fraile* published in the entertainment section an announcement of "Theater from the Frontier." The advertisement promised a great invasion of Indian actors "any day now," with stellar performances by the chiefs Catriel and Namuncurá and the minister of war, Adolfo Alsina. The price of admission was all the patron's property in addition to his or her skin.[44]

In literature of the era raids are frequently described as hellish scenes. The gaze of the narrator focuses on the Indians rather than their victims. There is no literature on the destinies of the women and children captured, no texts describing how they were bought and sold on the frontier. The iconography of the era reproduces the horrible moment of the attack, but silences the aftermath. What interests Prospero's civilization in Argentina is to define its enemy; the Indians attack the borders of the young nation, keeping them uncertain and confused, while what the nation requires is a stable sense of the limits between itself and its surroundings:

> Our own honor as a people obliges us to subjugate as soon as possible, by reason or by force, a handful of savages who destroy our principal wealth and impede our occupying definitively in the name of the law, and of progress, and of our security, the richest and most fertile territories of the Republic.

> Nuestro propio decoro como pueblo nos obliga a someter cuanto antes, por la razón o por la fuerza, a un puñado de salvajes que destruyen nuestra principal riqueza y nos impiden ocupar definitivamente en nombre de la ley, y del progreso y de nuestra seguridad, los territorios más ricos y fértiles de la República.

This is the message that Roca announced to the Congress in order to obtain necessary support for the final solution: to exterminate the Indians or cast them to the other side of the Río Negro. His intention was to launch an offensive by carrying out "a series of reverse raids" that reduced the number of indigenous by thousands (*HAC* 1:273). As is well known, Roca was more successful than his predecessor, Adolfo Alsina, whose fantastic proposal was to dig a ditch three meters deep and 300 meters wide, removing some two million cubic meters of earth from Córdoba to Bahía Blanca, as a defense for the line of forts that were connected to the urban centers by telegraph lines and railroad tracks: it was to be a sort of inverted Wall of China.[45] Although the idea of the ditch seems outlandish today, we have no way of knowing if this broad protection of the frontier would have been successful had Alsina not died before his plan was completed. It is also useless to try to imagine how the ethnographic map and the history of Argentina would have been different if individuals like Captain Rufino Solano had been given more freedom to operate. Solano, "with his good treatment and 'savoir faire,' maintained the peace within his territory during almost twenty years" (con su buen trato y "savoir faire" mantuvo la paz en sus confines durante casi veinte años), recovering captive women and negotiating with the respect of both sides between 1865 and 1880 (*HAC* 4:329).

These examples demonstrate that at the time there was little agreement on policy or personal conduct regarding the Indians; in consequence, to analyze this period from the present is not necessarily to impose foreign or anachronistic criteria. To defend the annihilation of the natives of any country of the world — and their dispossession — with arguments like the defense of borders and national identity, to find excuses in the values established during a given period (as if there had once existed ideological homogeneity on a national scale, or even among the different groups with access to power), is to misrepresent the past. It is more productive to try to understand why societies that consider themselves clear-sighted defend atrocious actions as a response to the violence of small groups, why the extermination of certain strata of the population is accepted as something natural, why coexistence seems impossible, why it is so easy to distance persons who are culturally different and ultimately to strip them of all rights.[46]

THE OBVERSE AND REVERSE OF TABOOS

The exclusion of blacks from history is documented in Andrews's book *The Afro-Argentines of Buenos Aires,* whose first chapter is titled "The Enigma of Disappearance." In *Indios, ejército y frontera,* one of the scarce studies on the "discourse of silence" or the cultural silence surrounding the extermination of the indigenous populations, David Viñas refers to the Indians as "the disappeared of 1870,"[47] suggesting a disturbing play of reflecting mirrors. The custom of "disappearing" social fringes that do not correspond to the self-image the nation desires was also exercised against thousands a century later in the so-called dirty war of the last military dictatorship. The concept of disappearance stubbornly returns again and again.[48] This elision of fragments of the past or present from the social or historical totality is a strategy for avoiding the negotiation that emerges from political interaction: the tragedy of the disappeared and the impunity of those responsible are utterly *negated*. Time and again a restrictive principle of organization is imposed: *nothing has happened here.*

The project of modernity that was carried out in the nineteenth century demanded a systematic ordering of the world. The separation between the civilized and the savage inherited from Enlightenment thought came accompanied by a scientifist discourse that created hierarchies among racial types. The idea of barbarism was in part an exercise of cultural distancing and a way of projecting, onto a foreign group, the fears that had to be controlled among the whites.[49]

In the case of Argentina, if the lettered society sought order, productivity, and law, it saw the Indians as the incarnation of disorder, laziness, and savagery. The Indians' communitarian social forms, with their chieftains and apparent lack of productivity, seemed monstrous and had to be mutilated in order to avoid a projective identification with this savage antimodel for self-control and progress. In reality, what was symbolized in Argentina — as in many other Latin American countries — was not the living Indian, but the conquered Indian, his lands modernized and distributed for private productivity, his community as such destroyed. The project of Sarmiento and his generation was to found agricultural and military colonies along the internal frontier, to create the seeds of stable towns that would bring about the productive development of civilization and commerce by combating the indigenous disorder and above all its nomadic life upon the territory. In Sarmiento's words, "the naked and insecure land is not wealth, nor has it any value as long as the hand of man does not make it produce" (la tierra desnuda e insegura no es riqueza ni tiene valor alguna mientras la mano del hombre no la haga producir) (*OC* 23:353). To develop this idea he publishes *Argirópolis* (1850), in which it becomes clear that the conquest of the *desierto* consists of its gradual occupation and urbanization. But not everything is industry and work in the plan of the illustrious Sarmiento; as for other great Argentine writers of the nineteenth century, for the man who would become president of the republic the captive women of reality mattered little: in the long disquisitions on problems of the frontier throughout his journalistic and literary career, they are scarcely mentioned twice. In contrast, his policy toward the Indian (despite favoring, in principle, the establishment of treaties), was for their extermination:

> In Buenos Aires there is an industry that feeds flies and they are the salters; there is another that feeds Indians, which is livestock. What recourse is there to finish off the flies? Cleanliness. What remedy will

extinguish the Indians? The settlement of our countrysides, since killing Indians is the same as trying to kill flies.

Hay en Buenos Aires una industria que cría moscas y son los saladeros; hay otra que cría indios, y es el ganado. ¿Qué remedio para agotar las moscas? El aseo. ¿Qué remedio para extinguir los indios? La población de nuestros campos, pues matar indios es lo mismo que pretender matar moscas. (*OC* 26:286)

The cohabitation of whites with Indians threatened the integrity of traditions and identities in the sense that the Indian, like every enemy of the nineteenth century, represented the nondomesticated. The captive woman — and her body as a metaphor for social space — was an expression of the signifying and founding system, a space of tensions so profound that they created one of the taboos of the national narrative. She herself became taboo because of the forbidden racial contact, taboo because the Miranda of the pampa had crossed a cultural frontier and to understand her would oblige the lettered elite to rethink its project of development. To approach her, to allow her to speak, would oblige the political, cultural, and economic elites to see themselves as if from the other side, an operation that was unacceptable because it would introduce nuances into a spectrum where writing defined good and bad as absolutes.

If the savage was despised and feared, the captives' carnal contact with him contaminated them and made them potentially contagious: according to the logic of the taboo, whoever has violated the prohibition becomes taboo in turn.[50]

As has been shown, the fears of the civilized — including the self-projecting ones — were concentrated on the barbarian; no taboo could be greater than the fear of becoming like him. And Freud said it well: every prohibition covers a desire. The play of identity and difference that constructs racism is founded not only on scorn for other, "inferior" races: desire and envy are also factors, even if they are not expressed.[51] During his expedition into indigenous territory, Colonel Lucio V. Mansilla, protagonist and author of *Una excursión a los indios ranqueles,* dreams repeatedly of becoming the emperor of the Ranquel, ruling over his own heart of darkness like a Creole version of Joseph Conrad's Kurtz.

To avoid or repress these ambivalences, racism suppresses the intermediate zones (like the captives, like miscegenation), reaffirming rigid and bipolar symbolic limits in order to make very clear who pertains to *us* and who are the *Others.* Sonia Montecino proposes a fascinating thesis that sheds new light on the bipolar opposition: if the white captives produced mestizos "in reverse," the indigenous captives were the agents of "obverse" racial mixing. "The right side of something," she says, "generally a cloth, is what appears to view, what is 'showable.'... The interior, the reverse, should not be shown since when it is made into a garment the seams, the hems, and everything that makes the right side appear as such are hidden. But also to 'turn something inside out' is to provoke disorder, to 'turn around,' is to show a face that is similar, but different from the accepted model."[52]

Within the lettered and liberal order, the intermediate space of *mestizaje* — the "contact zone," in Mary Louise Pratt's phrase — was unacceptable; the captive woman is covered in silence, and although in practice there were expeditions and negotiations of rescue, within the realm of the word she is ignored, deformed, negated.[53] The literature of the nineteenth century strips her of all importance. Nonetheless, the space of the frontier — that intermediate space between the barbarism within and the barbarism without, as Sarmiento said — was much less white than was commonly recorded. A good example is the composition of troops; as Ebelot said, among the women who accompanied the soldiers — known as the *fortineras* or the *cuarteleras*[54] — "all shades were represented, except white. The scale of tones began with light yellow and ended in chocolate" (estaban representados todos los matices, excepto el blanco. La escala de tonos empezaba en el agamuzado claro y terminaba en el chocolate). The soldiers, for their part, showed, "in their physiognomies, an amazing variety.... [T]he tints and profiles of all the races of the globe were displayed, from Irishmen to Kaffirs and from Kaffirs to Patagonians" (en sus fisonomías, de una asombrosa variedad.... [S]e reconocían los tintes y perfiles de todas las razas del globo, desde los irlandeses hasta los cafres y desde los cafres hasta los patagones).[55]

Is this the obverse or the reverse of the *discursively* white country?

WHO WERE THE CAPTIVES?

Although there were some ladies of "good families" torn from their settlements and ranches, the enormous majority were the humble women of the frontier: wives, mothers, daughters or sisters of gauchos, peons, shopkeepers, soldiers of the forts along the frontier. It may be necessary to explain that the words *frontier* or *internal frontier* do not refer to an impossible "line" that separates civilization from barbarism, but to a space that is dynamic — in geographic as well as ideological terms — with coexistence and exchange between cultures. "That internal frontier impeded the exact valuation of the territory and veiled its true limits. It was a fringe in constant movement, indefinite, the site of a war between two antagonistic human groups whose modes of life were found to be irreconcilable. This confrontation could only end with the destruction of one of the struggling groups," comments Ana Teresa Zigón.[56] This space on the margin or the periphery not only is transformed and eventually destroyed by the central power but also in turn transforms the dominant culture, obliging it to imagine itself from the periphery.[57]

Alvaro Barros makes clear enough the social distance that separated these victims from the powerful classes when he writes that

> The delicate woman of the cities shudders with fear upon hearing the lugubrious stories of country families. The citizen — enlightened, free, respected up to a certain point in his rights, and even a more or less direct participant in government — is also moved to think about the way to remedy such tremendous evils.

> La mujer delicada de las ciudades se estremece de pavor al escuchar las lúgubres historias de familias de la campaña. El ciudadano ilustrado, libre, respetado hasta cierto punto en sus derechos, y aun partícipe más o menos directamente en el gobierno, se conmueve también y piensa luego en el modo de poner remedio a tan tremendos males.[58]

Not all the captives were white, moreover, as we have seen among the female population of the frontier. Carlos Mayo attests that there were "diverse examples of black captives and also more or less Hispanicized Indians from other regions." He adds that "if, explicably, given the function that the captives were called to perform [referring to servitude and labor], the color of their skin seemed irrelevant, it is somewhat more surprising to know — against the wishes of a certain somewhat legendary tradition — that there were not only 'whites' among the women, but also indigenous."[59] Among the captive women — of varied colors, but predominantly white — the elegant wife of Prospero was rarely spotted: this should suggest another reason why lettered culture has not paid the captives more attention.

How many were there? It is easier to count up the cows, sheep, and horses that were stolen, or the economic losses caused by Indian raids, but informal witnesses generally remember the presence of at least thirty to fifty captives per tribe. Lucio V. Mansilla mentions between six hundred and eight hundred among the Ranquel Indians. Although imprecise, that number should be sufficient, given that each time a treaty was presented to the whites — as Santiago Avendaño recounts in his memoirs of captivity — the Indians would first send back some ten captives (sometimes against the women's will) as a show of good faith toward Buenos Aires.[60]

FROM PENELOPE TO MIRANDA

We should recognize that even less is known about the indigenous captives who became servants of the whites. The military expeditions to the internal frontier guaranteed "Generous distribution of *chinitas* for scullery or garden maids, in addition to land rights given in reward to the officials" (Generosa distribución de "chinitas" para criadas de antecocina o patio, además de bonos de tierra en premios a oficiales).[61] Indigenous servitude seems natural to civilization: the rules of the game were settled when Argentina was still a Spanish colony.[62]

The woman in the house was a guarantee of the lineage, of the genealogy of the nation. That was her genealogical imperative.[63] But the woman of the frontier was, in general, a problem. In the style of the first pages of José Hernández's *Martín Fierro*, the engineer Alfred Ebelot's memoirs recount the period in which he worked on the construction of Alsina's fantastical ditch:

> If Ulysses are frequent on the *pampa*, Penelopes are rare, if not unknown. The family is not composed as it was in Greece; there neither the household gods nor marriages are in order; absence has for that reason implacable consequences, and the return is as unhappy as the departure. The poor *gaucho* who one fine day returns to the places where his bedding was finds nothing of what he left. . . . His companion inhabits a new home, his children have followed her and carry the name of a different father, they are educated on another ranch as colts that form part of an anticipated inheritance: seed of nomads growing in the wind.

> Si los Ulises son frecuentes en la pampa, las Penélopes son raras, por no decir desconocidas. La familia no está constituida como lo estaba en Grecia; no hay ni dioses lares ni matrimonios en regla; la ausencia tiene por lo tanto consecuencias implacables, y el retorno resulta tan desdichado como la partida. El pobre gaucho que un buen día regresa a los lugares donde estuvieron sus petates no haya nada de cuanto dejó. . . . Su compañera habita un nuevo hogar, sus hijos la han seguido y llevan el apellido de otro padre, se educan en otro

rancho como potrillos que forman parte de una herencia anticipada: simiente de nómadas que crece a pleno viento.[64]

All of this creates an unstable nonurban population: itinerant men (perhaps in search of better jobs, perhaps because they were claimed by the army), women heads of households or companions of different men, children of diverse surnames, nomads growing in the wind. Perhaps this is the "elemental unit of our popular masses," of which Alberdi spoke. If we add to the scene indigenous nomadism, adventurers, unscrupulous traders, and the diverse fugitives from the law, the frightening kinesis of the frontier is nothing like Buenos Aires's dream of being Paris.

The "honorable" citizens themselves aided little in drawing the scene: their positions depended on the accumulation of goods (and, evidently, on legalizing their acquisitions through institutions) and not on their level of education. As Alfred Ebelot explains, the honorable persons designated by the government to carry out its operations on the frontier

> are made up of landholders and representatives of high commerce, rich ranchers who are residents of the city, great hide dealers, gatherers of dirty wool. Their great fortunes are esteemed sufficient guarantee of their honesty, their commercial activity as proof of their capacity.
>
> Están constituidas por terratenientes y representantes del alto comercio, ricos estancieros residentes en la ciudad, grandes negociantes de cueros, acopiadores de lana sucia. Se estima su gran fortuna como garantía suficiente de su honestidad, su actividad comercial como prenda de su capacidad.[65]

OF NOMADS AND OTHER DISAPPEARED

The life of the gauchos was not easy. As inhabitants of the pampas without title to property, they remained more or less tied to a patron or a geographic area, obliged to carry restrictive documents (internal passports, working papers, military registration). Losing these papers could mean being forcibly recruited by a justice of the peace or the landowners themselves, either to work their ranches or to serve in the military.[66] This aspect of Argentine history has been amply studied, besides being registered in the genre known as "gauchesque" poetry (*la poesía guachesca*). Colonel Daza writes:

It is an unfortunate peasant who doesn't get along well with the rural authorities or who would allow himself to vote against the official candidate in local elections. Those who did allow themselves to resist were persecuted and apprehended as vulgar criminals dangerous to society and were condemned to serve on the frontier.

Desgraciado el paisano que no se lleva bien con las autoridades rurales o que se permitiera votar en los comicios en contra del candidato oficial. Los que se permitían contrariar eran perseguidos y aprehendidos como vulgares criminales peligrosos para la sociedad a los que se condenaba a servir en la frontera.[67]

Property and lucre were law. Thus as the citizen of the frontier was duly measured by his titles to property, the poor of the countryside were the direct victims of indigenous aggressions. The landowners concerned themselves only with their profits, allowing cattle to pasture of their own accord, neglecting to invest in the culture of the land or the protection of the ranches. Leaving the ranches exposed to raid, they demanded the protection of the army. Sarmiento denounces the frontier ranchers for their opportunism and avarice:

Neither fence, nor corral, nor buildings, nor human beings even enter as production capital, as the overhead costs of this industry. They are ounces of gold scattered in a field; but ounces of gold visible from a league, and they walk where they are directed.

Ni cerco, ni corral, ni edificios, ni seres humanos siquiera entran como capital de fábrica, como obra muerta de esta industria. Son onzas de oro derramadas en una campaña; pero onzas de oro visibles de una legua, y que caminan para donde se las dirige.[68]

In an article from 1857, Sarmiento refers to the justice of the peace from the Ajó party to complain that

it is not possible that the poor peasants who have nothing go out to spill their blood on the frontier, while the landowning men remain to enjoy their homes as if they were dukes or marquises. This is a contradiction since we are republicans.

no es dable que los paisanos pobres que no tienen nada vayan a derramar su sangre a la frontera, mientras los hombres hacendados quedan disfrutando de sus casas como si fueran duques o marqueses, esto es un contrasentido pues somos republicanos.

Alvaro Barros provides another example of the atmosphere on the internal frontier, explaining that those recruited by the National Guard to serve on the frontier found that

> all guarantees are denied them, all the rights of man. They feel themselves fall to the bottom of an abyss from which they can leave only confused among criminals, and they desert because it is not possible to remain there. . . . At last there arrives a period in which the men who bear the stamp of *frontier* on their foreheads disappear like swallows in winter, and the campaign authorities run, rope in hand, uselessly, without locating enough men to tie up to make a contingent of wagons.

> les son suprimidas todas las garantías, todos los derechos del hombre. Se sienten entonces caer al fondo de un abismo de donde sólo pueden salir confundidos entre los criminales, y desertan porque allí no es posible permanecer. . . . Llega por fin una época en que los hombres que llevan sobre la frente un sello con la palabra frontera desaparecen como las golondrinas en el invierno, y las autoridades de campaña corren, cordel en mano, inútilmente, sin hallar hombres que amarrar para remitir un contingente de carretas.[69]

The figure who characterizes the internal frontier, the so-called pure gaucho (nomadic, nonintegrated, occasional resident of indigenous communities) crossing from one side to the other, himself an outsider to Prospero's culture, is also among those who disappeared during the Conquista del Desierto. With the extermination of the Indian a lifestyle was also swept away. Luis Campoy says that "the pure gaucho could withdraw from the norms of authority because he had the possibility of refuge in a neighboring nation"; the destruction of peripheral powers also meant the destruction of places of refuge.[70] In fact, the indigenous space described in Avendaño's memoirs is populated by every type of refugee from civilization; many of them, like Manuel Baigorria, had their own captives.

The erasure of the "authentic" gaucho is confirmed in Daireaux's recollections. After encountering a gaucho he asks, with characteristic irony: "What's happening? Is my vision disturbed? Or has my apparatus broken?" (¿Qué ocurre? ¿Se me turba la vista? O ¿se me ha descompuesto el aparato?). The incredulous succession of questions leaves room for the affirmation that the gaucho still exists, "but as different from the gaucho that I knew in 1880 as that one was from his predecessor twenty years earlier, the immortal Martín Fierro" (pero tan diferente del gaucho que he conocido en 1880, como lo era ese mismo, de su antecesor veinte años antes, el imperecedero Martín Fierro). And then he explains:

> Each time one must penetrate further into the still-unpopulated territories to find the genuine type of irreducible gaucho, refractory before any kind of discipline, hardened inheritor of the original nomadism. He has always retreated toward the wilderness, ceaselessly rolled along by the wave of population, and he will only disappear entirely, in his primitive type, when he no longer knows where to go without running into the advancing civilization.

> Es preciso internarse cada vez más en los territorios todavía despoblados, para encontrar el tipo genuino del gaucho irreducible, refractario a toda disciplina, heredero empedernido del nomadismo original. Siempre ha ido retirándose hacia el desierto, arrollado sin cesar por la ola de la población, y sólo desaparecerá del todo, en su tipo primitivo, cuando ya no sepa adónde ir, sin chocarse con la civilización que avanza.[71]

The gauchos' origin is racially hybrid, and as we have seen, for thinkers/governors like Sarmiento, miscegenation was not exactly the best thing that could happen to the Argentinean republic. It is true that Sarmiento expressed a certain admiration for the gauchos' natural abilities, but his description of the local population in the first chapter of *Facundo* is well known:

> [F]rom the fusion of these three families (white Spanish, Indian, black) has resulted a homogeneous whole that is distinguished by its love of laziness and industrial incapacity, when education and the exigencies of a social position do not come along to spur him out of his habitual path. The incorporation of the indigenous during colonization must have contributed much to this unfortunate result. The American races live in laziness, and show themselves incapable, even by means of compulsion, of dedicating themselves to hard and continuous labor. This suggested the idea of introducing blacks into America, which has produced such fatal results.

> [D]e la fusión de estas tres familias [blanca española, india, negra] ha resultado un todo homojéneo, que se distingue por su amor a la ociosidad e incapacidad industrial, cuando la educación i las exijencias de una posición social no vienen a ponerle espuela i sacarla de su paso habitual. Mucho debe haber contribuido a producir este resultado

desgraciado la incorporación de indíjenas que hizo la colonización. Las razas americanas viven en la ociosidad, i se muestran incapaces, aun por medio de la compulsión, para dedicarse a un trabajo duro i seguido. Esto sujirió la idea de introducir negros en América, que tan fatales resultados ha producido.[72]

The gauchos are probably the group most studied as an autochthonous product derived from these mixtures, but despite recognized evidence of their hybrid origin, writers of the stature of Ezequiel Martínez Estrada, Jorge Luis Borges, and Adolfo Bioy Casares have preferred to elide the roots of the racial equation in order to affirm that the gaucho "is not an ethnic type, but a social one" (no es un tipo étnico sino social).[73] It is significant that the lifestyle rather than the indigenous heritage of this Creole prototype is emphasized. The literary gaucho became a Creole icon only when the real gaucho began to disappear as such, absorbed by the ranches as a peon. Then his myth was erected to counteract the avalanche of immigration that threatened to deform the political-cultural panorama in the new century.[74]

Erasing the indigenous part. Many history books proceed in the same fashion. For example Juana Manso's *Compendio de la historia de las provincias unidas del Río de la Plata: Desde su descubrimiento hasta el año 1871* states that "these inhabitants of the New World, as it was denominated before taking the more characteristic denomination of America, were in general red-skinned, with the exception of the Mexicans, who were copper-colored, and of the Inca emperors, who were white"; in an unrelated passage she later affirms that "[t]he Argentines descend generally from Europeans, they are a strong race, manly and battlesome, qualities which without the direction of a wise education have nourished civil war for many years" (estos habitantes del Nuevo Mundo como se denominó antes de tomar la más característica denominación de América, eran de piel roja en lo jeneral, con escepción de los Mejicanos, que eran cobrizos, y de los emperadoras Incas que eran blancos. . . . Los Arjentinos descienden generalmente de Europeos, son de una raza fuerte, varonil y batalladora, calidades que no dirijidas por una sabia educacion han alimentado por muchos años la guerra civil).[75]

The captive woman raises more doubts about the precarious possessions of the Fathers of the Nation. If a woman represented the extension of the family, how could those literate, cultured fathers address the daughters through whom new lineages of indianized mestizo would be founded? This is not a rhetorical question. In *Una excursión a los indios ranqueles,* Lucio Mansilla reiterates again and again the presence of mestizo chiefs: the majority of the chiefs that he meets are the sons of white women. Perhaps his description is only a way to make these characters more sympathetic to his reading public, rendering them more similar, whiter and closer to the reassuring familiarity of Buenos Aires: but even if it is a narrative strategy, it is not a lie. The identity of these white mothers is never explained, but today we know that they must have been captives.[76]

The subject is uncomfortable: white women — the term "captive" implies, by historical tradition, a Christian woman in the land of infidels — carried off by force, disappearing from the society of "decent people." Indians disappear, blacks disappear, white women of the frontier also disappear from reality and from history. Nothing more is said of them.

Benedict Anderson, amplifying Renan's understanding of the need for oblivion in the constitution of nations, explains that the process of forgetting and remembering is a defense against the conflicts among the natural limits and the political aspirations of a nation. As Renan and Anderson suggest, the essence of a nation is that its individuals have much in common and that they have forgotten the same things. But, as we see, it is not a question of "all its individuals," given that vast social sectors have been swept away. In truth the identity of a nation is defined by means of its negotiations, its rituals, by the form in which its traditions are invented, by its social practices. And by its pacts of silence.

Identity is constructed over a negating self-definition, a problematization of the differences within the national subject. Rethinking that national identity today obliges us to elude the official frameworks in search of the remains, the traces, of a resistance that does not allow itself to be forgotten.

It is for that reason that Prospero's paradise on foreign soil is much less harmonious than it appears on the surface. There are fissures and tempests, vengeances and silences. For that reason we must rethink Prospero and Miranda, Caliban and the captives: reencountering them will illuminate the desire, the culture, the foundation of a nation, and the politics of an entire era.[77]

Chapter 3

NO ONE MOURNS FOR CAPTIVES: THE SOLDIERS

> *Sometimes the statues reopen the wounds within me or take on the color of the accusations that keep me from sleep. But there are proofs no one wants to see. ... Pry, pry into the place where your heart hurts most. It is necessary to know as if you weren't there.*
>
> *A veces las estatuas vuelven a abrir en mí ciertas heridas o toman el color de las acusaciones que me impiden domir. Pero hay pruebas que nadie quiere ver. ... Escarba, escarba donde más duela en tu corazón. Es necesario saber como si no estuvieras.*
>
> —Olga Orozco, *Dangerous Games*

The silence that covers the very existence of the Argentine captives of the nineteenth century is devastating: from the moment of the attack to today, captivity is synonymous with disappearance. The tales that exist are utterly insufficient to recuperate that reality or to reproduce in memory the experience of the encounter or confrontation between cultures, not to mention the nightmare that so many families lived on the internal frontier. This chapter is about the ramifications of silence; it tries to reconstruct the real situation of the captive women from the memoirs of soldiers on the frontier.

The real captives—not the idealized/invented captives of paintings or poems, but the flesh-and-blood captives—no one remembers. While they were subjugated among indigenous camps throughout the territory, the lettered elite (José Mármol, Juan María Gutiérrez, Domingo F. Sarmiento, etc.) created the high national literature, but the captives were not mentioned in it. Esteban Echeverría even managed to ignore them in a poem entitled *La cautiva,* as will be discussed in the following chapter.[1]

The next question is foreseeable: How many captives were there? The answer can only be more questions: What difference does it make if there

47

were three thousand or ten? Would either number justify silence or oblivion?[2] What is the measure of the dispensable: A hundred, a dozen, perhaps a thousand? Is there any figure for outrage or fear? What is the *desired standard of memory*? Which images does a community maintain as the desired origin, and which does it discard? Can this be done voluntarily? Do we construct our own memory, or is it constructed of experiences that happen to us?

If we cannot avoid being constituted by everything we have lived, there are — as Roger Bartra observes — rites of repetition and recuperation that reinforce some memories and reconstruct them according to the moment in which we tell them. Others we wish to forget, so we perform no rituals and preserve no structures to repeat them, hoping they will disappear. Preserving and disappearing were the responsibility of writers (of literature, journalism, history, political discourses), especially in the nineteenth century, when the autonomy of literary discourse was not yet established.[3]

The written word is equivalent to tribal ritual in the sense that it perpetuates roles, refreshes traditions, creates a sense of belonging and differentiation. There are memories that are never mentioned because they produce intolerable pain; others contradict the subject's vision of the world or the self. To act without register or rituals does not mean that they do not exist in memory; like traumas and taboos these silenced memories often say more about our identity than the signs seen on the surface. Then it is not a real oblivion but a way of covering, of defending oneself, of surrounding, of constructing around the Real.[4]

In general, to live with the absence of a captured relative, not knowing if she is still alive, if she suffers or lies in some anonymous grave in the desert, is a painful process, a process that brings with it mourning, fantasies, and guilt. Disappearance is difficult to discuss since the fate of the kidnapped person is unknown: no one knows how long to look for her or if they should mourn and say good-bye. And how do you say good-bye if the person may return? A kidnapping modifies many more lives that just the victim's. In the long run it is equivalent to the death of the captive, even if only in the realm of the symbolic.

On the other hand is the problem of the lack of collective mourning or, at least, evidence of such. When someone dies or disappears forever, quotidian reality and the sense or meaning of things are negated, suspended in time. The survivors are transformed by their numerous memories; little by little, the process of mourning allows them to defamiliarize the ordinary context of memory and begin to construct a representation of what is lost, to assimilate the definiteness of absence and to go on.[5] Mourning becomes reconstruction: the memory of the lost relative becomes the object of contemplation and not of tormented persecution.

I speak of the necessity of memories, of memory as a curative, even in the case of kidnapped persons whose whereabouts will never be known. This need is equally imperative at the social level: what is not elaborated remains as a ghost, refusing to abandon its place — intangible, yes, but just the same producing uneasiness, scars that never fully heal. It is a need like the one transmitted through generations of Holocaust survivors: "Remember, remember in order to continue living, remember so that it does not happen again."

Not only silence and oblivion. What happens if the dead return to life? When someone is rescued, does social responsibility include going beyond physical action and conversing, for example, and participating in what that person has to say? Must one *really listen to what she has to say?* Listening necessitates changing, carrying out response-ability: the capacity to share, to respond, to put oneself in the situation of the Other. But that capacity always seems to exceed societies. The captive who was one of *us* has become the *Other,* to be erased like the savages from the present and from history. *Listen?* No, it seems better not to.

NORTH AND SOUTH

In Argentina, unlike other countries where there were captives, there are no public registers of diaries written by the women; no testimonies written by the women themselves or dictated to others have become known. But even if the silence is less desolate in the rest of the continent, it cannot be said that the testimonies of captives abound in general in Latin America.

In the United States, in contrast, the first national best-seller was the diary of Mary White Rowlandson (1682), wife of a Puritan minister who described her eleven-week captivity among the Indians.[6] It was the foundation of a literary genre.[7] Another great best-seller, one that outsold even *Ivanhoe* and every other work by Walter Scott or James Fenimore Cooper, was the book Mary Jemison dictated to James Everett Seaver, in which Jemison admits to having loved her Indian husband and sketches her captivity within an idyllic landscape.[8]

Of course extensive territorial conquests, genocide, confinement of the surviving Indians, and a massive policy of European immigration were all carried out in North America in the same era as in Argentina. Despite the similarities, the literature of the United States developed a way if not to heal at least to confront the tensions of the frontier in captivity narratives like those of Mary Rowlandson, Mary Smith, and Mary Jemison, as well as the frontier adventures of Daniel Boone and Cooper's books (which so influenced Sarmiento). More recently the tradition includes films like *The Searchers* and *The Unforgiven* (in which Natalie Wood and Audrey Hepburn play captives), *The Last of the Mohicans,* and even Kevin Costner's *Dances with Wolves.*[9]

Mary Louise Pratt suggests that the tales of captives were — in general — a secure way to narrate the terrors of the frontier, given that they were written by survivors who had managed to *return,* and by returning reaffirmed the European and colonial social order.[10] Pratt's point, cogent as it is, cannot apply to Argentina, where the norm was silence, mitigation, and oblivion rather than recuperation as confirmation of the social order being established. The few Argentine fictions that do deal with captives do not have happy endings (as when Sleeping Beauty is rescued by Prince Charming; on the contrary, these "beauties" generally return to barbarism). It is difficult to explain why each country constructs its imaginary as it does, determining the uses of memory according to the style in which it imagines itself as a nation (see chapter 1). What does coincide in the foundational discourse of Argentina and the United States is the clear division between civilization and barbarism. In 1753, for example, Benjamin Franklin wrote to a friend in England that white prisoners of the Indians, no matter how tenderly they were treated, were always in the end so disgusted with their way of life that they sought the first opportunity to escape. On the other hand, the reverse never occurred: "When an Indian Child has been brought up among us, taught our language and habituated to our Customs, yet if he goes to see his relations and make one Indian Ramble with them, there is no persuading him ever to return."[11] Franklin was obviously so convinced of the benefits of civilization that he could not conceive of other forms of happiness.

Why are there no (or no known) memoirs, diaries, testimonies, or narratives of the captive women of Argentina, where there were apparently more captives than in the United States, where their texts were best-sellers? Bonnie Frederick asks the same question, wondering if there is material still hidden in some obscure archive, in a forgotten newspaper or an inaccessible private collection.[12] The question persists. The fact that after 150 years no text has been located or brought to light has its own implications.

While many women on the frontier were illiterate, others certainly were not, and the absolute absence of memoirs within the corpus of national traditions cannot be entirely explained by illiteracy. Another explanation for the silence is that the problem did not closely concern the lettered elite or the powerful individuals of the nation, or that the frontier population was dispensable. Susan Socolow attributes the "lack of reaction to the continuous loss of colonists"

> to the fact that those who ran most risk of capture were the rural settlers, people with little or no political power and education. Moreover, because the majority were women, their loss was not dramatically visible in the rural workforce. Nonetheless, the fear of captivity, without considering its reality, set frontier settlement back until the mid-nineteenth century.[13]

Scant political power, female gender, and nonurban location. The history of those women does not correspond to the image that the lettered elite held of themselves and their country. They are outside the frame of Prospero's vision of the pampas: within the spectrum of colonizer/colonized relations (civilization/barbarism?) they do not fit. They are invisible for the word founding national traditions.

The little that is known about the subject is due not to the creators of the so-called national literature but to the soldiers, English travelers, and itinerant priests. Never is voice given to the captives of reality, because to do so would have implied too profound a reform. Shoshana Feldman says that testimony is a discursive practice. Though she writes on the Holocaust, the idea is equally applicable to the victims of sexual abuse or other acts of violence to which society would prefer to turn its back. She opposes *practice* to pure theory, since to give testimony is to stand up and speak; it is to produce in one's own words material evidence of truth, to realize an act and not only a declaration.[14]

Incorporating those voices would be a performative act, a sort of conceptual offense against the organization of the white, Europeanizing national project. To tell about carnal contact with the Indian would transgress the system of domination or the white man's legitimating myth about the land. It is more comfortable to reject, negate, silence, and impose metropolitan conditions of citizen homogeneity, as contradictory as that concept is.[15]

But why look at the victims of the instability of the frontier, of the clash between human groups for the dominion of a territory, why look at them—I repeat—as a threat that must be forgotten?

BEFORE THE WORD

In March 1833, Juan Manuel de Rosas, supported by a group of ranchers looking to expand their possessions, undertook a thirteen-month excursion into Indian lands. The result of this expedition was the rescue of some thousand white captives (women and children) and an authorless document entitled *Relación de los cristianos salvados del cautiverio por la División Izquierda del Ejército Expedicionario contra los bárbaros, al mando del señor Brigadier General D. Juan Manuel de Rosas;* or, *Account of the Christians Saved from Captivity by the Left Division of the Expeditionary Army against the Barbarians, under the Command of Brigadier General D. Juan Manuel de Rosas.*[16]

There the captives are names, figures, dates, mere enunciations originally published in the Official Gazette. History would never again be troubled by them. The rest of the captives of the nineteenth century received similar treatment in the military documents, in treaties with the Indians, in literary texts: they lack texture, dimension, and importance.[17]

Rosas's document has no author and no introduction, and it is limited to recording the name, birthplace, age, parents, and a summary physical description of each person liberated.[18] Reading the text today provokes shudders. Examples, chosen at random: "José Leonardo. Buenos Aires, from the Guardia de Areco. Mother dead. Doesn't know her name or the father's. Age 12 to 14 years. Pock-marked, straight blondish hair, brown eyes. Captured at age five." "María Cabrera. Puntana, from San Luis, 39 years, married to Juan Francisco Espinosa, resident of said town. Has five young children with her, having left three in her country. Captured three years ago from the Morro ranch." "Juan Santos. San Juan, doesn't remember father's name, mother Antonia, 9 years old. Knows nothing else. No longer speaks Spanish" ("José Leonardo. Porteño, de la Guardia de Areco. Murió la madre. No sabe el nombre de ésta ni del padre. Su edad de 12 á 14 años. Picado de viruelas, pelo entre rubio lacio, ojos pardos. Lo cautivaron de cinco años." "María Cabrera. Puntana, de San Luis, de 39 años, casada con Juan Francisco Espinosa, residente en dicho pueblo. Tiene consigo cinco hijos menores, habiendo dejado tres en su país. Hacen tres años que la cautivaron en la estancia del Morro." "Juan Santos. Sanjuanino; no se acuerda del nombre del padre, su madre Antonia, de 9 años. Ignora todo lo demás. Ya no habla el castellano").

There are ninety-two pages in all. In them appear women of every age and civil status, with children and without, mute and unmemoried. When interrogated many mention families left behind, and although it may seem strange, no one mentions a previous rescue attempt. In Rosas's expedition into the desert there is a father who recovers his son; there is also a soldier who finds a missing cousin by chance. That is all. Studying the episode, Susan Socolow observes: "Some parents who firmly desired to free their children from the beginning warmly received their return from captivity and, possibly, helped them readjust to the Spanish world. But many of those liberated by Rosas could not reestablish ties with their families and were placed in the care of the Benevolent Society of Buenos Aires."[19]

The *Relación* ends with case number 634: "María Estanislada Díaz. Buenos Aires, Salado, Luján party: daughter of Manuel José and María del Tránsito Molina: 19 years of age, being 14 when captured; dark, black hair, brown eyes, pock-marks; has two moles on her throat" (María Estanislada Díaz. Porteña del Salado, partido de Luján: hija de Manuel José y de María del Tránsito Molina: 19 años, haciendo como 14 que la cautivaron; trigueña, pelo negro, ojos pardos, picada de viruela; tiene dos lunares en el pezcuezo). This last description, curiously, is one of the most complete; many captives are scarcely registered with their common name. Miracle and tragedy of a life, of hundreds of lives, converted into three to five lines each, in a list of incomplete names, birthplaces, approximate ages, and some other distinctive trait: the name of the parents, a mole on the throat. The shudder is brought on by the void of these descriptions, the most complete known inventory of the group rescued.[20]

THE MOST DREADED HELL: SEX?

The captive women of reality never had voices. Unless some soldier decided to give them one in his memories, which was never the norm. On the contrary, if some captive slips into a text from the nineteenth century, she does it through the gaze of the narrator and, obviously, through his frame of reference and interpretation of the world. It is always Prospero's gaze that organizes the tale: the disgust and the scorn that he professes toward Caliban would tarnish his relationship with Miranda if his own valued daughter had spent a season in the slave's cave.

One of the writers most distinguished in describing the life of the captives is Estanislao Zeballos — fierce enemy of the indigenous and Roca's executing arm in the Conquista del Desierto — who, without naming any captive in particular (as is the norm), describes a dreadful panorama in *Painé y la dinastía de los zorros* (Painé and the dynasty of the foxes):

> Mounted upon wasted, quixotic nags that suddenly fall when they trip on the brush grasses, the captive women bear the knocks of the beasts, whose rough burden scratches them, the laborious and intolerable march of the old horses, the cruel and implacable fury of the jealous Indian women, the blows and wounds they inflict in

their erotic delirium when they believe the captives have provoked the attention of the men, and the horrors of a captivity subject to the insatiable caprices of the most audacious barbarians.

Montadas en quijotescos rocines, que caen a menudo al tropezar en las matas de pastos o extenuados, las cautivas soportan los choques de los cargueros, cuya carga escabrosa las hiere, la marcha laboriosa e intolerable de sus matalones, la cruel e implacable furia de las indias celosas, los golpes y heridas que éstas les infieren en su delirio erótico, cuando creen que ellas provocan la atención de los indios, y los horrores de una cautividad sujeta a los caprichos insaciables y feroces de los bárbaros más audaces.

As if it were a mirror-image of "La vuelta" in José Hernández's *Martín Fierro,* he continues:

The spectacle of beloved persons immolated, of tender infants snatched from their very arms and speared within sight or given away to Indians who take them off to distant villages, the memory of the fire that demolished their homes and of the shed blood of their beloved protectors, bury their souls in the anguish of supreme martyrdom.

El espectáculo de los seres queridos inmolados, de las tiernas criaturas arrancadas de sus propios brazos para lancearlas a su vista o para regalarlas a indios que se retiran a sus tolderías lejanas, el recuerdo del incendio que devoró sus hogares y de la sangre en ellos vertida por sus defensores queridos, hunden sus almas en las angustias del martirio supremo.

He goes on, accentuating the horror:

In the afternoon, when the tribe camps, they fall fainting from the horses, with no real knowledge of what surrounds them, and as in a dream weep a precious wealth of tears, moaning for outraged virginity, or for the immolated flesh of their guts; and when they hide their pain and the shame that burns their scorched faces in the straw, seeking asylum in the bosom of the mother of us all, they receive from a *china*[21] the pails with which they must bring water from the distant laguna, through the spines of cactus, through the grasses and the trees that break against their delicate flesh.

A la tarde, cuando la tribu acampa, caen de los caballos desfallecidas, sin el conocimiento real de cuanto las rodea, y como en sueño derraman el precioso caudal de sus lágrimas, gimiendo por la virginidad ultrajada, o por la inmolación de la carne de sus entrañas; y cuando ocultan su dolor y la verguenza que queman su rostro abrasadas a las pajas buscando asilo en el seno de la madre de todos, reciben de una china los baldes con que deben traer agua de la laguna lejana, a través de las espinas de los cactus, de las yerbas y de los árboles, que se quiebran en sus delicadas carnes.[22]

I cite Zeballos extensively because, in the first place, such detail is rare in the history books and archives; second, because he uses that wealth of detail to paint an infernal scene. The images are so sharp they leave no fissures even to imagine that some captives did not wish to return to "civilization" (as occurred more than once). Third, the text contains all the commonplaces of those who wrote on the subject: from violence to invasive eroticism, icons from Christian martyrology, hostile nature, shame over "outraged virginity," the Hispanization of the white women (imagined essentially as mothers), nostalgia for a lost order, the atrocious cruelty of the savage, the strong textualization of bodies (absent from almost all the literature of the nineteenth century), a narrative voice that is white and expressive of urban and domestic values, inclined toward commercial development and private property, and directed to a reading public waiting to find exactly these images to confirm its ideas about the world of the frontier.

The fragment from Zeballos, especially in its descriptions of horrific indigenous behavior, seems like a combination of Esteban Echeverría's *La cautiva* and "La vuelta" ("The Return") from José Hernández's *Martín Fierro*. More crucial than establishing who read whom first is discovering the common articulations among literature and military documents of the same period and tracing, above all, a concrete *epistēmē*, a poetics of memory: how it is written, how it is silenced, how the images to be remembered are constructed.

The norm was to silence what happened to the lives of the captives on the other side of the frontier and to assume from the beginning that it could not be other than as Zeballos described. Beginning with a preconception (life among the Indians had to be hell), the rest was an ellipsis: this is doubtless what occurred in the *Relación de los cristianos salvados del cautivero por la División Izquierda del Ejército Expedicionario contra los bárbaros, al mando del señor Brigadier General D. Juan Manuel de Rosas*.

Among the few documented cases the most complete is the story of

Dorotea Cabral, rescued by a military contingent years after her kidnapping. The soldiers had discovered her existence when her Indian son was captured by the army and confessed. Colonel José Daza writes that Dorotea Cabral was "white, pink, with brown hair, pretty green eyes"; she had been captured from her ranch south of Villa María by chief Cañumil in 1864:[23]

> At that time, when the raid occurred, Dorotea was fourteen years old, and she witnessed the sacrifice of various members of her family, killed with spears, while others managed to escape thanks to their good horses; from that time on she had no notice of those who died, nor of the others who managed to escape.

> En esa época, cuando dieron el malón, Dorotea contaba catorce años de edad y presenció el sacrificio de varios miembros de su familia, muertos a lanzadas, mientras que otros consiguieron escaparse gracias a sus buenos caballos; desde ese tiempo no tenía ninguna noticia respecto á los que habrían perecido, ni de los que salvarse pudieron. (228)

The chief "treated her well" and, although Daza uses the word "obligation" in reference to her married life, he admits that Dorotea loved "with all the effusion of her soul" the three children born of her union with Cañumil. Until now, only the moment of capture seems disastrous, not captivity itself. Nonetheless, Daza takes the same position as all the others who wrote on the subject:

> *To describe* the journeys and the vicissitudes that she experienced during the long captivity to which misfortune had condemned her, suffering in the deserts, an educated girl who had been wrenched from home, deprived of parental affection and the comforts that civilized life affords, forced to share and make a common life of a life of orgies and dissipation with the barbarians, is impossible; it is enough to say that she felt she had been reborn from the moment she was returned and incorporated into civilization.

> *Relatar* las correrías y peripecias que pasó en el largo cautiverio á que se vió condenada por el infortunio, á sufrir en los desiertos una niña educada y que había sido arrebatada del hogar, privándola de las caricias paternas y de las comodidades que proporciona la vida civilizada, para ir á compartir haciendo vida común en vida de orgías y disipación con la barbarie, es imposible; basta decir, que creía haber

nacido de nuevo desde el momento que fué reducida é incorporada
á la civilización. (229)

To describe ... is impossible. The reticence of the narration is the true mark of
eloquence. A cliché so generalizing that it already shapes an imaginary (in
the literal sense: it is like a sculpture of effigies) is repeated. Or it happens,
much more frequently, that the texts are silent, that their authors look the
other way and dedicate their pages to speaking about customs in the forts,
about horses or Indians.

On the one hand silence, on the other stereotype: orgy, savagery. And in
the middle, an uncomfortable gray zone that makes narrative impossible.
Not only was Dorotea treated well as the wife of a chief, not only did she
confess to loving her Indian children — she committed the most intolerable act in showing herself a sexual and unfaithful woman. Is that what
makes the story impossible? When Dorotea is rescued by the whites, she
disappears anew for several days. Finally they discover that she has escaped
with a subaltern. Mortal sin: Dorotea is forcibly returned to her town of
origin and her family, without anyone asking if that is what she wishes, and
the subaltern is so severely punished that he retires from military service.

Dorotea's history — the only or one of the only reconstructions of
the life of a real captive who returns to civilization — illustrates that of
many other captives who managed to adapt to their life on the other side
of the frontier and did not have the least intention of returning to their
original families. When these women were "saved," they already had ideas
or desires of their own about their bodies or their destinies; such desires
were intolerable and their will was never accepted. Within the reasoning of white civilization, the good damsel had been saved in every sense,
even from her own appetites. Or on the contrary, if the ending is taken
into account, the story demonstrates instead that the captive is seen as
incorrigible, irredeemable.

Sexuality interferes again and again, like a conflict that the texts know
not how to embody: it is certain that in the moment of kidnapping the
captive is generally naked or stripped from the waist up, which increases
the desire of the savage. The problem is when the woman responds to her
captor. Such is the case of Francisca Adaro, another of the privileged few
who have survived the vicissitudes of History with a first and last name.
The story is reproduced by Zeballos, but this time the narrator cannot
restrain his own desire toward the captive, admitting that his eyes "lit up
with a burning passion upon discovering the delicate form of a naked
woman who, in the safety of the others' sleep, washed her body almost

hidden, like the swan in its nest, by the *achiras* in bloom" (se iluminaron de una pasión candente al descubrir las mórbidas formas de una mujer desnuda que, al amparo del sueño de todos, lavaba su cuerpo casi oculta, como el cisne en su nido, por las achiras en flor).[24]

In the narratives the one who spies on this aquatic Venus is normally a savage (as occurs in the legend of Lucía Miranda), but in this case it is none less than Zeballos himself. All to explain that Francisca (or Panchita) already has a past: before her capture, "she had conceived a profound and desolating passion for a gentle youth," but because he was married, "hysteria began slowly to devour that robust and fresh organism of a country damsel" (habia concebido una pasión profunda y desoladora por un gentil mancebo el histerismo comenzó a devorar lentamente aquel robusto y fresco organismo de doncella de campaña).[25] It is worth remembering, as George Mosse suggests, that in the nineteenth century hysteria was tied to female sexuality, nervousness was considered a vice — including among men, whose virility depended upon self-control — and what was expected of good citizens (especially females) was the practice of virtues that would exalt the nation and transcend sensuality.[26] Evidently Panchita did not demonstrate any of those virtues, not even when she lived among the civilized — or at least not as her history was registered by persons unable to see her adventures through other than their own codes of life.

On the advice of the town doctor Panchita's father took her on a trip so that the "change of air" would "calm" the girl, but on the road they met with the misfortune of a raid. Panchita, instead of fainting as often occurs in the tales, suffered an epileptic seizure. Though a slight variation from the norm, the result is that she remembers nothing, and upon awakening finds herself

> in the arms of the chief, who carries her on the back of his horse, affectionately pressing her against his body. From that day on she was Painé's favorite, obliged to devour her sorrows and to hide the nauseating disgust that the fetid breath of the sturdy Araucanian caused her.

> en brazos del cacique, que la conducía sobre la cruz de su caballo, oprimiéndola cariñosamente contra su cuerpo. Desde ese día fué la favorita de Painé, obligada a devorar sus dolores y a ocultar el asco nauseabundo que le causaba el aliento fétido del macizo araucano.

The matter of the breath and the disgust is the opinion of the soldier Estanislao Severo Zeballos. But the episode confronts the teller with a dimension of reality that escapes from his hands. At the end he lets slip out that as the wife of the chief, "Pachita's nerves were cured" (Panchita sanó de los nervios).

What part of this scene could literature not narrate? The desire of the illustrious, supposedly sublime (or civilized) soldier for a woman who is modestly trying to bathe in privacy? Or the consciousness that a woman achieves, among the Indians, what white civilization will not allow: "curing her nerves," or, as our psychoanalyzed society would say, healing the hysteria brought on by her long abstinence and frustrated desire for a married man? Or the idea that a white woman of known father would *enjoy* her sexuality on the other side of the frontier? Or is all this just the tip of a racism so total that it prefers to obliterate history rather than accept the material existence of mestizo children, bearers of cultures and lifeways different from those being imposed? As Michael Taussig explains, racism is a procession in which the civilized rehearse a love-hate relationship with their own repressed sensuality.[27]

Many and all — whites, Indians, mestizos, blacks, captives of various colors, immigrants, rich, poor, illiterate, and lettered — shared the same territory. But those for whom writing and publishing were real possibilities lived as if only their group were alive and the rest howled around like incomprehensible (but aggressive) ghosts.

Taking into account the morality, customs, and sexual repression of the era, the scene of a young white girl, beautiful and nude, happy thanks to her satisfied sexuality, was certainly not an image to leave a white man unaffected. And it must have been even more damaging to his civilized psyche to confront the fact that that satisfaction was produced among the Indians: this was the highest outrage. The convictions (and the projection of repressed desires and fears) of Zeballos (and those of the others who, like him, left their memories in writing) could carry him to heroism on the battlefield. But it would have been too much to ask him to confront also his own masculine anxieties. In *Painé y la dinastía de los zorros,* Zeballos's desire for Panchita — now one of the wives of the chief — increases intolerably until, after eight years among the Indians, he decides to escape with his beloved, who faces death in the tribe now that Painé has died and his son has ordered the sacrifice of his widows. Zeballos's tale reaches such heights of fantasy that not only does he manage to avoid the execution — itself an impossibility, considering the description in *Memorias del ex cautivo Santiago Avendaño* (Memoirs of the former captive Santiago Avendaño) — but Panchita herself accompanies him, completely enamored of Zeballos. She will reappear as heroine/victim of *Relmú, reina de los pinares* (Relmú, queen of the Pinar), captured again and the wife of another chief. Sexuality produces a short circuit in this text, belying its fictional content despite the many citations and footnotes intended to create historical verisimilitude; the excesses of fiction run the risk of neutralizing Zeballos's accounts, the only ones that pause to tell with interest and detail the life of the captives. For example, after giving proper names and places of origin — which, as we have seen, do not abound in texts from the nineteenth century — he writes:

It was not unusual to see from time to time among the Indians, distinguished women from Argentine high society, like the Cordovan nun, niece of Governor López, surprised and captured on the horrible voyages of the coaches of the time. The unhappy captives would quickly die in the martyrdom of the Araucanian seraglio, in the midst of the sanguinary hatred of the Indian women whose place they occupied, at times completely, in the sensuality of the barbarians.

No era extraño que aparecieran de cuando en cuando entre los indios, mujeres distinguidas, de la alta sociedad argentina, como la monja cordobesa sobrina del gobernador López, sorprendidas y cautivadas en los horribles viajes de las mensajerías de aquel tiempo. Las infelices cautivas morían pronto en el martirio del serrallo araucano, en medio del odio sanguinario de las chinas cuyo lugar ocupaban a veces por completo en el sensualismo de los bárbaros.

He adds:

Many of them would have preferred suicide; but they were watched scrupulously. Nonetheless, the blows and the wounds that the jealous Indian women inflicted, the invincible repugnance produced by the greasy horse-meat, the raw blood they were given to drink, and the supreme disgust caused by the caresses of the repugnant Indians consumed their delicate organisms and prepared them for a death which they received as gladly as the mercy of Heaven.

Muchas de ellas habrían preferido el suicidio; pero las vigilaban escrupulosamente. Sin embargo, los golpes y las heridas que les inferían las chinas celosas, la repugnancia invencible producida por la grasosa carne de yegua, la sangre cruda que les daban a comer y el asco supremo causado por la caricia de los indios hediondos, minaban profundamente sus organismos delicados y las precipitaban a una muerte que recibían gozosas como la misericordia del Cielo. (128)

Zeballos remained captive to the image of Panchita naked, with an "inextinguishable fire of the soul, that dries my lips and makes my eyes shine" (fiebre inextinguible del alma, que seca los labios y abrillanta mis ojos), with an anxiety that draws "the spring-time bellow of the tiger and hurls upon the fainted captive the panting assault of the Indians" (el bramido primaveral del tigre y arroja sobre la cautiva desmayada el asalto jadeante de los indios) (160). That wet body, stripped of clothing, inhabiting forbidden territory, confuses his imagination:

> In my soul this passion reached unconscious manifestations of delirium, and my existence shook with mortal shudders, pulled to the edge of the abyss, whose only exit is suicide, against which struggled the heavenly and infinite hope of my mother's kiss!
>
> ¡Esta pasión alcanzaba en mi alma hasta las manifestaciones inconscientes del delirio, y mi existencia tenía estremecimientos mortales, arrojada a veces al borde del abismo, cuya única salida es el suicidio, con el cual luchaba la esperanza celestial e infinita de un beso de mi madre! (160)

Passion and delirium, heaven and mother: these are the two poles in which images of femininity are usually contained. In *Painé y la dinastía de los zorros* there is more passion: the protagonist, against logic, exposes his own life for the sake of hers. "Our bodies were united, tied by an immense embrace and our lips came together instinctively with the delirium of savage passion and the supreme martyrdom of eight years" (Nuestros cuerpos se unieron, ligados por un abrazo inmenso y nuestros labios se juntaron instintivamente con el delirio de la pasión salvaje y del martirio supremo de ocho años) (190). But she must be lost in the confusion between Unitarios and Federales on the frontier, to be found again almost by chance in Chile, converted into an irresistible but ailing Venus in his next book. Time and again the captive will be desired flesh, traded on the frontier; years may pass and husbands change, but the captive continues to embody this function of "mysterious creature of unknown origin, of pilgrim beauty, such as even the oldest Indians who had crossed most territory had never seen in any tribe" (misteriosa criatura de origen desconocido, de una belleza peregrina, como no recordaban haber visto en tribu alguna los indios más viejos y que más tierras habían corrido) (287). This legendary white woman who speaks the Indian language perfectly and awakens delirious passions in whites and Indians alike must remain young and charming. Perhaps most strangely—following the logic of the narrative — she must never be a mother, despite having been the wife or lover of at least three men. Revered among the cushions of blue cloth and fur (302), watched over by the Indian women, or dirty and starving during her attempted escapes, Panchita always remains the wet and naked woman of the frontier, whom the trappings of civilization will never really redeem since her destiny is, if not to be taken captive again, to continue to embody masculine fantasies of the forbidden.

In the text the author of *Painé* declares that he was witness and protagonist of the pampa civilization until 1847, the year of his flight "in search of my home and my country" (80), and constantly refers the reader to his other works, which contain facts he cannot recount in this book. This first-person identification of the authorial voice — in the terrain of the document, the memoirs, and the confession — produces another short circuit in the reading by ascribing to the text a degree of verisimilitude that clashes with the fantastic logic of the tale itself. The date of the events narrated also makes a testimonial stance impossible, since Zeballos was born at least a decade after the events described. Since Zeballos was a public figure, charged by President Avellaneda with writing narratives about the frontier to favorably dispose public opinion toward the Desert Campaign, the reader of the time would have known that the man who in the 1880s was chancellor and deputy could not have been old enough to be the protagonist of these events in the 1840s. The testimonial posture so well achieved in *Callvacurá y la dinastía de los piedra* is compromised here.[28]

SIX HORSES FOR A WOMAN

Narratives like Zeballos's — so detailed in the order of lust, cruelty, and daily life among the Indians — are true exceptions, to be patiently tracked through public and private archives, in decrepit books, and especially in the photocopies of photocopies that pass from hand to hand in a closely restricted circulation. Zeballos's text is, to a large extent, a fictional tale based upon readings and documents that were in his control, as were the memoirs of Santiago Avendaño.[29]

The silence covering the captives does not mean that there has been no information about them. Writing did not leave the captives out entirely: if such were the case, the imaginary would have filled that space almost by the force of gravity, following the same law that Argentine literature postulated regarding the desert — the void must be filled with words.

What occurred is worse: from time to time the captive is dedicated one paragraph or another in a book of memoirs or appears in article 4 or 5 of military treaties signed with the Indians, as part of the exchange of horses, cows, money, and services. Chapters are not dedicated to the captives in the history books, they appear in no index; but if one looks carefully they can just be discerned, glimmering from a line or two.

We do know their exchange value. Price was determined according to the quality of the rescued woman: the average cost of each person was "six unmarked horses, twelve cows, a lance-pole, a braided lasso, and a pair of silver spurs" (seis caballos sin marca, doce vacas, una caña de lanza, un lazo trenzado y un par de estribos de plata).[30] What had happened to these women was neither known nor asked.

They are one more cipher of the frontier. An example: in 1833 an attack against the village of Yanquestruz left in the power of General Aldao

> 51 captive women..., 133 Indians of the common rabble, 200 service horses, 120 colts and tame mares, 48 untamed, 352 head of cattle, from small to large, and 10,000 head of sheep and goats.

> 51 cautivas..., 133 indios de chusma, 200 caballos de servicio, 120 cabezas entre potrillos y yeguas mansas, 48 cabezas chúcaros, 352 cabezas de ganado entre chico y grande, y 10,000 cabezas de ganado lanar y cabras.[31]

In the best of cases the woman is a cipher. The travelers note them, but the majority are more interested in their texts in describing the customs of gauchos, outlaws, or chiefs. Sometimes they are rescued, true, and they are even invoked among the justifications to carry out a *final solution* to the problem of the Indian — the Conquista del Desierto — but no one wants to get too close to them.

Here I read Michel de Certeau, reading in turn the humanism of Emmanuel Levinas: to understand the suffering of another, or simply to understand his experience, it would be necessary to leave everything behind *to be able to see*.[32] True knowledge is not the imposition of one's own power over the other person, nor is it considering his existence a threat. But such ties of empathy and solidarity are not, obviously, what enter the game when nations are consolidated: it seems communities fortify themselves more in distancing the *Others* than in revising the true sense of *us*.

Of course nationalism is a process of exclusions, of inclusions, of negations. As Rosaldo would say: "Who was not in the room on the day consensus was achieved?"[33] Continuing the figure: I do not know the exact names of those who were in the room when national traditions were invented, but I am sure that blacks, Indians, and mestizos were not invited. Of the captive women, perhaps only a few were reluctantly included, with a magnanimous gesture of tolerance, as long as they remained virginal and Spanish-speaking (but mute), as long as they did not seem like Indians in European clothing, as long was they were anything but true captives.

HISTORY FALLS SILENT

Statistics were the basic source of official misinformation: just as Argentine blacks did not appear in the census, neither did the captives. Twice — in the period spanning from 1830 to the end of the century — they figure as a rubric in the national government's list of annual expenses: the budget of 1833–34 registers a "Subsidy of prisoners, refugees and captive women" of 1,573.6 pesos, while more than 187,000 pesos are dedicated to friendly Indians and 58,000 to slaves; one year later the figure has risen to 7,000 pesos, but after that it vanishes from the budget. The rescued captives are attributed — for two years, although the problem of kidnapping lasted more than a century — the status of prisoners and slaves. Later they don't get even that much.

I always speak of the captives as women because men were rarely ransomed: they were more often killed. The children who remained in the Indians' possession were considered of little importance: they do not appear in the iconography or in the military treaties.[34] Their destiny is uncertain, but assimilation into indigenous customs is probably the true reason for their omission: they became Indians. For the white culture in which they had been born, the captive children (the boys, since the girls pertain to the same category as the women) seem to have had no more value than as appendages of their mothers; the alternative was being considered culturally dead. In other words, after a time the boys were definitively transformed into Others, into Indians. They became the white Indians, no less fierce or frightening than the rest, described with neither emphasis nor inquiry into their origins by soldiers like Colonel Mansilla, author of *Una excursión a los indios ranqueles.*

The little that is told is slanted and one-sided: thus is history constructed out of images, manipulated, incomplete images sifted by the interests of the one who composes them. It has always been this way, it is true, but here the voices are especially one-sided.

If anyone suffers in these tales, it is the whites.[35]

Gauchesque poetry re-creates the situation in its own way. Chapter 13 of Ascasubi's *Santos Vega* describes Indians killing the old women and distributing the pretty girls whom they marry "in their way":[36]

> And there was a captive who lived
> fifteen years among the Indians,
> from whom, at last, she escaped
> and with a son she came;
> he, when grown, remembered
> that he was an Indian
> and so returned to his own kind;
> back came he with the others
> and in one of their massacres
> set his mother free.

> Y hay cautiva que ha vivido
> quince años entre la indiada,
> de donde, al fin, escapada
> con un hijo se ha venido;
> el cual, después de crecido
> de que era indio se acordó
> y a los suyos se largó;
> y vino otra vez con ellos
> y en unos de esos degüellos
> a su madre libertó.

A later stanza about the captives adds that they have managed to escape from the desert, only to meet a terrible end: "her own children have killed her / later in a scouting party / because they found her beaten, / or did not recognize her" (sus propios hijos la han muerto / después en una avanzada / por hallarla avejentada, / o haberla desconocido). Attention focuses on the captive: the son is already so lost from civilization that he becomes a matricide. Ascasubi himself sings the history of the Lunareja, to whom he dedicates six chapters. She lives through the horror of the raid, the murder of her husband and brother-in-law, but in the midst of the horror, in contrast to the captive of *Martín Fierro*, in *Santos Vega* she and her young son are protected by Chief Cocomel, who "enthralled, carried her off / to marry her on the pampa, in love" (se la llevó muy prendado / para casarse con ella a lo pampa enamorado). The poem goes on to say that "her son the captive, / when he was sixteen years old, / . . . there among the savages / was the renegade chief" (su hijo el cautivo, / al cumplir dieciséis años, / . . . allá entre los salvajes / fué el cacique renegado).

As occurs in the story of Dorotea, the narrative falls silent regarding the Lunareja's life among the Indians, but it must not have been too bad if she returns to live among the whites bearing a message of peace and friendship from Cocomel, "without the mistrust of the Indians / or having aggrieved anyone" (sin recelos de los indios / ni haber agraviao a naides).

In contrast to cultured literature, gauchesque poetry does allude to the scene of the frontier and, for that reason, the captive women as well; nonetheless, this literature was invited into the national pantheon only when the world it represents was already receding.[37]

Texts and documents are crossed by contradictions. Rather than describe the suffering of the Indians and the cruelty of the "civilized," they submerge these in a silence even vaster than that which covers the captives. The traffic in children and the killing of Indians are mentioned by the English travelers J. P. and W. P. Robertson, who deny that the Indians killed men, women, and children in their invasions and affirm instead that Francisco Bedoya, commandant of the Corrientes troops, had massacred the inhabitants of a small village a few weeks earlier and that the people of Corrientes feared a retaliation.[38]

The apparent bias of the texts forces us to remember that the indigenous raids were the official excuse for the extermination of the Indians. In order to justify the violence against them — not to mention their exclusion from the nation — the Indians were represented in terms of a single attribute: cruelty. In that sense the term "barbarian" serves two purposes, since it also registers the horror of power itself; by condemning the violence of the barbarian one ends up supporting the notion of the savage.[39] It is a mirror of attribution and counterattribution: the "civilized" attribute the worst to the Indians. In the attacks both sides kidnapped women and children; if the Indians did it, it was called theft; if the whites did it, it was a civilizing act. Supported by such a noble cause, the whites did not have to confront the true reasons that impelled territorial expansion. The Conquista del Desierto, for example, is easily explained by the economic-financial crisis, brought on by partisan rivalries, that necessitated the increase of cattle exportations in the 1870s. Indian attacks along the frontier drained "men, cattle, and money" and impeded the occupation of new territories, occupation that was necessary "since [the territories] already in use, in particular those of the province of Buenos Aires, showed signs of exhaustion" (pues las [tierras] ya utilizadas, en especial las de la provincia de Buenos Aires, mostraban síntomas de agotamiento).[40]

(UN)HAPPY CAPTIVITY

It is difficult to say how much the captives suffered among the Indians. The stories are contradictory. The Robertsons, for example, relate the curious story of the Cordovan named Ascensión, whom a chief handed over to his wife to work as her servant, adding that she was "not [to be] treated harshly." During her stay among the Indians, the woman witnessed cruel murders. When she encounters the same Indians again soon after her rescue, the whites fear that she will be recaptured; Ascensión, curiously, is unafraid because the Indian women are pleased to see her, "as if she were a sister," and visit every day that they remain in the area.[41]

The central issue was not the children. The documents speak of women: having them combined power and desire. In the end, "to captivate" has another connotation too: to charm, to seduce. But we are in the nineteenth century and sexuality is elusive.

Alvaro Barros explains in his memoirs:

> [The Indians] invade our settled camps and carry off with them as much as they can to use or to trade for the objects they need. They take women and children, to make use of them or to sell them, they kill the men and destroy by instinct, by custom, what is useless to them or cannot be carried.

> [Los indios] invaden nuestros campos poblados y se llevan cuanto puede servirles para mantenerse o para permutar por los objetos que necesitan. Llevan mujeres y niños, para servirse de ellos o venderlos, matan a los hombres y destruyen por instinto, por costumbre, lo que no les es útil o no pueden llevar.[42]

R. B. Cunninghame Graham, perhaps because his loyalties were divided between Britain and Argentina, perhaps because he spoke of the Indians after their extermination, offers a more explicit account:

> [A]s they came to plunder, not especially to kill, they wasted little time upon such places, unless they knew that there were young and handsome women shut up in the house. "Christian girl, she more big, more white than Indians," they would say, and woe betide the unlucky girl who fell into their hands.

> Hurried off to the *toldos*, often a hundred leagues away, they fell, if young and pretty, to the chiefs. If not, they had to do the hardest kind of work; but in all cases, unless they gained the affections of

their captor, their lives were made a burden by the Indian women, who beat and otherwise ill-used them on the sly.[43]

Despite accounts like this one it is difficult to know how badly the captives were treated among the Indians, given that the scant extant information comes from the pens of white men and generally soldiers whose mission was to combat the indigenous. Most concur that the Indian women mistreated the new arrivals out of jealousy and that the abuse ceased when the captive became a mother. Most agree that the majority were not raped: their masters tortured them physically by imposing hard labors, but nothing indicates that the captives were abused sexually. It may be that many were, but their consent seems to have been necessary on the whole. There are tales — though they are never given more than a few brief lines — that affirm that some, not unyielding, were resold to other Indians or to gauchos in the area.

The minimal space that masculine and white imaginations dedicated to the subject has left us the scene of the captive in a sort of Calgary. Thus, for example, says Estanislao Zeballos in *La conquista de quince mil leguas* (The conquest of fifteen thousand leagues): "Moving were the scenes those unfortunate captives offered upon finding themselves suddenly alleviated of their suffering and of the martyrdom they had so long experienced" (Eran conmovedoras las escenas que ofrecían aquellos desgraciados cautivos al encontrarse de repente aliviados del sufrimiento y del martirio que por tanto tiempo habían experimentado). There is no reason to doubt Zeballos's honesty, though it is clear that he could not have borne the sight of a beautiful white woman who was angry enough to throw rocks at the men who had conquered fifteen thousand leagues without asking if she wished to be conquered yet again.

I don't mean to say that it was a happy captivity; that would be absurd: the situation of captivity and, moreover, captivity in a foreign culture can hardly be considered happy. But it is unclear whether the captives were treated well or badly by the Indians, or if they had the right to express an opinion in choosing a partner: there is no way to hear their voices. The majority were captured when very young and forced to work alongside the Indian women in the weaving, in domestic chores, the care of the animals, the curing of leather, and the setup of the tents; unlike the few captive men, they often married the chiefs or warriors, which was not necessarily a real privilege given that the arrangement could perpetuate the dynamic of captivity: master-slave, torturer-victim.

I do suggest that it must have been insufferable for a white man to admit the possibility that there were captives who, after a time, preferred to live among the Indians or had fallen in love with one of them. The French Alcide D'Orbigny cites the testimony of an engineer named Parachappe in Bahía Blanca in 1828, recounting that

> We flattered ourselves thinking to rescue those prisoners (racially white women and children) for the price of a few colts, the currency ordinarily used in this kind of exchange, but the thing was difficult to bring about. The most notable problem came from the captives themselves, who had grown close to their Indian owners. After Colonel Rauch's expedition against the tribes of the South, a large quantity of white women who had been captured by the Indians escaped to return to them. During the nocturnal marches they slipped over the haunches of the soldiers' horses that carried them and were lost in the darkness.

> Nos lisonjeamos pensando rescatar estos prisoneros (mujeres y niños de raza blanca) al precio de algunos potrillos, moneda ordinariamente empleada en este tipo de intercambios; pero la cosa se hizo con dificultad. Lo más notable fue que provino de las mismas cautivas, que se habían apegado mucho a sus dueños indios. Después de la expedición del coronel Rauch contra las tribus del Sur, una gran cantidad de mujeres blancas que habían sido raptadas por los indios se escaparon para volver con ellos. Durante las marchas nocturnas se dejaban caer de las ancas de los caballos de los soldados que las llevaban y se perdían en la oscuridad.[44]

Reflecting on the captives who preferred to remain among the Indians, Socolow says: "this behavior was inexplicable for the European men, who could only interpret it as a sign of sexual passion and feminine weakness."[45] About why the number of women among the fugitives was so low, she adds, "it is doubtful that these women, victims of 'Indian captivity and sensuality,' would receive a warm welcome when they returned to Spanish society, with or without half-raised children."[46] The easiest way, doubtless, was to degrade and discard them forever as "indecent women." The men in their situation were in contrast labeled traitors or fugitives, either of which was more dignified than the charge of licentiousness. Thus "Viaje al Río de la Plata y Chile (1752–1756)" (Journey to the Río de la Plata and Chile), by an anonymous author, says that these women preferred "to live as slaves and satisfy thus their passions, than to reside among those of their race (so corrupt is human nature)" (vivir como esclavas y satisfacer así sus pasiones, que residir entre los de su raza [tan corrupta es la naturaleza humana]).[47]

The masculine anxiety suggested by the choice of representation or decision to omit these experiences altogether and the relationships between master and slave are subjects too complex to resolve here. But it is worth saying that the few times a text accepts the existence of a captive who refuses to return to civilization, it tries to justify her decision with the bonds of motherhood: she refuses to abandon her children. The simple reason that many stayed because it was the only world they knew (having been captured as girls in the vast majority of cases) seems to be thinkable only in the historiography of a century later.

MISTRUST, ON TOP OF EVERYTHING ELSE

If anything has remained constant with regard to the captives, it is society's incomprehension of the person who crosses. Incomprehension, mistrust, perhaps fear.[48] The frontier, more than a place of encounter, is a place of loss (in various senses), an abyss that marks the individual forever. Cristina Iglesia has developed Julia Kristeva's theory that the abject is all that that disturbs a system or an identity, that does not respect limits or rules, all that is ambiguous or mixed, especially indecipherable eroticism:

> From the side of her origin, the captive is the woman who provokes the love of the enemy, the one who may come to love him, the one who perhaps may also come to love a land which is not her own. It is a question of something dangerous, difficult to conjure because the forced character of the capture is always tainted with guilt, with provocation, and for that reason, the captive becomes a figure for the desire of the other that cannot be made explicit but that can be expanded and should, for that reason, be socially repressed. From the other side, that of her captors, be she loved or scorned, she will always be someone who can betray, who spies, who watches with different eyes.[49]

Laura Malosetti Costa, for her part, summarizes the situation well:

> The Christian woman who has remained long years in captivity and has had mestizo children is definitively condemned. Once she has crossed the frontier she no longer pertains to one world or the other: among the Indians she will always be a prisoner, she will live trying to escape or hoping to be liberated. Later she will find no escape in

the world of the whites. The captive is no longer a chaste heroine who has managed to preserve her "purity" despite it all.... She is now a figure of the frontier, a woman without identity (without name), condemned for her transgression, no matter that it has been involuntary or forced.[50]

The lack of name is a revealing constant; in fact, there are few texts that give names and surnames to the captives. The condemnation to oblivion is so irrevocable that they are denied even the recognition of their individual identity. The transgression — or perhaps the abject state of being between two worlds — is not erased, and the captive who manages to return to her own will never again inspire confidence (see chapter 1).

In *Tipos y paisajes criollos,* for example, Godofredo Daireaux writes the story "Ha sido indio" (Has been an Indian), in which he describes the destiny of a few survivors of "the great assault that from 1875 to 1877, with Alsina first and Roca after, finished sweeping the savages off the Pampa, [in which] thousands of Indians, of all ages and sexes, were dispersed" (la gran ráfaga que de 1875 a 1877, con Alsina primero y Roca después, acabó de barrer al salvaje de la Pampa, millares de indios, de toda edad y de todo sexo, quedaron dispersos). According to the text, those who resisted were killed; others received lands so that "they would cease to be the nomads of before and begin to civilize themselves through work"; others were incorporated into the army and "many, many Indian children...were turned over to families that requested them, remaining among them as servants" (muchísimos niños indios...fueron entregados a las familias que los pidieron, quedando en ellas como sirvientes). Be they diligent or lazy, in the end "they are still Indians" as if "by atavism": "Indian he had been, Indian he had remained" (indio había sido, indio ha quedado). He describes a reverse captive, that is, an Indian woman among the whites:

A chief's daughter, adopted by her masters, educated and endowed by them, admirably instructed, seduced with her exotic grace a gentleman of European high society, who made her a countess; and some there, certainly, in aristocratic salons, did not cease to whisper: "She has been an Indian."

Una hija de cacique, adoptada por sus amos, educada y dotada por ellos, admirablemente instruida, sedujo por su gracia exótica a un gentil hombre de la alta sociedad europea, que la hizo condesa; y algunos, allá, seguramente, en los salones aristocráticos, no dejaron de cuchichear: "Ha sido india."[51]

Atavism remains, even though an Indian who comes "from this side" may one day be a count; a white woman who goes toward the other side will never cease to be a savage or a madwoman.

In "The Captive" Graham relates the story of a woman rescued by a white man after eight years of captivity; she had been trapped during an invasion of San Luis in which her father, mother, and siblings died. She had three children with Chief Huichán; "the Christian women pass through hell amongst the infidel," he writes.[52] Little by little she gives up the name of Lincomilla along with her Indian clothing to become a Spanish woman called Nieves. One of the most interesting elements of the story has to do with sexuality: while she responds to the (Indian) name of Lincomilla, she assumes she has to serve all the needs of her white captor, but he is inhibited from the beginning, perhaps because of the whiteness he senses in her. When she become Nieves (a white woman), the abyss between them grows and the captor—or savior—is awed with respect and becomes almost her servant. Contradicting the initial assumption that she has suffered in captivity, Nieves-Lincomilla asks for permission to return to her children and her Indian husband. The white man accompanies her, without speaking, as when he brought her, and she departs at a gallop for the desert.[53]

A little-considered aspect of the problem is the political situation of the country, which was divided not only between whites and Indians, but also between Federales and Unitarios. There were captives who, having the opportunity to return, preferred life among the Indians to the one that awaited them if they returned to the cities. Thus, for example, when Manuel Baigorria decides to live with the Indians, he tells the girl who has accompanied him to return to her home. But she refuses, crying.

> Baigorria responds: "you don't know what you're doing: if anything happened to me, you would remain a captive among the Indians." Then, wiping her tears with a handkerchief, she said: "I would rather be a captive than a servant of the Federales, especially since my brother was killed by them."

> Baigorria replicó: "tú no sabes lo que haces; si yo fuese desgraciado, tú quedarías cautiva entre los indios. Entonces, limpiándose las lágrimas con un pañuelo, dijo: "prefiero ser cautiva y no sirvienta de los federales, más cuando mi hermano ha sido asesinado por ellos."[54]

Some preferred to maintain their position as wives of Indian leaders instead of facing the rejection they would face if they returned. In chapter

65 of *Una excursión,* Mansilla reproduces a dialogue with Chief Ramón's wife Doña Fermina Zárate, whom he invites to return with him: "Oh, sir!" she answers bitterly, "and what am I going to do among the Christians?" ("¡Ah señor! . . . ¿y qué voy a hacer entre los cristianos?"). He suggests that her family in Carlota must miss her, but she refuses to leave her children. She adds:

> "Furthermore, sir, what life would be mine among the Christians, after so many years away from my people? I was young and attractive when they captured me. And now you see, I am old. I look like a Christian because Ramón allows me to dress as they do, but I live like an Indian; and, frankly, it seems to me I am more Indian than Christian, although I do believe in God."

> "Además señor, ¿qué vida sería la mía entre los cristianos, después de tantos años que falto de mi pueblo? Yo era joven y buena moza cuando me cautivaron. Y ahora ya ve, estoy vieja. Parezco cristiana porque Ramón me permite vestirme como ellas, pero vivo como indio; y, francamente, me parece que soy máas india que cristiana, aunque creo en Dios."

Even more revealing is Mansilla's response:

> "Despite being a captive you believe in God?" "And Him, how is it His fault that the Indians took me? The blame belongs with the Christians who don't know how to take care of their women and children." I did not answer; such high philosophy from the mouth of that woman, the retired concubine of a barbarian, humiliated me more than the windbag's sudden soliloquy.

> "¿A pesar de estar usted cautiva cree en Dios?" "¿Y El qué culpa tiene de que me agarraran los indios? La culpa la tendrán los cristianos que no saben cuidar sus mujeres ni sus hijos." No contesté; tan alta filosofía en boca de aquella mujer, la concubina jubilada de aquel bárbaro, me humilló más que el soliloquio a propósito del fuelle.

Mansilla's construction of opposites is interesting: high philosophy is set against the lowest person imaginable (the "retired concubine of a barbarian"), and the contrast generates surprise. Aside from this detail, the episode resembles the story of María López, a beautiful Spanish actress, "comedienne of the language," kidnapped by the Indian Catriel when she and her companions were shipwrecked en route to Buenos Aires. Ciro Bayo explains that

The Indians are polygamous and show a preference for white women; so the Spanish woman, a girl of twenty, was an appetizing morsel for the pampa. He made her cut her hair as a sign of captivity and entrusted her to the other women to teach her to spin and to make *chicha*. Once instructed, she became his favorite.

Los indios son polígamos y muestran preferencia por las mujeres blancas; de modo, que la española, joven de veinte años, resultaba para el pampa un bocado apetitoso. La hizo cortar el cabello en señal de cautividad y la confió a las demás mujeres para que la adiestraran a hilar y a hacer chicha. Una vez adiestrada la hizo su favorita.[55]

With time she adopts the customs of the Indians and shares with them the attacks of the whites, while, in contrast, there is no rescue attempt. When the country is pacified, she survives to recover her Spanish name. The narrator offers her a chance to return to the whites, saying: "You are free, you are an Argentine citizen." She refuses because she has two sons with Catriel and, like Doña Fermina Zárate, because

Here I am the chief's wife, the queen; in Buenos Aires I would be a detestable *china* whom they would lock up in an asylum. My destiny is to die in a hut and be buried on the pampa.

Aquí soy cacica, la reina; en Buenos Aires sería una china desprecia-ble, que encerrarían en un asilo. Mi destino es morir en una ruca y que me entierren en la pampa. (30)

The story, of course, does not end so sympathetically. Since the only thing that María López asks of her potential (and failed) liberator is some firewater, she becomes the object of his scorn: "In a moment that woman lost all the interest that I had felt for her; thirty years of captivity and contact with the Indians had made the unhappy woman a miserable being who found her nirvana in the brutalization of alcohol" (En un momento perdió aquella mujer para mí todo el interés que sentía por ella; treinta años de cautiverio y de roce con los indios habían hecho de aquella infeliz una miserable que encontraba su nirvana en el embrutecimiento del alcohol). As in Daireaux's story "Ha sido indio," the contamination of the *Other* remains like a sort of incurable atavism. At least Bayo ends up trying to explain to a gaucho why the Spanish woman prefers to be a *china*: "Haven't you heard it said that we all like to command, even if only a flock of sheep?" (¿No ha oído usted decir que a todos nos gusta mandar, aunque sea un hato de ovejas?) (31).

CAPTIVES AND THE WICKED

The existence of the captive herself is too uncomfortable to elicit any other reaction: she is one of us who has crossed a boundary and is no longer I nor they. She ceases to be recognizable, decipherable, or even capable of reproducing the pure white lineage that the nation desires for itself.

The texts written between 1830 and 1870 do not try to imagine what kidnapping can mean in the life of a person, the loss of her life and normalcy, servitude or captivity. Representing the frontier itself was hard enough for a nation with a project of homogeneity: the frontier was the margin of the possible, the place of contagion, populated not only by Indians but by every kind of gaucho, adventurer, and fugitive of the law. It was an intolerable place of disorder, of the untenable, of the unclassifiable.

It is not surprising, then, that in one of the last peace treaties, the 1878 accords between the national government and the indigenous tribes headed by Chiefs Epumer Rosas and Manuel Baigorria, the Indians are offered money, sugar, tobacco, soap, and whisky in exchange for pursuing "the Indian Gaucho robbers" and delivery of "the wicked Christians," the deserters and "all the captives, men, women or children, who inhabit or arrive at their lands or birthplace" without passports or license written by a frontier authority (a los indios Gauchos ladrones . . . a los malévolos cristianos . . . a todos los cautivos, hombres, mujeres o niños que asistan o lleguen a sus tierras o pagos).[56] The objective was to normalize the space with a recognizable and, above all, uniform project; in fact the language serves to maintain order and to suppress the arbitrariness and contingency of events. To classify is to give the world structure, to name is to divide and omit; to do so is always an act of violence perpetrated in the world and requires the support of a certain quantity of coercion.[57]

In writing, the captive women are equivalent to thieves, wicked ones, deserters: they are beyond the pale. Nor is it strange that soon after the signing of this unequal treaty the Conquista del Desierto began exterminating the Indians and every form of intolerable heterogeneity.

The problem of the captives is resolved: not because they are recovered and saved, but because the frontier has also been eliminated as a register of the existence of these women. The captive is no longer anywhere. The captive is no one.

I look in the *Merriam Webster's Collegiate Dictionary,* trying to define so many key words for this analysis. DISAPPEAR: to pass from view, to cease to be: pass out of existence or notice. The same word in Spanish, in the dictionary of María Moliner, also means to sweep away, to make vanish, to let the devil take it (*llevarse el diablo*), to dissipate, to eclipse, to bury, to obscure, to evaporate, to reduce to nothing. Such is the relation between cultural mechanisms of memory and oblivion, between the (in)existence of the captives and the disappeared of the dictatorship of the 1970s. I also look up OBLIVION: the fact or condition of forgetting or having forgotten; the Spanish *olvidar* has the additional meanings of to sepulcher, to omit, to abandon, to unlearn, to erase. NEGATE: the origin of the word ties negligence to negotiation; according to the dictionary it is to deny the existence or truth, to cause to be ineffective or invalid. All words related to the fate of a group of abandoned women who, in the end, embodied the fears and fantasies of a national project.

Another uncomfortable hypothesis explaining the disappearance of the captives is that the silence surrounding the past "implies culpability or bad conscience toward an individual or a stage that is uncomfortable to explain." On the disappearance of the Indians, Viñas says:

> Guilt or uneasiness [were] evinced by a silence that could be seen as the desire to hide the Indian one carried within. And a victorious elite cannot feel shame before retrospective doubts; if that group has God on its side, all that happens on its account is canonized, even its oldest perversions are considered exalting.[58]

Perhaps it would have been necessary to silence the Indian, the black within, or the horrific cries of pain for what was lost: the children, the identity, the sense. All that is different must disappear, must be negated, silenced, forgotten. Or as the dictionary says, let the devil take it.

Chapter 4

FRONTIER BODIES:
ESTEBAN ECHEVERRÍA'S *LA CAUTIVA*

Theories are everything; deeds in themselves matter little.

Las teorías son todo; los hechos por sí solos poco importan.

—Esteban Echeverría

Identity is a social construction, a creation, a system of interpretation or representation that is produced through the word, through images, through the repetition of collective rituals. The Bible describes this creative gesture of filling/creating the world: "In the beginning was the Word, and the Word was with God and the Word was God. He was in the beginning with God, and without Him was not anything made that was made."

I can find no better abstraction than the Bible's with which to approach the foundation of a national literature with Esteban Echeverría's *La cautiva* (The captive [1837]), a poem about a couple kidnapped by Indians on the Argentine frontier in which nothing is as it appears.[1] The Bible summarizes contemporary theories about nationhood and subjectivity, theories that are created by disciples or critics of Freud, Foucault, or Althusser. Word and Power, Word and Nation, Word and Knowledge. Language orders daily life, gives sense and meaning, marks the coordinates of society.[2] Through language the individual and the community think and understand: they are (we are) through it. As Heidegger said, Language is the House of Being. Identity inscribes itself in language: we speak and we are spoken. Interpellation and ideology.

Drawing the landscapes and protagonists of the frontier, Echeverría's *La cautiva* reproduces Prospero's gesture upon arriving at the island and taking possession of the territory as well as its barbarians. This is the gesture of the creator: "In the beginning God created the heavens and the earth. The earth was without form and void," and God filled the void. God filled the void with light, stars, waters, twilights, plants, animals, men; writers filled the space with words. The void of the desert is covered with representation: this does not mean that the enormous space of the pampa was literally empty, but that in the process of re-creating it through the Word the pampa was appropriated, interpreted, and invented under a selective gaze. We will see at what price.

The nation is, in the end, also a narrative strategy. In an era of confrontations as absolute as that between Rosas's Federales and the Unitarios of the lettered elite, one and another throw themselves into the project of writing the nation. Each side proposes cultural differences and identifications of class, race, gender; each side uses writing as a *performative* instrument, invoking these identifications in the historic present. Adolfo Prieto maintains, in fact, that Rosas's caesarism forced the genesis of the Asociación de Mayo.[3] Writing against writing: Don Juan Manuel de Rosas — whose hegemony would last from 1829 to 1852 — ceaselessly circulates his "messages," increasing the weight of censorship as his own power grows. Between 1836 and 1837 his intellectual underling Pedro de Angelis publishes no less than seven volumes of the *Colección de Obras y Documentos Relativos a la Historia Antigua y Moderna de las Provincias del Río de la Plata* and responds to the anti-Rosas propaganda of the *Revista de Dos Mundos* through *El Archivo Americano* and *La Gaceta*.[4] Over a century later, the confrontation between narrative versions is still fascinating, in particular because Rosas's great force was not enough to triumph in the long run as the constitutive image of History.

The nascent Argentine nationalism of the postindependence period is obsessed with the two ideas: the conflict between civilization and barbarism and the project of filling/creating with words.[5] This chapter reflects on the concealments of language, or how the discursive field can *deform* realities by describing them — imagining them, reinventing them, repeating one version: *it is as I say, no matter how it is or was before I spoke of it.* To write, to repeat, are in this sense *performative:* cultural acts, critical perspectives, political interventions.[6] Writing is a way of culturally transmitting (and constructing) social memory. Which version of the present will remain for posterity? Which will be accepted within the macronarrative of national identity? Few cases are so clear as this one: Rosas's enemies were doubtless much more capable in the construction of monuments of memory, understanding as such texts like Esteban Echeverría's *La cautiva* and "El matadero" (The slaughter-house), José Marmol's *Amalia,* or Sarmiento's *Facundo: Civilización y barbarie.* Their works became part of school curricula, while de Angelis is read today only by specialists.[7]

In the beginning, then, is the Word. The Word is the matter, a sort of "filling" that explains and allows thought, but only within the conditions of that word. Knowledge, Being, the opposite of Nothing. Latin America can offer few examples that show as clearly as Argentine literature this relationship between reality and the word, writing and identity, the word and power. Sarmiento may be the best example to explain the generative function of the intellectual; not far behind is Esteban Echeverría, who went so far as to attest in the sentence cited as this chapter's epigraph: *"Theories are everything; deeds in themselves matter little."*[8]

Throughout the nineteenth century, the lettered elite founds the national literature: the representation of identity. In the verbiage of *Facundo: Civilización y barbarie* or Echeverría's "El matadero" and *La cautiva* we find, in some way, the nation.[9] Through the generative force of these texts other sculptors of the word have been launched, modifying, displacing, actualizing these representations that summarize (order, engender) the identity of the nation.

AN ASIDE: IDENTITY AND LANGUAGE

Again and again the organization of the word — the Knowledge of the Nation — tends toward the same system: civilization and barbarism. If social thought is essentially collective memory that survives because of the repetition of the same scene in anecdote after anecdote and text after text, then the self-image of that community always operates within a very precise frame. It is like what happens during early childhood: we remember the anecdotes that the family repeats about each of us; the rest remains hazy. What is not there, what is not part of the literary repetitions, the official and pedagogical rituals, has nowhere to take hold. What is left out of the order of the word (historical enclaves, undesirable areas of reality) remains in the margin of the foundation of identity, of culture. That of which no one speaks (captive women, blacks), that which has no mourners, no words and no monuments, is lost: collective memory exists through the force of narratives. It is also clear, however, that what is excluded still remains, even in the very act of exclusion. Language manipulates and constructs, and — speaking — it silences.

ANOTHER ASIDE: IN THE BEGINNING WAS THE ENEMY

In the formation of national cultures an originative mechanism is found: it is a scheme of confrontations. To define who I am (as a community, as an individual), I construct, delimit, define the enemy, the Other, the one who is different from me.[10] This makes my own being more clear: I am not that.

To the extent that it is valid to summarize the history of a country in the schematization of two figures, the simplest would be the representative binarism Sarmiento/Rosas — signifying the oppositions civility/violence, education/savagery, presidency/dictatorship, elites/people — that still holds sway over Argentine culture today.

Nonetheless, considering the question more carefully, the figure that orders nineteenth-century thought, paradoxical as it may seem, is Juan Manuel de Rosas, the bête noire of lettered Argentines (and of Sarmiento himself: *Facundo* was also a political pamphlet against the dictator). It is as if all the great literature were created as a reaction to or against the Restorer, as if Sarmiento could not have existed without Rosas. The simplified notion that to recognize the concept of Good, one must also understand Evil is both unacceptably Manichaean and inadequate; here the figures in play (these two antitheses) participate in the dance of Power. The rest neither matter nor have been invited to the discussion.

More than racial confrontation, what is *verbalized* in Argentina is a political conflict between power-groups with different projects (Federales/Unitarios, conservatives/liberals). This is another reason why the customary practice of eliminating minorities and all those who are different remains outside the discursive field. Within such a polemicizing culture, this is one of the disappearances of History and Culture, and in this sense the captive women join the Indians, blacks, and the presumed militant political opposition of more recent history. The word centers on the internal debates of those who have access to public space (and fill it with their versions); and the right hand does not know (or does not care) what the left hand does. The word re-creates only some fragments and silences others: those referring to the minorities and the different, to the poor, the laborers, the illegal immigrants.

Rosas's dictatorship is the context of the writing of *La cautiva*. Almost all the writers of the century were in one way or another affected by the Restorer: they were persecuted and exiled, they censored themselves or were complicit with the regime. Rosas remains even twenty years later as an indelible presence in the works of his nephew, Lucio V. Mansilla. Only the consolidation of the liberal State by the Generation of 1880 would reduce Rosas's shadow to normal size. Or at least reduce it.

It is, then, a literature written as a polemic *against,* a cultural identity constructed *against.* Every enemy acquires the same tint: gauchos, Federales, raiding Indians; Rosas is the demon, and every other fringe to be eliminated is given, through concomitance or obsessive association, the same treatment. It is a supreme confrontation of will between sides: literature seems only to care about which project will be imposed not only upon the Other, but upon reality as a whole. This obsession explains, to a large extent, the writing of Esteban Echeverría.

INEVITABLY ROSAS

The Desert Expedition of 1833 was carried out under the nominal command of General Juan Facundo Quiroga. As he became ill, he delegated command of the divisions to Brigadier José Féliz Aldao and Generals José Ruiz Huidobro and Juan Manuel de Rosas; the last of these had obtained all the support for the expedition and was the most successful. The expedition lasted thirteen months and, in addition to producing the document *Relación de los cristianos salvados del cautiverio por la División Izquierda del Ejército expedicionario contra los bárbaros, al mando del señor brigadier general D. Juan Manuel de Rosas*[11] and liberating captives by force or trickery, served to cement Rosas's ascent to power. Tulio Halperín Donghi explains:

> [Rosas's] incursion into Indian territory allows him, . . . as he desires, to be simultaneously present and absent during the development of the political crisis. Balcarce's government, to whose detriment the business is planned, nonetheless finances it (nothing seems more reasonable than the jewel of the province undertaking a campaign organized to benefit the collective interest). Rosas, on the other hand, watches with a jealousy some of his supporters judge excessive his successor's willingness to sustain financially such a meritorious undertaking: between 1833 and 1834 it was to receive $3,368,590, of which $1,197,406 is personally entrusted to the expedition's leader.[12]

Success not only produces a juicy compensation (Rosas received seventy leagues of territory in payment for the liberation of the captives), but also reaffirms Rosas's image as the only leader strong enough to unite sectors, establish control, and advance the interests of the landholders.[13]

When Esteban Echeverría writes *La cautiva* in 1837, he is writing, among other reasons, to answer or question the success of Rosas's desert expedition and its documentary product, the *Relación* delivered to public knowledge just two years before. We must remember that in the nineteenth century the indigenous raid was a symbol of barbarism, of instability; to subdue the Indians was to establish order. For that reason Rosas's political strategy was extremely effective because he debilitated the government and at the same time appeared as the conqueror of the frontier. For his lettered enemies, however, the political order embodied in the tyrannical figure of Juan Manuel de Rosas was too much to tolerate, and dramatizing the savagery of the raids in the poem *La cautiva* was a way to reestablish the Unitarios in the collective imagination. The frontier is actualized, the danger continues, the subject is current. Not only has Rosas failed to conquer the frontier, he embodies it.[14]

Echeverría, who would later write "El matadero" (The slaughterhouse) — in which Rosas appears as a character — uses the raid to create an allegory of current barbarism: the protagonists Brián and María, like the elegant Unitario horseman captured by the hordes in "El matadero," are the avant garde of the civilizing project that falls victim to the unbridled masses. In both texts the protagonists embody the white, civilized paradigm that the Unitarios were trying to impose; in both texts, as Francine Masiello notes, masculine discourse is feminized as a form of "civilized" resistance to barbarism.[15]

It is curious that, also in both texts, the death of the protagonists is not directly produced by the enemy, but occurs instead as a consequence of their savage customs. The Unitario in "El matadero" dies almost out of pride, incapable of resisting the violence of the offenses against him, while in *La cautiva* the heroes die during their flight across the desert, when they are no longer among the Indians. The allegorical implications of the impossibility of *coexisting* with the Other (whether that Other be Rosas's followers or the Indians) are clear: coexistence leads to the death of the fatherland. Civilization or barbarism. Identity and difference.[16]

THE POEM AND THE DESERT

Of course, Echeverría's success in his own day was not based on describing exactly what his enemy's document omitted. The enormous approbation of *La cautiva* was due to the poem's marking a path that had seemed impossible for the skeptical lettered party: as Juan María Gutiérrez and brothers Florencio and Juan Cruz Varela noted at the time, its merit was to find elements worthy of poetry in what were considered a desolate landscape and a dubious human nature.

The canon is born: this is the first "national poem." Although the poem effectively renews the lyric with romantic effects — effects which Noé Jitrik has thoroughly examined — its force is not really due to metric variations, the epic narration of anonymous heroes, and the poeticization of an overwhelming reality.[17] What awes the generation of 1837 is the incorporation of the landscape. Even when Domingo F. Sarmiento publishes

Facundo — the book that has most marked the way in which Argentine culture imagines itself — years later, the first chapters ratify the importance of Echeverría's achievement.

Sarmiento, fascinated by the idea of taking descriptions to the "limit between barbarous and civilized life," acclaims the "Argentine bard" for finding the key to imagining a national literature by looking to the desert, the limitless immensity, "the solitudes in which the savage wanders" (las soledades en que vaga el salvaje), "the distant region of fire the traveler sees approach when the countryside ignites" (la lejana zona de fuego que el viajero ve acercarse cuando los campos se incendian).[18] As Echeverría himself said in the prologue to his *Rimas:* "The Desert is ours, it is our richest patrimony" (El Desierto es nuestro, es nuestro más pingüe patrimonio); that is, in it one finds "our aggrandizement and well-being" and also "our national literature" (nuestro engrandecimiento y bienestar ... nuestra literatura nacional).

La cautiva founds a national literature whose discursive practice is anchored to space. The frontier of fire, the empty landscape clamoring to be possessed, the limit between civilization and barbarism: more than simple tropes, they are the foundation, the very engineering, of the great Argentine literature of the nineteenth century. And it must be understood that "desert" does not mean dry or sterile territory, but rather open and fertile land: it is the immense pampa, the void that must be filled with words and, at the same time, must be militarily possessed — national wealth and literature.

La cautiva synthesizes subjects scarcely touched previously — as Carlos Altamirano and Beatriz Sarlo explain — "through which it responds, in the realm of the imaginative, to questions effectively present in society: the relationship between urban, Christian-European civilization and the barbarous countryside, where the limits between the organized rural world and the desert world, that is Indian space, are erased, limits that culture repeats again and again in the frontier towns, and that the raid makes permanently contentious." They add, "Over the iconography of the desert the virtues of culture are drawn, over the cruelty of Indian space, the qualities of the Creoles of European origin, over the force of arms, the spiritual force of a new feminine archetype."[19] In this way, then, the landscape of *La cautiva* functions as "a metaphor of collective belonging,"[20] while her body serves as a map of exclusions.

This discourse of space is constructed over the notion of limit and the space of the margin: the unstable periphery (the frontier) serves a discourse of the strong center (the city).[21] Desert, limit, periphery, margin: frontier.

A PAPER GEOGRAPHY

The concept of a "discourse of space" is problematic in the case of the concrete corpus of Argentine literature that spans from the Generation of 1837 to the 1870 writing of *Una excursión a los indios ranqueles* by Lucio V. Mansilla, the author who in turn most influenced the Generation of 1880. It is problematic because with the exception of Mansilla's, none of the texts included in this temporal arc is really about a journey to the frontier or, for that matter, a text of intercultural encounter.

If the internal frontier is the very essence of *the writable,* then to write it, to draw it as a void, as a wilderness that waits to be reached by the word and by progress, is to eliminate it as such. The text of the landscape of the national is ordered, manipulated, designed. The ambivalent and the undefinable are eliminated: it is not coincidental that *Una excursión a los indios ranqueles* ends with a map of the territory drawn by Mansilla himself.

That *Desierto,* the counterpoint of the nation about to be designed, does not function as the contact zone that Pratt has described, nor as the space of journey James Clifford understands as a place where bipolarity is eliminated; much to the contrary, its invocation will allow the construction of clear notions of friends and enemies.[22] *La cautiva* and its design of the desert as a place of the abject are worthy examples. The abject is the frontier, *mestizaje,* barbarism, uncontrol, the sexualized body, the Other. And there, between one side of the frontier and the other, the uncontrollable short circuit occurs: the raid.

Few images could embody the fears of the white project as well as the raid. In *La cautiva* it represents at least two levels of meaning: in the textual space, that of the Indians and the whites; in the extratextual space, the "noble" Creoles versus the rest (blacks, mulattos, Indians, and Rosistas). Echeverría describes the landscape, but later it is pure sound: the "thunderclap," "distant rumbles," "deaf and confused clamor" are heard; the wind howls with such noise that it produces "terror" in the "brutes" (*EOC* 456). Later comes the trembling of the ground, the rising dust, flying spears, heads, "And like naked forms / Of strange and cruel aspect" approaches the "insensible throng" that "with its shriek disturbs / the silent solitudes" (Y como formas desnudas / De aspecto extraño y cruel... la insensata turba... con su alarido perturba, / las calladas soledades). The textual violence grows:

> Where do they go? Whence do they come?
> What is the source of their pleasure?
> Why do they shout, run, fly

Clutching their spurs into the brutes,
Without looking around?
Look! at their fierce postures.
As spoils, hanging from their spears,
They carry human heads,
Whose inflamed eyes
Still breathe fury.

¿Dónde va? ¿De dónde viene?
¿De qué su gozo proviene?
¿Por qué grita, corre, vuela
Clavando al bruto la espuela,
Sin mirar alrededor?
¡Ved! que las plantas ufanas.
De sus lanzas, por despojos,
Llevan cabezas humanas,
Cuyos inflamados ojos
Respiran aún furor.

This Christian nightmare, complete with virgins, martyrs, and demons, shows, more than the foundation of Argentine romantic poetry, the definition of a country that will not tolerate cultural or racial differences. The language grows increasingly extreme in *La cautiva:* during the celebration the captive women, "all young and beautiful," are juxtaposed with drunken Indians, hitting each other and taking directly into their mouths the blood that bubbles out of the neck of a freshly slaughtered mare (*EOC* 457). The poem says of the Indians, literally, that "like thirsty vampires, / they drink, suck, savor / The blood, murmuring / And with blood fill themselves" (como sedientos vampiros, / Sorben, chupan, saborean / La sangre, haciendo murmullo / Y de sangre se rellenan...), given over completely to "the vile pleasure / of the sabbath celebration" (al torpe gozo / De la sabática fiesta). A footnote by the author explains: "Nocturnal gathering of malignant spirits, according to tradition communicated to the Christian peoples by the Jews" (Junta nocturna de espíritus malignos, según tradición comunicada a los pueblos cristianos por los judíos) (*EOC* 458).

Returning to the design of spaces: the *Desierto* will be outside (the negative). Inside (the urban modernizing project) will be positive.[23] The *Desierto* will be invented as landscape and populated by savage enemies: the Indian can be inscribed in this space of the Other, but so can the gaucho cavalry — according to the era — and, of course, Rosas. Multiple forms of violence play across the physical space; and in the monologic writing produced there is no place for the captive and her polysemic body, the disturbing, real flesh of the frontier.

More than thirty years have passed when Mansilla cites Echeverría's nature descriptions. Mansilla refers to Echeverría despite having, on previous pages, contradicted his assertions. Mansilla declares, for example, that on the pampa there are no *ombú* trees, and in doing so cancels the powerful final images of *La cautiva*'s epilogue, in which a humble cross and a gigantic *ombú* of "verdant tresses" are said to signal the place where the protagonists are buried.

The *ombú* negated by Mansilla is not the only thing that abounds in the nature that all proclaim as the locus of their culture — or perhaps more accurately, the locus of what can be "literized" and made their own.[24] What is paradoxical is that, as has been said, Echeverría's contemporaries celebrated *La cautiva* for its ability to represent the national landscape: it is paradoxical because that space is not entirely real.[25] Echeverría mythifies the desert as a sterile wasteland, "exalting only its negative aspects."[26] It is the same desert, of course, for whose extraordinary fertility farmers and soldiers fought, beginning with Rosas himself. The extermination of the Indian, the consolidation of the rural estates, the disappearance of the gaucho: none of this originated in a sterile wasteland. That is the mere allegory of barbarism.

In the beginning was the Word and its exclusive vision of the world. The rest does not matter.

EQUIVOCATION AS CANON

La cautiva establishes several Argentine literary traditions: the European quotation as the narrative's frame, the landscape more textual than real, the imperative to fill the spatial voids, to make the gauchesque cultured, to show the barbarian as the extreme of horror.[27]

But the most important of the traditions *La cautiva* founds is in the way the poem arms itself through a chain of equivocations. The real captive is not María, the *cautiva* of the title who manages to escape from her captor, but her husband, Brián, a *cautivo*: "Captive he is, but he sleeps; / Immobile, forceless, disarmed" (Cautivo es, pero duerme; / Inmoble, sin fuerza, inerme) (*EOC* 461). The feminine title, in other words, is already a mistake: it gestures toward the wrong gender, completing a purely symbolic function of deus ex machina.

In addition to the title, whose arbitrariness Ezequiel Martínez Estrada noted decades ago, Brián's captivity is itself equivocal. According to the testimonials of the time, the Indians preferred to retain women and children, and killed the majority of the men.[28] A. Guinnard confirms:

> In their expeditions, the Indians do not respect women of age or men: they murder them. They do not forgive absolutely anyone but the young women, whom they make their privileged wives under affectionate relations. The very young children become slaves, charged with the care of their animals, when they are not sold to Indians of distant tribes.

> En sus expediciones, los indios no respetan a las mujeres de edad ni a los hombres; los asesinan. No perdonan absolutamente más que a las mujeres jóvenes, de quienes hacen sus mujeres privilegiadas bajo la relación del afecto. Los niños muy jovenes pasan a ser esclavos, a cuyo cuidado confían sus animales, cuando no los venden a los indios de tribus alejadas.[29]

Vicuña Mackenna describes a raid:

> There was the most coveted portion of the spoil, which is the woman, because the savage of the pampa counts his glory by the number of his captive women and his power by the number of sons they give him. Like packs of wolves on the defenseless sheepfold they fell on the families, who, kneeling in terrified tumult, directed entreaties to the Virgin in their affliction; and in a moment each one of those unfortunate females had a fierce master who separated her from her mother, from her children, from her immolated husband. More than two hundred fifty women and a great number of children were taken in this way.

> Allí estaba la parte más codiciada de su botín, que es la mujer, porque la gloria del salvaje de la pampa se cuenta por el número de sus cautivas y su poder por el número de los hijos que éstas le dan. Como cuadrillas de lobos en el indefenso redil cayeron sobre las familias, que arrodilladas en pavoroso tumulto, dirigían a la Virgen plegarias en su aflicción; y en un momento cada una de esas desgraciadas tuvo un dueño feroz que la apartaba ya de la madre, ya de los hijos, ya del esposo inmolado. Más de doscientas cincuenta mujeres y un gran número de niños fueron tomados de esta suerte.[30]

Carlos A. Mayo explains that there were two kinds of captured men: recently taken adults who might manage to flee, mistrusted by the Indians as potential traitors, and those who would ultimately be adopted and even join the raids against the whites. But the male captives' average age was only thirteen, while the women — who numbered twice as many — averaged around twenty-one years of age.[31]

Brián is a majestic soldier, "accustomed to conquering" (*EOC* 471). He is described more as a heroic icon of the Independence Wars than one of the many soldiers recruited to protect the frontier. "The Andes saw my steel / Resplendent with honor / Oh din of arms! Oh intoxication of victory! Oh lances of combat!" (Los Andes vieron mi acero / Con honor resplandecer / ¡Oh estrépito de las armas! ¡Oh embriaguez de la victoria! ¡Oh lances del combatir!) (*EOC* 472). Another impossibility, given that the ranks of the army sent to the frontier essentially consisted of vagrants and gauchos in trouble with the law, who chose between prison and military service.[32] Brián's name is another equivocation, and its English resonance has more than once caused confusion in a critical reading. It has also been suggested that the protagonists are a pair of colonists (?), an Englishman married to a *criolla,* who are captured with their young daughter; the truth is that in *La cautiva* there is no daughter, only a male child.[33] Verses written by Lord Byron appear as the poem's epigraph: the allusion to the English poet contributes to the confusion about the nationality of the hero, whose name, "Brián," may be an anagram for "Byron."[34]

In the poem, to focus on a concrete example, María and Brián are captured by a raid, but it is she who organizes Brián's rescue. Somehow — her actions are not described — María gets hold of a dagger, murders an Indian in the middle of the night, and awakens her unconscious husband. Then, invested with a supernatural, masculine strength, María initiates their defense and escape, acts that are futile since the debilitated Brián will inevitably die. María's strength is so great that she crosses the pampa carrying Brián like a child and defeats a tiger with her glare. Another of the narrative's incongruencies arises when Brián dies: only then does María remember that she must also rescue her young son. She dies of desperation when the troops inform her that the boy has been killed by the Indians.

More could not be asked of a woman: supernatural strength to save the others and maintain her own virtue, defenselessness at the hour of surviving for herself alone. Sarmiento will later explain the role so clearly demonstrated in the character of María in the expectations of feminine behavior outlined in *Recuerdos de provincia* and his articles for the magazine *La moda:*

> Mothers of families one day, wives, they would have said to the barbarism a government blows forth: do not come near my door,

thinking you would extinguish with your breath the sacred fire of civilization and morality that twenty years ago was confided in us.

Madres de familia un día, esposas, habrían dicho a la barbarie que sopla un gobierno: no entraréis en mis umbrales, que apagaríais con vuestro hálito el fuego sagrado de la civilización y la moral que hace veinte años nos confiaron. (*Recuerdos,* 91)

The sacred fire of civilization and the family, in the hands of this woman who more than a wife seems the protective mother of her debilitated husband. Echeverría confirms this by beginning the poem with verses by Lord Byron: "Female hearts are such a genial soil / For kinder feelings, whatsoe'er their nation, / They naturally pour the 'wine and oil' / Samaritans in every situation." The author himself translates the verses as: "En todo clima el corazón de la mujer es tierra fértil en afecto generoso; ellas en cualquier circunstancia de la vida saben, como la Samaritana, prodigar el óleo y el vino."

The announcement of the death of the son, which weighs heavily as the narrative ending of the poem, is nevertheless part of the chain of equivocations: the boy's death is actually announced in the third section, when María first appears ("of my tender son and my mother / Unjust death to avenge" [de mi hijo tierno y mi madre / La injusta muerte vengar] says the protagonist [*EOC* 462]). The information is reiterated in the eighth canto, when Brián tells his beloved: "'You know? His hands were washed, / with hellish exultation / in the blood of my son'" ("¿Sabes? — sus manos lavaron, / con infernal regocijo, / En la sangre de mi hijo") (*EOC* 470). This is the very canto that produces the equivocation when it ends with Brián's dying words to María: "'Goodbye, in vain I afflict you ... / Live, live for your son'" ("Adiós, en vano te aflijo ... / Vive, vive para tu hijo") (*EOC* 472), a command that she obeys until the following canto, when soldiers inform her that her son's throat has been cut (*EOC* 474).

The place of the equivocation is the true space of the founding: a frontier that is mentioned and invented, but not seen (much less visited), characters who do not exist (the beginning of the poem states that the raid killed the couple's child, but the dying Brián tells María, "'Live, live for your son, / God imposes that duty upon you'" ["Vive, vive para tu hijo, / Dios te impone ese deber"] [*EOC* 472]), enemies who are caricatures of savagery, mixed styles. A literature that locates itself on the internal frontier (not an international border), a literature that misreads and is misread. A literature, perhaps most importantly, that leaves aside the captive herself, her never-described body, her never-told reality.

THE CAPTIVE BODY

Who, then, is María? Brián's origin and the equivocations it produces have been discussed, but who is the poem's protagonist? It is safe to suppose that if *La cautiva* alluded to the internal frontier scourged by indigenous raids, the "angels" like María inhabited a space defined in the nineteenth century as diseased: "on the threshold of the pampa was our internal leprosy. There our movement was paralyzed; there we lost without recovering. That region of our body was sick" (en el dintel de la pampa estaba nuestra lepra interna. Allí paralizaba nuestro movimiento; allí perdíamos sin recuperar. Aquel contorno de nuestro cuerpo estaba enfermo).[35] What inhabitants could occupy that diseased space of the nation? Certainly not the "decent people."

Reflecting on mobility and stasis in textual representations of women, María Lugones asks why they move, who moves and where, whom they meet, why they wish to go there. Each response is different according to the woman, her social class, and race. Each person in the society has a point on the map, with roads that go from one to another; many are prescribed, but always to someone's benefit.[36] Following this logic, which point on the map does María occupy? Which roads does she find, and who travels them? Who benefits?

Contradictorily or not, the "Angel" of the text, extrapolated from the text to the space of historical reality, was one of the many women who accompanied the troops, the *fortineras* or *cuarteleras,* as they were called: as the wife of a soldier María is probably one of these. I find the temptation to reconstruct the scene of the raid that precedes the poem *La cautiva* — the event Echeverría neglects to describe — irresistible. A group of ragged soldiers, not having received in weeks their rations of cookies, mate, soap, and cigarettes, sleep with their wives in the stifling heat, their dogs and mules left as sentinels. Howls awaken them late at night: the raiding party is already upon them, ravaging the camp. Brián and María are taken captive, along with many others.

María, then, the famous María of the poem, must have been a *cuartelera:* a drawing-room lady would not have married a soldier destined for the frontier. As Alfredo Ebelot wrote of these women:

The frontline corps recruit and take in tow during their peregrinations through the provinces almost as many women as you count soldiers. The State tolerates and even encourages this custom. It willingly provides these women with rations in the camps and horses in case of journeys, and concerns itself with the education of their children.

Los cuerpos de línea reclutan en sus peregrinations a través de las provincias y llevan consigo a remolque casi tantas mujeres como cuentas los soldados. El Estado tolera y hasta favorece esta costumbre. Provee a estas criaturas de buena voluntad con raciones en los campamentos, caballos en caso de viaje y se ocupa de la educación de sus hijos.[37]

Ebelot adds:

[T]hese skirted recruits rapidly assimilate the *espirit de corps,* take pleasure in the barracks and do not leave it. I have seen a toothless old woman... following on horseback, with her skinny legs, the end of a marching column, receiving the same attentions — and perhaps more — than her young companions: they were veterans.

Esas reclutas con polleras asimilan rápidamente el espíritu de cuerpo, le toman gusto al cuartel y no lo dejan más. He visto una anciana sin dientes... seguir cabalgando con sus piernas flácidas, a continuación de una columna en marcha y ser objeto de las mismas atenciones — y tal vez más — que sus jóvenes compañeras: eran veteranas.[38]

We can assume, then, that prior to the raid María, like all the *cuarteleras,* washed Brián's uniform, cooked turnovers and fried cakes, cared for the animals, gave birth, and perhaps even offered advice as a healer.

This versatile and heroic woman, without whose presence and that of others like her the troops would have lost morale, is totally absent from *La cautiva.* The *cuarteleras* neither exist nor have their own points on the map, even though they had gone to the frontier to fight along with their husbands or companions. But neither the roads nor the texts benefited them, those women who were unknown forever whether or not they lived out their days as captives.

The captive is, in Echeverría's poem, another literary cliché. Her body is scarcely mentioned: at the beginning of the poem it is a shadow that murders, acts, and speaks, but only a shadow. The scant physical descriptions that the text allows her arise only at the time of Brián's death and correspond to clichés of Spanish womanhood, repeating the typical gestures of narratives about captives. Echeverría's decision to leave aside the captive herself, despite the poem's title and the fact that she is, in practice, its heroine, is the most revealing aspect of the text. Because it is one thing to caricature the Other/enemy (the Indian as drunken demon) and another to face the unnamable, the unspeakable, the unclassifiable: the captive woman is one of ours who no longer pertains to us. In the third canto the protagonists, María and Brián, appear for the first time. It is unclear whether she was with the other captives or has come from outside, after the celebration, to rescue Brián, whose capture has already been narrated.

The poem must ascertain that María is not a captive in every sense of the word — a white woman possessed by an Indian — so that the diegesis may continue: only if she does not bear the stigma of rape can there be a narrative. María, the timid damsel whose dagger drips indigenous blood, cuts Brián's bonds and kisses him awake from his faint. Love has made her pass through innumerable trials, but Brián does not recognize her: he says, "'Are you some soul / that I can and should love? / Are you an errant spirit, / Good or fallen angel / Part of my fantasy?' / 'My common name is María, Your guardian angel am I'" ("¿Eres alguna alma / que pueda y deba querer? / ¿Eres espíritu errante, / Angel bueno, o vacilante / Parte de mi fantasía?" / "Mi vulgar nombre es María, Angel de tu guarda soy").

They kiss and soon, "as if in his soul sprung forth / a horrible idea" (como si en su alma brotara / horrible idea), Brián says to her, "'María, I am unhappy, / You are no longer worthy of me. The obscenity of the savage / Must have spoiled the purity / Of your honor, and sullied / Your body sanctified / By my affection and your love; / It is no longer my lot to love you'" ("María, soy infelice, / Ya no eres digna de mí. Del salvaje la torpeza / Habrá ajado la pureza / De tu honor, y mancillado / Tu cuerpo sanctificado / Por mi cariño y tu amor; / Ya no me es dado quererte").

Who is not worthy of whom? According to the poem, if María had been stained, that is, if she had been raped or had sexually cohabited with an Indian, even if by force, she would no longer be worthy of Brián. It does not matter that he, the heroic soldier, has been stripped of his honor by allowing himself to be beaten in combat by a savage: it matters that she has suddenly lost her identity (guardian angel, good angel), that she has become unrecognizable, unlabelable, that she no longer adequately fills her role. The process is familiar: the guilty, stigmatized party is the victim herself: if she has been unable to resist, she is abominable.

If Echeverría had intended to fulfill the poem's title, *La cautiva,* the narrative would have paused here to tell her true history, the history of the frontier between cultures. But the text does not take it up, as no Argentine work of the nineteenth century takes it up. For the text to continue, María must be normalized, must be made clearly one of "ours" for the national project. So she immediately responds: "'listen / On this steel is written /

My purity and my joy, / My tenderness and my valor / Look at this bloody dagger / And your proud heart / Will leap with pleasure'" ("advierte / Que en este acero está escrito / Mi pureza y mi delito, / Mi ternura y mi valor / Mira este puñal sangriento / Y saltará de contento / Tu corazón orgulloso") (*EOC* 461–62). She goes on to explain that Chief Loncoy failed to seduce her and died, murdered by her; it is curious that at the time of this dialogue the son (and thus maternity) has already been killed, although his death is withheld from the logic of the tale until the end.

The first dialogue of the poem serves to signal that María's body is not stained, to approve it, to erase the suspicion of stigma and of an ir-redeemable *mark* (the sign of her belonging to the other world), and to affirm the unvanquished body of the woman or the body of the frontier. A body marked by the Indian (a woman's body, because for a man there is no visible stigma but language and customs, signs that can be erased, substituted) is a body lost, a body that is best forgotten, left behind, unrecognized.

The poem affirms in its title, *La cautiva,* something that the body of the text denies: the text is a body that denies another body the right to exist in its insistence that the captive cannot be a *cautiva.* That foundational gesture of negation, and the contradiction of describing as "civilized" something that in reality has already been condemned as barbaric, will occupy the Argentine imagination of the nineteenth century. The captive (the real individual called a captive) ceases to exist: no one knows where to put her, in which part of the story (or the narrative of history) to deposit her; no one knows how to tell her story, nor does anyone seriously try to know her.

It is worth remembering that this period also saw the initiation of an entire series of visual representations of the Indian raids and the taking of captives. Probably the most representative case is that of the German painter Rugendas, who repeatedly painted kidnappings. This does not mean that the captives of reality would have found a place in the paintings; Rugendas, after all, painted from his reading of Esteban Echeverría's poem. The poem, in turn, was later published with Rugendas's illustrations, in a cultural contamination in which what each imagined was reproduced in the other like a play of mirrors.[39]

The painter's gaze reproduces (and reinforces, in the sense in which every cultural artifact, every space in visual culture, every monument of memory does) a system of ordering the world. In *Pehuenches: The Raid, Parley for the Exchange of Captives,* from 1838, for example, the painter has incorporated even the idiom of the colonial era by representing the white men as conquistadors; the captive women are perhaps lashed, in the indistinct background, perhaps extending their hands begging for help on the left, to the right one seems to cry.

In *Pehuenche: The Taking of a Captive,* also of 1838, the visual axes of the scene converge on the bosom of the captive, a bosom that is contradictorily uncovered, but apparently not naked. This strange image occurs obsessively in all of the tales.

In *Pehuenches: The Raid, Combat,* of the same year, once again the visual lines converge on the captive, or on her breast. Here disorder prevails; all is so confusing that it is unclear if the lances belong to gauchos or Indians; we assume that it is a drawing of an Indian raid basically because our cultural prejudices provide information the painting leaves out: that the captive is a white, Spanish victim of evil, that the disorder is only attributable to the savages, that these beseeching figures cannot be other than persons who beg to be rescued by the good people, that is, the whites. But if we look closely, the scene may just as well depict a raid by whites, especially if we remember descriptions like the following:

> The cavalry, like an avalanche of soulless men, came crashing onto the villages of the Argentine countryside, slaughtered the flocks, sacked the habitations and carried off the women; and from the orgy of the celebration that lit up the camps and the lighted roofs, departed victors and vanquished, men and women, possessed by the same vertigo of pillage and blood to which some had just fallen victim. The women fought like furies in the struggle.

> La montonera, como avalancha de hombres desalmados, se desplomaba sobre las villas de las campañas argentinas, degollaba los rebaños, saqueaba las habitaciones y robaba las mujeres; y de la orgía del festín que iluminaba los campos y las techumbres incendiadas, partían vencedores y vencidos; hombres y mujeres, poseídos ya del mismo vértigo de pillaje y de sangre de que acaban los unos de ser víctimas. Las mujeres peleaban como furias en los combates. (*Recuerdos,* 103)

Rugendas's best-known image is without a doubt *Pampas: The Taking of the Captive*. It adds, like the others, to the chain of confusions. We have here the very synthesis of the imaginary of capture: mobility, confusion, animality. It is unclear whether the black dog pursues the Indian or accompanies him; the kidnapper is dark and diabolical, but the face in shadows could have a beard, which confuses his real identity — only the historical context could assure that the figure is an Indian. It is unclear whether the figures running behind are fleeing Indians or avengers. The white woman gazing up to heaven like a Renaissance Virgin is fascinating. The cultural code is clearer than ever: a Christian martyr, tied and already lost — the detail of the slipped shoulder of her dress is enough to indicate chaos, unspeakable sexuality. This white face is an autonomous value for the reader of the era to defend: the painting as a whole depicts captivity as an allegory of evil and perdition. This woman would have represented the future of the nation if natural and savage forces had not destroyed her purity and her destiny. The tropes are consistent in other artists' paintings, such as Angel della Valle's oil painting *The Return of the Raid* (*La vuelta del malón*), after Rugendas's probably the best-known painting of the subject.[40]

The eroticism of Rugendas's paintings, eventual companions of the first national poem, was recognized by Sarmiento:

The infinite pampa and the cloud effects of the background, partially confused with the clouds of dust raised by the half-tamed horses the savage rides; his long, unkempt hair blowing, and his coppery arms grasping the white and pallid victim he prepares for his lust. Floating garments that lend themselves to all the demands of art; groups of riders and horses; naked bodies; violent passions, racial contrasts among characters, contrast between the civilized dress of the victim and the barbarism of the captor, all are found in Rugendas, in this favorite subject of his spirited brush.

La pampa infinita y los celajes del cielo por fondo, confundidos en parte por las nubes de polvo que levantan los caballos medio domados que monta el salvaje; la melena desgreñada flotando al aire, y sus cobrizos brazos asiendo la blanca y pálida víctima, que prepara para su lascivia. Ropajes flotantes que se prestan a todas las exigencias del arte; grupos de jinetes y caballos; cuerpos desnudos; pasiones violentas, contrastes de caracteres en las razas, de trajes en la civilización de la víctima y la barbarie del raptor, todo ha encontrado en Rugendas, en este asunto favorito de su animoso pincel.[41]

Observe the language: lust, nakedness, violent passions, barbarism. The women of the scant narrative on captives, beginning with Echeverría's María, are young married women in the apogee of their love, as if to assure their respectability beforehand.[42] Frederick proposes that the texts of captives — in which the paintings may be included — functioned as a warning to the reader, who would decode their religious imagery. It was hoped that the woman, a beautiful and brave angel, would escape "from the guilt that is attributed to the supposed complicity of the victim of a rape," because that situation — that of "allowing" herself to be violated — could lead to the despised *mestizaje*.[43]

THE BODY AS FRONTIER

Here is another of the reasons for the omission of the figure of the captives. In the writing of the nation there is no contamination between groups who confront one another or cohabit on the internal frontier, or at least there should not be any: there should be only certainties. To speak of the real traffic in the bodies of captives would imply accepting, for example, that the border or frontier is not only an expedition of conquest and a voyage in a single direction; it would mean accepting that the border or frontier can also be a return journey laden with signifiers, mysteries, and perhaps sympathies; it necessitates accepting the creation of new forms of relationship and exchange, accepting the impossible.

Cristina Iglesia explains, in one of the most beautiful paragraphs written on the drama of the captives:

> The captive is a body in motion, a body that crosses a frontier. The kidnapping, from this perspective, is a possible form of feminine journey. A body in motion contrasts that with the woman tied to the earth and sustenance. A body that does not wait for the man but follows him. An equivocal body that equivocates the direction of its desire. Doubtless the captive does not choose her itinerary, and she travels toward a landscape she does not know. For that reason, while she does it, moved by terror and curiosity, she begins to fall in love with her own nostalgia for an almost impossible return journey that restores her to her ever-more-distant order, to her landscape. Marked by this double voyage, the one that distances and the other that draws her near to her dreams, the captive will always be the symbol of no place, of not being there, of not belonging.[44]

There was not the slightest risk of "racial contamination," since the "decent people" preserved the racial hierarchy carefully maintained since Spanish legislation of the colonial era. Heritage gave the right to an unquestioned superiority over nonwhites, and the liberal project itself was, as is known, to replace the racially mixed population that was considered a depository of the worst defects of its progenitors.[45] The figure of the captive was totally inappropriate to this national project: contaminated by her contact with the Indians, she would have demanded that the bourgeois society establishing itself question the values that supported it with regard to the legitimacy of lineage, the family, sexuality, and well-being. In this way,

> if the journey of the captive realizes the inversion of what is meant by "civilization," if the journey is made toward barbarism, backward in history, if the body of a woman prepared to be a dominion of civilized man is corrupted by the barbarous body of her captor, then the impurity, the degradation, will change her into the abject: a body that engenders mixing with the barbarian other.[46]

In the foundation or delineation of a style of national identity, bodies are used to trace clear frontiers, to demarcate spaces, and to leave well differentiated who is who. No exaggeration is excessive when trying to discredit the enemy camp; no recourse of the imagination that represents reality in gray, ambiguous, blended tones is used. In the constitution of the Generación de Mayo is the dichotomy that determines the national subject: the modern and civilized citizen is designed with a strong inclination toward European culture, especially French and English, but above all, in a spirit of rejection. The opposite of what is desired is in the space of chaos, in obscurity, in the frontier between the urban project and the rural.[47] Against the background of the body of the captive, the map of the abject and the discourse of progress are drawn; upon her (textual, pictorial) body the identity of what we are not and do not wish to be is constructed.

"The violence the Indian exercises against her would in itself justify all violence against the captor."[48] The captives who made it into the collective imaginary — since the captives of flesh and blood did not — were in reality an instrument, an excuse, another justification to brandish in the fight against barbarism and to legitimate a political project. To that end Echeverría's María not only must remain chaste, but also must die almost immediately: in this way civilization is not subjected to the "threat" of her returning contaminated. In this way she appears only as an absolute victim, incapable of defending herself without her husband: unfailingly resistant for the honor of her people and her family, but vulnerable enough to provide the "civilized" with a victim to avenge. Meanwhile the bodies of those who did survive, who adapted to their subjugation among the Indians or served as material for the political and mercantile trade of the frontier — those captives' bodies (undifferentiated from the frontier to be eliminated) remained submerged in the abject, an abject constructed thanks to their legend.[49] In the end, as Echeverría said, "Theories are everything; deeds in themselves matter little."

Chapter 5

THE RETURN OF THE FORBIDDEN:
THE WOMEN WRITERS

There is a rape at the very origin of Argentina. Not the ritual rape of the subjugated indigenous woman by the Spaniard, but the reverse: the violation of a married, Catholic, Spanish lady by a chief of the pampa. At least that is what is told time and again through decades of literature that alludes to that origin as to sin: silencing it, covering it over with virtue, transforming it into something else.

The legend is known by the victim's name: Lucía Miranda, a sort of Spanish Helen of Troy who along with her husband, Sebastián, came to live in the fort of Sancti Spiritu around 1532. The desire she sparks in two indigenous chiefs, the brothers Siripo and Mangoré, leads to the massacre of the fort's inhabitants. Ruy Díaz de Guzmán is the first to describe the event, which he writes about between 1598 and 1612.[1] In the many rewritings of the myth that follow throughout four centuries of Argentine literature, a half-nude Lucía is kidnapped by the Indians and the fear of imminent violation paralyzes her so that she faints. What happens next depends upon the text, but the basic story line is that Mangoré dies and Siripo tries vainly to seduce Lucía, offering her marriage, power, and even an Indian woman to satisfy her Spanish husband, but Lucía and Sebastián prefer to die as martyrs.

This allegory of Argentina's first captive woman dramatizes the violence of the Conquest, from the point of view of the whites who believe that one of the first colonization attempts failed because the colonists trusted in a tribe of perfidious Indians. The treachery of the savages is counterpoised with the purity and loyalty of the Christian martyrs Lucía and Sebastián. Lucía and Sebastián become emblems of the frustrated foundation of a lineage: he, a brave and handsome soldier who leaves Spain for America; she, a devout and beautiful girl who uncomplainingly sacrifices everything to accompany her husband, to help him establish himself in the New World and catechize its inhabitants.

Ruy Díaz de Guzmán's chapter "De la muerte del capitán don Nuño de

98

Lara, la de su jente, con lo demás sucedido por traición de indios amigos"
(On the death of Captain don Nuño de Lara, that of his people, with
the rest that occurred because of the treachery of their Indian friends) is
the origin of a concatenation of literary narratives. It describes the couple's relationship with the Timbú Indians and Chief Mangoré's increasing
"admiration" of Lucía. The passionate Timbú tries to seduce Lucía with
presents and the "assistance of food" and tries to "corrupt" her husband
by inviting him to go "to entertain his people."[2] When Sebastián Hurtado refuses, the Indian sees that he cannot defeat "the composure and
honesty of the wife, and the rectitude of the husband" (La compostura y
honestidad de la mujer, y el recato del marido), and so "he comes to lose
his patience, with great indignation and mortal passion" (vino a perder
la paciencia con grande indignación y mortal pasión). He orders, then,
the Indians' betrayal of the Spanish: he decides that they will go to the
fort, carrying food as if making a friendly visit. After the banquet they
will surprise and kill the Spanish and carry off Lucía. Night and feigned
friendship will be the cloaks that conceal their betrayal.

In this first version, after the terrible massacre of the Spanish in the
fort of Sancti Spiritu, a total of five captive women and "some three or
four boys, who because they were children were not killed but held as
captives, making a mountain of loot to divide among all the people of
war" (unos tres ó cuatro muchachos, que por ser niños no los mataron y
fueron presos y cautivos, haciendo montón de todo el despojo para repar-
tirle entre toda la gente de guerra), are carried off. The information is
as uncertain as writing about the captive women of reality. Ruy Díaz de
Guzmán writes that Sebastián Hurtado returns to the fort, sees the traces
of what happened there and tries to rescue his wife, falling captive to the
Indians himself. Mangoré has died in the assault and his brother, Siripo,
also in love with Lucía, remains with her to make her his wife. Instead
of killing Sebastián, Siripo offers him indigenous concubines in hopes of
arranging an exchange of women. The gesture is curious because Siripo, as
lord and master of the place, has no need to ingratiate himself with Hurtado; nonetheless, the exchange would serve in some way to legitimate his
transgression of the pact of friendship and the laws of Christian marriage.
In fact, if Lucía had agreed to be his wife and Hurtado accepted the concubines, the rules of the game would have been rewritten according to the
logic of the Timbú.

In the original Díaz de Guzmán version, the loving Spanish spouses
agree to the exchange because it is the only way to preserve their lives.
Sexuality—or at least an insinuation of sexuality—lurks on each line. A

furtive encounter between husband and wife is the cause of their death sentence: sometimes — depending upon the author rewriting the legend — there is a jealous Indian woman who denounces Lucía; in other versions Siripo discovers the pair himself. Siripo is indignant at the betrayal because Lucía and Sebastián have broken the pact with their Indian partners, and perhaps because the Indians have not managed to replace the "true love" of the whites. In his anger Siripo condemns Lucía and Sebastián to be burned at the stake and shot with arrows: exactly the manners of death chosen for the early Christian martyrs whose names they bear.[3]

THE SYMPTOM THAT NEVER DISAPPEARS

The recurrence of the legend in Argentine literature after the end of the colonial period has the scent of a symptom. One rewriting is layered upon another. Guzmán's chronicle is taken up again as sacred epic by Father Lozano in his *Historia del Paraguay.* Later — I cite only the most important landmarks — it reappears as the first Argentine drama: Manuel José de Labardén's *Siripo* (1789). And, even more interesting, once independence from Spain is achieved, the image of Lucía Miranda returns more forcefully: Pedro Bermúdez's *El Charrúa: Drama histórico en verso y en cinco actos por el sargento mayor de caballería* (The Charruan: Historical drama in verse and in five acts by the sergeant mayor of Cavalry, 1863), Alejandro Magariños Cervantes's *Mangora: Leyenda histórica, 1530–1536* (1864), and novels entitled simply *Lucía Miranda,* written by Rosa Guerra (1862), Eduarda Mansilla de García (1862), Miguel Ortega (1864), and Celestina Fúnes (1883). The subject was taken up again in the twentieth century by Catholic nationalists like Hugo Wast.[4] Lucía, the Spanish beauty, is captured time and again over the centuries. Like a bad dream that returns night after night and never plays itself out, each of the texts falls silent in its most awful moment — the capture of the first literary captive. The text falls silent, the protagonist faints, the sleeper awakens without wanting to know any more. Silence and unconsciousness, negation and rewriting, as if behind the story there were a traumatic social division that cannot be symbolized and, for that reason, remains unresolved.[5]

There is one clear fact in the first version that disappears from all the others. In Ruy Díaz de Guzmán's seventh chapter, Lucía cannot dissimulate her great misery at finding herself *possessed* by a barbarian. Her husband, to save his life, has taken an indigenous woman for his wife; both Lucía and Sebastián will soon die for having offended and betrayed their new partners by continuing to love each other. In the abstract, the tale dramatizes an exchange of women that goes back to the oldest tribal customs, registering the ancestral pact among human groups: the traffic in women.[6] The exchange of wives marks the union between groups. The problem is that the image of this union is unacceptable within the Argentine social formation we have been discussing: the abjection of the origin is located in the body of a woman.

TO RAPE A WOMAN

To besiege a city: in historiographic discourse, a legitimate act of military power. To besiege a woman: in art and literature, a metaphor for the conquest of peoples. In bed or on the battlefield, the man dominates with physical force, political power, and language: the body of the woman — in the texts, in Culture — is no more than a mute metaphor for a will to power. Or a collective trauma, a memory no one wants, a desire for oblivion.

The loss of an outpost of civilization because of the uncontrolled desire to capture a white woman — the legend of Lucía Miranda — is not an individual and private story of the destiny of tragic lovers in the early colonial years, but rather the allegory of a public conflict. The stolen body of Lucía Miranda functions as a dialogue of social antagonisms, as an allegory of confrontation between cultures that represents the virtues of loyalty, Christianity, friendship, and chastity while condemning the savage. Her body, adored by the Indian as well as the white, sacrificed to save her soul from the barbarians, is — according to Walter Benjamin's definition of allegory — a record of history and the human fall. If allegory is "in the realm of thought, what ruins are in the realm of things," then the kidnapping of Lucía Miranda is like a living and mediated image of social conflicts, as when history is read through ruins.[7] The violation of her domestic and familial space, the violation of her Christian body by an Indian, repeated so many times in the cultural history of Argentina, shows that, at bottom, the negation of racial conflicts did not resolve them.

If we follow Benjamin and read Lucía as an allegory for Argentine society's tense relationship to its origin, then Paul de Man's theory of allegory is also illuminating: as a symbol postulates the possibility of an identity or an identification, allegory marks distance with relation to its own origin. Allegory renounces nostalgia and the desire to coincide, establishing its language instead in the void of temporal difference. This means that the repetition and variations of the Lucía Miranda story do not speak of the captives of reality, but instead are a way of perpetuating the racial conflict in collective memory and avoiding identification with the Other. Allegory is the recognition of difference: Lucía's body, kidnapped and later killed to maintain honor and fidelity, marks only the enormous distance between white culture and the representation of the indigenous as Other.[8]

Rape is usually concealed. What remains is a conspicuous absence: sexual violence against women is the origin of social relationships and narratives, but the act itself, significantly, is always elided.[9] Ernesto Laclau and Chantal Mouffe write that every ideological formation constitutes itself through and against an antagonism and should be understood, for that reason, as an effort to cover over or suture together a combination of contingent relationships.[10] In this case, despite the use that has been made of the myth, it is significant that what reappears so many times in history is precisely the traumatic face most difficult to re-create: the humiliation of the conqueror.

We should pause on this idea. Within the naturalizing mechanism of national traditions — such as can be supposed — the Spanish conquistador triumphs over competing images. The conventional naturalization of reality is demonstrated in a letter of 1545, in which Alonso Riquelme de Guzmán proudly states that the Spanish of Paraguay have enslaved the Guaraní and produced with the women "more than four hundred mestizos, male and female" (más de cuatrocientos mestizos entre varones y hembras). The author adds another line to the letter, written to his father in Argentina: "so that you see if we are *good populators* when *not conquistadors*" (para que vea vuestra merced si somos buenos populadores lo que no conquistadores).[11] Riquelme's violent boast, accentuated by the jocose tone, does not mention that the situation in Paraguay was a war like the struggles of prehistoric peoples, two groups confronting one another for the possession of the land and the seed that will grow on it, battling for survival and the ability to impose servitude upon the other. The conquistador's gaze is "natural."

The anecdote acquires weight when the letter's signer and addressee are identified: it was written by his son to Ruy Díaz de Guzmán, author of the book that ruled in its own way as the patriarch and primogenitor of Argentine historiography.[12] And Díaz de Guzmán is also the author of the most famous version of the myth of Lucía Miranda, the only white captive woman who reappears over and over again in literature. The letter gives an idea of the intellectual atmosphere in which Díaz de Guzmán would a few years later write his *Anales del descubrimiento, población y conquista del Río de la Plata* (Annals of the discovery, population, and conquest of the Río de la Plata [1598–1612]) and summarizes one of most atrocious practices in ethnic struggles even today: the affirmation of power through possession of the female body.

It is significant that the father of the author of that ironic letter about the Spanish conquistadors as *populators* has been the only one capable of contemplating, in the legend of Lucía Miranda, the possibility of rape and cohabitation. Contact (sexual possession) disappears from the later versions, despite Ruy Díaz de Guzmán's clarity on the matter: when Lucía, now the wife of Siripo, heard that the chief planned to kill Hurtado, she "begged *her new husband* not to execute him, before she had begged him to spare his life, so that both could be employed in his service as true slaves, for which they would always be grateful" (rogó a su nuevo marido no lo ejecutase, antes le suplicaba le otorgase la vida, para que ambos se empleasen en su servicio como verdaderos esclavos, de que siempre estarían muy agradecidos). As early as Dean Funes's version, the chiefs of the Timbú are capable of the worst crimes and betrayals — even between brothers — but not of offending the Spanish woman's honor, which remains untouched.[13]

For some reason the subject is taken up again by the first national poem of what is considered Latin America's only "white" country: the poem, of course, is Esteban Echeverría's *La cautiva* (1837).[14] This foundational poem is also a text of the frontier, in which a Creole woman of Spanish origin, Catholic and married, is the victim of a raid. Echeverría's María is part of the same traumatic dream as Lucía Miranda: both have been in the arms of the indigenous raptor; both reject his violent desire and end tragically, avoiding sexual cohabitation and servitude to the Indian. The heroine's death, like every beautiful woman's, makes the preservation of dominant cultural values exigent. Over her dead body — Lucía's, María's — the norms are reconfigured and secured: she must be sacrificed if the danger her presence presents is to disappear.[15] Dead, she cannot be subjugated by the enemy, but this way of representing the problem of the frontier hides the reality of the white captives, the flesh-and-blood captives, the mothers of so many "white Indians."[16]

The María of the poem and the repeated figure of Lucía Miranda — the two captives of Argentine literature — are married women of such perfect loyalty that they do not hesitate for a moment before sacrificing themselves to save the men they love. Their bodies, exposed to the desire of the enemy, are in reality as white and impenetrable as stone tablets. These bodies, on the border of sin (María is accused by her husband of having cohabited with the infidel after the raid, while Lucía pretends to love her captor to save her life and Hurtado's), are bodies that as literary representation, dressed or half-dressed, serve to regulate and contain the sexual/social female body. In the representation of this married body the apertures have been closed so that "marginal material [does not] penetrate the frontiers that divide the inside of the body from the outside, the I of space from the other."[17] In contrast, the true captives, unimmaculate flesh and blood of the frontier, symbolically threaten the processes of formation of the I, of order, of the separation of the Other, and for that reason are silenced.

Lynda Nead writes: "If the female body is defined as lacking containment and issuing filth and pollution from its faltering outlines and broken surface, then the classical forms of art perform a kind of magical regulation of the female body, containing it and momentarily repairing the orifices and tears." This means that the representation of the nude in the plastic arts is a way of reinterpreting and controlling sexuality. But the achievement is fleeting because "the margins are dangerous and will need to be subjected to the discipline of art again . . . and again."[18] It is for that reason that the mythified image of a captive looking up to heaven like a Renaissance virgin returns to the paintings, the poems, and the dramas; so that there is a protagonist in the texts this captive must be represented time and again as Lucía/María.

If the moment of the kidnapping can be summarized as that of the consummation of the violence of desire (preceded by massive deaths: Eros and Thanatos), the lady is represented through all the codes for noncontamination: she is of purely Spanish aspect (not Creole, so there is no question of prior contamination), married (the woman clearly "belongs" to one particular man), and she is not a mother (there is no risk of proliferation: Lucía's marriage with Hurtado is sterile, while the son of Brián and María dies under ambiguous circumstances). The nation is saved, at least according to the national narrative being constructed. But since the achievement is fleeting, it will be necessary to tell the story again. Again and again.

THE GAZE OF NARCISSUS

It should be said that no one has proven that the characters of the tragedy of Lucía Miranda existed historically. The legend may have developed to cover up an error of the conquistadors, since the destruction of the fort was in reality due to the inexperience and cowardice of a Spaniard, Gregorio Caro.[19] Rather than recognize Spanish responsibility, the early colonists began to develop a mythology accusing the indigenous. Over the space of what was to be conquered and domesticated, the tale of the abject was constructed — the abject, or treachery, sensual unrestraint, savagery, heresy.

The legend of Lucía Miranda — the story of subjugation and cohabitation with the *Other* — is uncomfortable: in Argentina not only has the mestizo origin been diluted, buried below strata of literary and historical versions and masses of European immigrants, but Culture has tended to omit these originary violations, representing them as if contact with the Other had been occasional, sporadic, and insignificant, rather than foundational. These disgraced bodies of women, hidden among the layers of eroticism, "of sanity and of politics,"[20] found practically no space of representation in the culture, not even after Argentina's independence: they scarcely filter into Esteban Echeverría's equivocal poem, into a few lines by Lucio V. Mansilla, and into the stories and plays about Lucía Miranda. The legend, set in the sixteenth century, is too distant in time for any author to have utilized it to make the real captive women a place in the field of what was writable and, for that matter, of what was conceivable in the public sphere of nineteenth-century Argentina.[21]

As a construction of identity, it would seem that the Fathers of the Nation have left a void that corresponds to the concept of *narcissisme blanche.*[22] *Narcissisme blanche,* according to André Green, is the other face of primary narcissism (searching for the Other, the alter ego). White narcissism is neutral: it tends toward inexistence, toward anesthesia, toward indifference. Although Green uses the term *blanche* more in the English sense of *blank* (neutral, void) than the French *blanc* (white), when applied to cultural processes the idea inevitably acquires a very significant racial connotation. It is a negating psychosis.

If *narcissisme blanche,* as I use it here, denies the gaze to determinate parts of reality, that does not mean that such a reality does not exist. As with certain traumas or bad memories that refuse to disappear, something in that negated origin pressures the imaginary. Every so often, over four centuries, sometimes in the margins and sometimes near the lettered center, the image of the chief of the pampa who subjugates a married, Catholic, Spanish lady in the early years of Argentina's colonization reappears. That image, that tale, always has the same name: Lucía Miranda.

The legend of Lucía Miranda is a metaphor for the tensions of the frontier and of the sexual order. Of course, in the nineteenth century, a period in which many of the rewritings were produced, sexuality had to be controlled to preserve the white national project. In a society as unstable as that one, nothing was better for keeping faithful and pure wives at home. The impulse behind sexual regulation was not only the influence of the Catholic Church, the bourgeoisie, and the reflections of Victorian values in South America: racial conflicts also necessitated family unity and, more particularly, guarding the body of the woman to preserve the purity of the lineage. Furthermore, the problem of prostitution was not uncommon: before it was legalized in 1875, the government treated city women accused of "suspicious conduct" like unemployed gauchos and vagrants; they were arrested and sent to lend sexual service to the troops of the frontier.[23] The ideal family was transformed into the symbol — and women its guardians — of the continuity and immutability of the nation.[24]

THE TRAUMA OF ORIGINS

In a country that proposes to exterminate the indigenous inhabitants, the return of the legend of Lucía Miranda in such dissimilar texts is intriguing: What is hidden? What is plotted? What is there of fascination or irresolution in this story that returns and returns?[25] Each new version of the fable produces a new covering, so that the legend organizes itself in strata — not of meanings, but of denials of meanings, or searches for tolerable meanings. It is one layer of inventions upon another, silencing violence and constructing oblivions, protecting the integrity of *narcissme blanche*. The repetition of the trope from the past helps to construct a historical present; it is the discursive *performance* of identity; it is the legitimization of a ruling class through archaic traditions.[26]

One of the explanations for the resurgence of Lucía Miranda in the nineteenth century is the convenience of the myth for the racial project: the story represents, with the weight of History, indigenous savagery as a threat to the white, bourgeois, Catholic project of territorial expansion that will culminate in Roca's Conquista del Desierto and the extermination of the Indians. In this stage of national construction the myth appears more often. The icon was apt: "Lucía Miranda...existed at a safe distance in the past, she was from the 'correct' race and class, and she was virtuously married — altogether a safe, unproblematic hero," as Bonnie Frederick writes.[27] The indigenous figures were convenient as retrospective and renarrated myth: Mangoré represents the potentially civilizable Indian, the one who could have embodied agreement between Indians and whites if he had not succumbed to sexual desire for the white woman and violently demolished the only space of civilization. If the attractive and conflicted Mangoré represents the defeated pact, Siripo is the real Indian, indomitable, deformed, vengeful, and repugnant, the Indian who remains a threat in the present.

On the other hand, the omission of the captive women from real history is like a black hole that must be filled. It is a threat to the integrity of identity and, as such, demands some form of representation, even if totally allusive and elusive. Ironically enough, the threat of contact is less horrific if it is represented as violence and violation than if cohabitation and miscegenation are depicted as such: Lucía is carried off by force, in the midst of terrifying scenes of death and destruction.

It is another symptom of the trauma of the origin: as in the Genesis story of Eve and the apple, there is an original sin that cannot be spoken; in this case the forbidden fruit is not the Knowledge of Good and Evil, but the carnal sin. Worse yet, the sin is committed by the genealogical parents of the nation. Their sin reveals the desire and hatred between racial groups; it involves sexual violence and, worse still, the consequences of contact: ethnic and cultural contamination. But this sin is itself omitted: the myth covers over but cannot make it disappear: on the contrary, Lucía Miranda reappears many times in Argentina's literary history. But never as an invited guest. She never acquires the prestige of Facundo or Martín Fierro; Lucía Miranda may be present at the national banquet, but she always enters through the back door.

Coexistence/collusion with the Indians is a sin of a different nature, registered in terms of the betrayal of the (white) propertied class. In fact, another legendary woman appears after the Lucía Miranda episode in Ruy Díaz de Guzmán's book of origins, *Anales del descubrimiento, población y conquista del Río de la Plata*. The second story would be less fascinating if it formed a part of any other Culture's history: it is that of La Maldonada, a Spanish woman who decides to escape from the fort where all her companions are dying of hunger. According to Díaz de Guzmán, La Maldonada helps a lioness giving birth and later goes to live among the Indians. Discovered ("rescued") by the Spanish, she receives a frightful punishment: she is lashed to trees a mile from the fort and left to be eaten by wild animals. The lioness protects her and finally the woman is able to return to the fort. But this character, whom Díaz de Guzmán claimed to have known personally and who, in her own words, should have been called "Biendonada" (*Anales*, 130),[28] represents Lucía's exact opposite: she is a woman who does not appear to belong to the weaker sex, the only one who finds a way to survive. La Maldonada, endowed as her name suggests with evil gifts, makes a pact with the savages (including the beasts) and does not suffer any violence because of it, but comes out winning; such an attitude is considered a grievous betrayal. What has prevailed as the culture's supreme value, in contrast, is wifely abnegation, the sacrifice of a martyr (Lucía) before an irreducible world of enemy Indians, a world that can only be destroyed.

FEMALE VERSIONS

There was nothing more to consider than the disappearance of the captives from the bosom of the family: after the raids it was necessary to produce narratives that represented the interests of society as a whole. But to renarrate their history (to understand it, to resolve the anxiety) would necessitate rethinking the values upon which the family, bourgeois sexuality, and the national racial project are based. The problem becomes still more complicated when we consider that mourning for these disappeared white women could not be encouraged as a cultural practice. Mourning — the articulation of grief that is necessary to recover from a loss — in this case implied unveiling the layers that covered over the kidnapping of the captive. To articulate grief is to renarrate, to raise these layers: both gestures would in the end question the policy of the State.[29] There is no mourning: there is disappearance and silence.

How are we to interpret, then, the gesture of the women who rewrite the myth of Lucía Miranda? In 1860 the raids have increased, but Rosa Guerra and Eduarda Mansilla ignore the current situation to re-present in the public sphere a legend, distant in time and space, about a beautiful Spanish woman who inspires indigenous passions and is able to defend — as a woman — the space of progress: family, culture, civilization.[30] In other words, the *criolla* subjugated on the frontier is not described, but rather a remote Spanish lady. The present era is not represented, but rather a distant failure of the whites. A policy (or lack thereof) is not denounced: instead a legend with the weight of History is consecrated, a legend in which the reconciliation between whites and Indians is impossible.

Analyzing the works of Rosa Guerra and Eduarda Mansilla, Francine Masiello notes that these authors were more preoccupied than their contemporaries with strengthening the tie between civilization and barbarism, making marriage and the domestic the place for those opposed forces to converge.[31] Guerra and Mansilla are the first to take up the legend in the period after the Rosas government, and both focus their tales on the character of Lucía. In the same decade, Pedro Bermúdez concentrates on Hurtado and Siripo (*El Charrúa,* 1864), while Alejandro Magariños Cervantes pays more attention to the Indians (*Mangora*, 1864). Miguel Ortega's drama *Lucía Miranda* (1864) is closer to the traditional axes, but is completely disparaging toward the Indians.

In literary terms Rosa Guerra's *Lucía Miranda* is probably the best of the versions. It is also the most modern, in the sense that Lucía Miranda is not locked into the female stereotypes of romantic literature and that she, the woman, is the mediator between cultures. It is she who evangelizes, performs works of charity, and manages to save Mangoré's soul before he dies. Rosa Guerra, a journalist, depended upon the good will of Miguel Cané to publish this book that, at first glance, is a paean to marital fidelity. (In fact, Guerra claimed to have written it as a wedding present to a friend.)[32] But the novel is more than a romantic drama and brings to the discussion the transformative powers of language as mediator between different cultures. The savages are likable and Lucía learns to speak their language. Guerra shows how silence and incomprehension of cultural signs can lead to tragedy; in fact, the drama unfolds through the misinterpretation of an intercepted letter.[33]

Eduarda Mansilla de García, the niece of Juan Manuel de Rosas and sister of Lucio V. Mansilla and later a well-known children's author, was also a journalist. Mansilla attempts a much more ambitious and extravagant version, re-creating Lucía's past in Spain in such detail that the legend itself occupies only a third of the book. Mansilla invents Lucía Miranda a lineage of legendary loves, gives her a childhood in Spain, makes her a great reader, and accompanies her throughout the trajectory that will take her to Argentina. Once there Lucía becomes the translator between Spanish and Indians and, most notably, the axis of a network of female friendships that becomes the basis for the involvement between the two cultures.

There is not space enough in this study to describe the delirious exoticism of Mansilla's *Lucía Miranda,* in which Lucía uses her own rituals against the tricks of a witch, nor can I detail the fantastical orchard where Rosa Guerra locates the romantic sufferings of the spouses.[34] What must be described instead is the version of yet another journalist, Celestina Funes, who as late as 1883 — after the Conquista del Desierto — rewrites the legend of Lucía Miranda in verse. In her text the fascinating ambiguity expressed by Guerra and Mansilla is lost, as if the historical elimination of the raids has made it more necessary than ever to create images of savagery that justify the extermination of the Indians and emphasize the importance of maintaining the family values of the white tradition. If Guerra locates Lucía Miranda in an Edenic Argentina, Funes re-creates the point of view of the early Conquest, when America was the promise of limitless riches: "With Rivers of silver with sands of gold / Over beds of rich minerals; / And seas of gleaming sapphires / Of magnificent painted corals / And crags of nacreous pearls" (Con Ríos de plata con arenas de oro / Sobre lecho de ricos minerales; / Y mares de zafiro fulgurantes / De pintados magníficos corales / Y peñascos de perlas nacaradas) (51). Since Celestina Funes writes not in the sixteenth century but at the end of the nineteenth, she warns that "With mad and fantastic ideals / And burning with thirst for gold, / They dug into the bowels of the earth / To extinguish their fever for riches: / Longed-for treasure / Which the greedy, sepulchered in the abyss, / Left everywhere / Beneath the limpid brilliance of the sky / Of fecund America, whose soil / Valuable as Oriental riches / Only in exchange / For honorable labor would be given" (Con locos y fantásticos ideales / Y ardiendo en sed de oro, / Cavaban de la tierra las entrañas / Para apagar su fiebre de caudales: / Anhelado tesoro / Que al sepultarse en el abismo, avaros / Dejaba por doquiera / Bajo la lumbre límpida del cielo / De América fecunda, cuyo suelo / Orientales riquezas á porfía / En cambio solamente / De la labor honrada le daría) (52). The legend of Lucía Miranda allows Funes to exalt the value of work as opposed to the illusory search for easy wealth.

Returning to the versions of the myth of Lucía Miranda from the decade of the 1860s — when the problem of Indians, real captives, and raids was still current — and specifically those of Rosa Guerra and Eduarda Mansilla, it should be said that the body/garden is the topography of the text, the silenced body/map, the invented geography. More than the frontier, the body of the captive woman is the site of displacement in these texts; her body is the place of the border, of hybridity and struggle, and the space of the unacceptable transgression; the garden of a past before innocence was lost.

Neither of these two writers caused the rupture that giving voice to the real women of the frontier would have entailed, but they do demonstrate a displacement of content and of the gaze itself, especially if they are compared with the rigidity of another work of the time: in Manuel Ortega's text the traditional ethos of the story is preserved and Lucía's attitude toward the savages is consistently deprecating. In the cases of Guerra and Mansilla — despite differences between the texts — in the midst of the wars of national reconstruction the words caress Lucía with sensuality, pausing over her voluptuous shoulders, her uncovered breast, her nude baths in the lake, her beauty rituals, her diminutive feet, or her partial nudity at the moment of kidnapping.

Sensuality, curiosity, ambiguity: I would almost say nostalgia. Although the endings of Guerra's and Mansilla's texts are as tragic as any, their versions of crossing the frontier hold a mirror up to the Other and allow the reader to consider both the image reflected and the mirror itself, the crossing. The waters are not so clearly divided as in Manuel Ortega's drama, in which Mangoré is a stupid savage, incapable of accepting Lucía's absolute scorn. In contrast, Guerra's and Mansilla's texts are ambiguous regarding the relationship with Mangoré: there is a sort of identification with the realm of the abject, of the excluded, of the unrepresentable. There is pleasure in representing desire and the body; there is fear and pleasure in describing exchanges with the Indians.

Why do the women writers get involved in Mangoré's emotional conflicts? Why do they imagine confusion in the reading of signs (he misinterprets Lucía's sisterly friendliness)? Why do they trouble themselves with friendship with the Indian women, with Siripo's jealousy? They have involved themselves in the territory of the nonsubject. They do not violate the limits, it is true, but just the same they make their incursion into a region that was socially unacceptable: the frontier. They may neglect the present, but their writing conveys a sensual curiosity toward the forbidden. Rosa Guerra writes:

> Although a barbarian, Mangora, chief of the Timbú, gathered in his person all the pride of his race, the beautiful raiments of a gentleman.... He was tall in stature, and of a strong nervous musculature, his forms slender; and although copper-colored like all the Indians, his nose was not flat; his eyes were sparkling, and all his continent knew he was ruled by passions at once strong and tender. Better said, Mangora was one of a special kind among the Indians, described by the celebrated Hercilla in his Araucana.

> Mangora, cacique de los Timbúes, á pesar de ser bárbaro, reunía en su persona toda la arrogancia de su raza, las bellas prendas de un caballero.... Tenía alta talla, y era de fuerte nerviosa musculatura, sus formas esbeltas; y aunque de color cobrizo como lo son todos los indios, no tenía aplastada la nariz; sus ojos eran chispeantes, y en todo su continente se conocía era dominado por pasiones fuertes y tiernas á la vez. Mejor dicho, era Mangora uno de esos tipos especiales entre los indios, descriptos por el célebre Hercilla en su Araucana. (18)

Of Lucía she writes:

> She was of the true Spanish type, beautiful like the first woman God gave to man as his companion, slender as the most beautiful tree in paradise, seductive as our loving mother Eve.

> Era el verdadero tipo español, hermosa como la primera mujer que Dios diera por compañera al hombre, esbelta como el más bello árbol del paraíso, seductora como nuestra amorosa madre Eva. (19)

Rosa Guerra dedicates more than a page to the "delicacy [*morbidez*] of her body," of her feet, her waist, her throat, the shape of her vein-laced shoulders, her eyes, her perfect and voluptuous mouth, shapely nose, and even the down that covers her fresh cheeks. The tension between the bodies of Mangoré and Lucía signals an anxiety different from that of the male-authored texts, even if the basic facts of the narrative remain within the institution of matrimony and reinforce the conventional values of duty and sacrifice. Lucía is ambiguous, provocative, victimized; Mangoré, on the other hand, with his colorful feathers and his young, half-nude body is represented as remarkably *similar* to the whites. Lucía even tells him, "if Sebastián had not been my husband, I would have been the wife of Mangoré" (si Sebastián no hubiera sido mi marido, yo habría sido la esposa de Mangoré). Her confession is all but unheard-of from the heroine of a legend whose traditional allegorical function was to differentiate between whites and Indians.

In Rosa Guerra's text, to continue with what I believe to be the best of the narratives, the proximity of the bodies breaks the bonds of physical restraint. I will concentrate on the scene of the kidnapping itself. The attack surprises Lucía: "she had not had more time to cover herself than to throw around her naked shoulders a great black shawl adorned with furs" (no había tenido más tiempo para cubrirse que echarse sobre sus desnudos hombros un gran manto negro guarnecido de pieles) (52). There is a hellish, demonic noise, the sound of wind, rough and wild surf, children's cries, the clamor of the women, moans of the dying, savage howls of the barbarians. Mangoré appears

> adorned with his showy feathers, with his crown full of precious stones, and rich strings of coral and pearls that encircle his neck and fall upon his bloody chest, soiled not with the blood of his wounds, but with the Spanish blood of his victims.... With his imposing attitude, he was arrogant, more than a man he was an exterminating angel — he was beautiful. Lucía, seeing him, gave a cry and fainted away.

adornado con sus vistosos plumajes, con su diadema llena de piedras preciosas, y ricas sartas de coral y perlas que rodeaban su cuello, y caían sobre su ensangrentado pecho, no con la sangre de sus heridas, sino con la sangre española de sus víctimas.... [S]u actitud imponente, estaba soberbio, más que un hombre era un ángel exterminador — estaba hermoso —. Lucía al verlo, dio un grito y cayó desmayada. (53)

This is not the first time in the novel that Lucía faints at the sight of Mangoré's body. The barbarian "grabs her in his arms" (la coje en sus brazos). The blanket that covers her "has fallen from her shoulders, and her soft breast, like her beautiful back would have been exposed to the profane gaze of the savages, if her beautiful ebony hair had not covered her almost entirely, leaving in sight of the greedy eyes of the barbarians only her white and well-turned arms" (ha caído de sus hombros, y su mórvido seno, así como sus hermosísimas espaldas estuvieran espuestas a las miradas profanas de los salvajes, si su hermosa cabellera de ébano, no le cubriese casi toda entera, dejando solo a la vista de las codiciosas miradas de los bárbaros, sus blancos y bien torneados brazos). He carries her off from among the dead as the storm rages:

At the horrific roaring of the storm, feeling a shudder in her person, he fixes his gaze on her in the flashes of lightning, her long hair floats on the wind, her chest and back exposed in all their nudity.

Al estampido horroroso del trueno, ha sentido un estremecimiento en su persona, fija una mirada en ella a la claridad de los relámpagos, flota al viento su larga cabellera, su seno y espaldas quedan en toda su desnudez. (56)

Believing she is dead, Mangoré, "convulsive and passionate," embraces Lucía, and "the ardent lips of the infidel profane the lips of Hurtado's virtuous wife" (convulsivo y apasionado ... los ardientes labios del infiel profanan los labios de la virtuosa esposa de Hurtado) (56).

After the sexual vehemence of these descriptions, the narrative maintains that Mangoré dies repentant, swearing he has preserved "the dignity" (el decoro) of Lucía (62). Lucía must then confront the savage Siripo and die a martyr to conjugal duty.

In chapter 41 of *Una excursión a los indios ranqueles,* Lucio Mansilla mentions the *via crucis* of the captives, the place where they are detained and forced to work; anyone who resists may be beaten to death. He allocates only a few lines to the information. But even for Lucio Mansilla, the body of the captive woman (the body of the frontier) is an opportunity for eroticism; while describing the wounds on the arms and the breast of a captive who has approached him (chapter 45), a confession seems to escape from his pen: "I was disgusted by that unfortunate woman, whose eyes were beautiful. She had a provocative lewdness in her physiognomy" (Me dio asco aquella desdichada, cuyos ojos eran hermosísimos. Tenía una lubricidad incitante en su fisionomía). He admits that she was "slender and graceful," but he cannot avoid, at the same time, a measure of disgust.

Horror and desire. Lucio's sister, Eduarda Mansilla de García, prefers to adhere to literary tradition. In her lengthy version of the myth of Lucía Miranda, Mangoré spies while Lucía bathes "her nude body in the pure current of the river" (su desnudo cuerpo en la pura corriente del río); "he devours her in silence with ardent gazes" (la devora en silencio con ardientes miradas); he looks on as she dresses in her bedroom. But he never takes her in his arms: a treacherous blow, planned by his own brother, kills Mangoré during the attack on the fort. Lucía is carried off by Siripo, once again "hair loose and scarcely dressed, with her beautiful head hanging over the Indian's shoulder" (suelto el cabello, y apenas vestida, con su hermosa cabeza colgando por sobre el hombro del indio). Once again she falls "unconscious in the arms of the fierce chief" (exánime en brazos del feroz cacique). She will awaken the following day in a miserable hut, her naked body "scarcely covered by light, crushed garments, [as] the horrible reality presents itself in all its palpable truth" (cubierto apenas por lijeras y estrujadas ropas, la horrible realidad se le presenta en toda su más palpable verdad) (154). The first thing she sees is the deformed body of Siripo, who announces that from now on, "you belong to me alone" (me perteneces a mí solo).

The ambiguity, sexual desire, and feminine curiosity in these episodes stand out more if they are compared to another contemporary version, Miguel Ortega's drama *Lucía Miranda*. The characters are the same, but there are no fissures in Ortega's text. Siripo becomes a victim of desire very late in the drama, and the action unfolds instead through his activity as a leader of indigenous resistance and his belief that Mangoré's weakness for a Christian woman will make him a traitor to the Indians. The moment of the kidnapping is not even represented: the drama is an epic confrontation between opposing soldiers who desire an unapproachable and incorruptible woman. Celestina Funes's version, written almost twenty years after those of Guerra, Mansilla, and Ortega and already almost a justification for the extermination of the Indians, negates the eroticism of the kidnapping: "And the tribe, replete with killing, / Carrying off the senseless women, /

Among which was the unhappy Lucía, / They returned to their village / With their rich booty" (Y la tribu, repleta de matanza, / Llevando las mujeres sin sentido, / Do se contaba la infeliz Lucía, / Volvió á su tolderia / Con su rico botín) (67). That is all. In this poem it does not matter what happens to the other captives; the center of the text is conjugal love and the construction of the image of a woman, "Beautiful like dreams" (Bella cual ensueños) (56), all light and harmony, with a magical voice, "which if it vibrated / With heavenly music / Intoxicated the ear!" (que si vibraba / Con música del cielo / El oído embriagaba!), and a "seraphic beauty of the soul" (belleza seráfica del alma). The Lucía Miranda of this poem leaves behind her loving family — siblings, mother, and friends — out of loyalty to her husband, and for him she suffers "with Christian patience, the bitterness / Of an isolated and uncertain existence, / Vulnerable to barbarous outrages / And the constant danger / Of living surrounded by savages" (con cristiana paciencia, la amargura / De una existencia aislada é insegura, / De la suerte los bárbaros ultrajes, / Y el constante peligro / De vivir rodeada de salvajes) (57). For a woman there is no greater happiness than sacrifice (58), writes Celestina Funes, omitting all eroticism and dissolving the scene of the kidnapping by generalizing it with references as vague as "the tribe" and "the senseless women." Around 1883, the national State has begun to consolidate; the raids are a part of the (albeit recent) past; and urban modernization, immigration, and poverty press upon the elite, which closes ranks to protect itself. The Otherness of the Indian is no longer a seduction (at the level of symbolic fantasy) for the female subject.

But in 1860 neither the space of identity nor the space on the map was so definite: this is why the two women writers who take up the figure of the captive — even if only through the remote Lucía Miranda — and offer glimpses of a distinct and disturbing subjectivity are so fascinating. Lucía Miranda's faints in the texts of Rosa Guerra and Eduarda Mansilla de García speak their mute language. In the climax of passion and terror, the texts fall silent. How else could the rhetoric of the nation be satisfied? The female versions of 1860 show glimmers of something that remains in the shadows: the proximity of the bodies of Mangoré and Lucía produces all kinds of alterations, confronting desire, temptation, and duty with such tension (and guilt) that the silenced violation is represented as an exit.

Sexual domination of another person is, furthermore, a discursive symbol instrumental in reproducing other meanings. Anne Laura Stoler presents the problem graphically when she sarcastically asks if the sexual domination of some over others is perhaps a substation on the trajectory of

Power by demonstrating who is "beneath and who is on top of whom."[35] Because sexual images illustrate the iconography of Power, an Indian "possessing" a white woman seems inconceivable within the symbolic networks of the nation.

These women writers are on the verge of original sin. Like the biblical Eve, they attempt to feed the white Narcissus fruit from the Tree of Knowledge. But not even they dare to bite the forbidden fruit. They escape the attraction that resists symbolization only by blaming the enemy for violence and disorder: if anything happened between the Indian and the *española,* it was his fault. But nothing really could have happened.

With their curiosity, with veiled fantasy, Guerra and Mansilla have opened a tiny breach in racism's logic of exclusions: incurring into the terrain of the abject, they discard the horror of violation and deliver themselves to a more romantic fantasy through which they filter, perhaps for the only time, a desire for the Other *without disgust.* Something could have happened after the attack on the fort: Lucía cannot be held responsible for what happens to her in the strong and young arms of the captor, because she has fainted. The abominable rape becomes a hiatus in the text, creating uncertainty as to whether it was really abominable or a rape. What happened during Lucía's unconsciousness remains open to romantic fantasy: in her conscious world everything is in order, no one has been stained. In the conscious world, in the world of the speakable, the Spanish lady becomes once again the indignant wife, the martyr of conjugal love. Although it appears to be a story about humiliation, the trauma is in fact resolved: there is no contamination, neither miscegenation nor enslavement.

This nocturnal breach closes to make way for the rationalizing discourse of civilization. Silence returns: in less than twenty years the campaign to exterminate the Indians will begin. That campaign will eliminate the uncomfortable presence of the real captives, the flesh-and-blood women who were as disturbing as every frontier body. Lucía Miranda will not appear again until the ultranationalists need her, in the 1920s and 1930s, to bury with words a reality contaminated no longer by Indians or blacks, but by another threatening Other: immigrants. Meanwhile, the nineteenth-century canon is constructed around Echeverría's "El matadero," Sarmiento's *Facundo,* and José Hernández's *Martín Fierro.* Rosas remains the common enemy, even if only for memory.

The broken body of the captive, the violated and enslaved body of the frontier, today produces nothing more than puzzlement. If she had followed the course of nineteenth-century history, Lucía Miranda might have been widowed, spent several years among the Indians, and then returned alone to work as a servant wandering from house to house, unable to find a better occupation or a home in which the lady saw her as more than a "useless" woman "of bad habits" (que no sirve para nada, de malas costumbres), a woman "ruined" (echada a perder) among the Indians.[36] Lucía—and the same could have happened to Miranda, Prospero's daughter in *The Tempest*—would have spent the rest of her days scrubbing floors and ruing the day she decided to run away, leaving behind her mestizo children and her position as a white queen in the eyes of her ugly but loving Siripo.

Chapter 6

CAPTIVE TEXTS:
THE ETHICS OF REPRESENTATION

My father just found out that a raid attacked and nine Indians are missing, if they've got any taken alive let's see if we can get a few captives out.

Mi padre acabó de saber que an asaltado un malon y faltan nueve yndios sin an tomado algunos bibos que los tengan haber si le sacamos algunos cautivos.

— Chief Mariano Rosas

I am extremely afflicted by the news ... that they have brought a little girl to Via de Mersedes to exchange for the sister of the white Indian, if this is true, do me the favor of answering as quickly as you can.

Estoi sumamente afligida por una noticia ... que han traído una niñita a Via de Mersedes para el cambio de la hermana del indio blanco, si esto es verdad, hagame el fabor de contestarme lo mas pronto que pueda.

— Gregoria N. De Freites, mother on the frontier

Be careful that Eve may tempt Adam. Women have always been the instrument that the common enemy has used to the perdition of many, with the exception of Holy Mary and a few others.

Cuidado que Eva tiente á Adán. Las mugeres siempre han sido instrumento de que se ha valido el comun enemigo para perdicion de muchos, á escepcion de Maria Santísima y otras pocas más.

— Brother Marcos Donati, the "Redeemer of Captives"

[C]ompadre I also write to say on my word what they gave me for a woman captive they gave me a hundred pesos silver five shirts five pair of Consoillo five shawls a woolen poncho a silk kerchief and something else I ask you one hundred pesos more you Compadre know I am so poor with So much family as I have.

[C]ompadre también me mando desir depalabra lo que me daba por una cautiva me daba sien pesos plata sinco camisas sinco pare de Consoillo sinco rreboso un poncho de palo un pañuelo desea un sombreo y algomas yo le pido sien pesos mas ya he Usted Compadre de que estoy tan pobre Contanta familia que tengo.   —Chief Manuel Baigorria, also called Baigorrita

This unfortunate lady would like to get out of captivity, and hopes that someone buys her, or at least to know of her family.

Esta desventurada señora quisiera salir del cautiverio, y espera que alguien la compre, o por lo menos saber de su familia.   —Brother Marcos Donati

The Ladies of Beneficence are quick to sacrifice anything they can to buy even a pair of captives.

Las Señoras de Beneficiencia estan prontas a sacrificar lo que pueden para comprar siquiera un par de cautivas.   —Brother Alfonso María Alizeri

Don't forget what I have always charged you with, one or two Indian women, I have a very good location for them. . . . [N]eedless to say I don't want them to be old.

No ce olvide, lo que ciempre le he encargado, una o dos indias, tengo una mui buena colocacion para ellas. . . . [E]s escusado decirle a Ud. que no quiero que sean viejas.
       —Bernardo Lacase, intermediary for Pedro Lavase, "rich proprietor of Calamuchita"

Late yesterday Mariano's son Lineo died and since he came Ilenchuger and Carionao are sick I think it must be the plague I have nothing to do in Similar conflicts.

Ayer tarde murio un hijo de mi hermando Mariano llamado Lineo, y desde que bino Ilenchuger y Carionao estan enfermos Creo sera la peste no ayo que aserme en Semejante conflictos.   —Chief Epumer Rosas

The Indians that come here are treated well and lodged in a good hut. If they complain it's because they want to.

Los indios q'bienen aquí son bien tratados y estan alojados en una buena ramada. Si se quejan es porque quieren.   —Colonel Julio A. Roca

Doña Angelita Roca wrote to tell me she would take charge of a little captive girl that had no kin, that was and will be if you want to place one there for Rita's daughter, years ago she had a little black girl who died of chicken pox, I am certain that they treated her well.

Doña Angleita Lopez me escribio diciendome que se haria cargo de alguna cautivita que no tuviera deudos, era y será si Ud. quiere colocar allí una para su hija de ella Rita, tuvo años pasados una negrita que le murió de viruela, me consta que le trataba bien.　　　　　　　—Brother Moysés Álvarez

Lieutenant Colonel Cayupan is in prison, they say because he barbarously abused a woman captive in his control.

[E]l teniente Coronel Cayupan está preso, dicen que su prision es motivada por un maltrato bárbaro que ha dado á una cautiva que tenia en su poder.　　　　　　　　　　　　　　　　—Father Marcos Donati

I am preparing for the Indians a thousand butchered cows and two hundred steers. . . . Send me a list of the fees so I know what is needed.

Estoy preparando para los indios mil vacas al corte y doscientas yeguas. . . . Mandemé una lista de los sueldos para saber lo que se precisa.　　　　　　　　　　　　　　　　—Colonel Julio A. Roca

I'm sorry I could not get the women on board the train, it was too dangerous, the train being in motion.

Siento no haber podido dejar entrar en tren las mujeres, era demasiado peligroso, tren siendo en movimiento.　　　—Chief of the Río Cuarto Station

[S]ince I know you buy captive women, I present her to you to offer you one for sale.

[C]omo se que Ud. compra cautivas, la presentees para ofrecerle una en venta.　　　　　　　　　　　　　　　　　　—Baigorrita

The little Indians of the School are doing very well they already know the Christian doctrine by memory. I go on Saturdays and explain them one or a few chapters, although it may be like talking Greek to them at least something must stay with them.

Los indiecitos de la Escuela van mui bien ya saben la doctrina cristiana de memoria. Yo voi los sabados y les esplico alguno o algunos capítulos, que aunque sea como hablarles en greigo pero algo les hade quedar.

—Brother Moysés Álvarez

In this mission 56 infidels have been solemnly baptized; during various epidemics *in articulo mortis,* also they have rescued 295 captives from the power of the barbarians.

En esta misión se han bautizado solemnemente 56 infieles; en varias epidemias *in articulo mortis,* también se han rescatado del poder de los bárbaros 295 cautivos.

—Brother Moysés Álvarez, Prefect of the M. of Córdoba and San Luis

Eleven or twelve years ago the Indians captured my only sister named Marta Mujica.

Hase 11 o 12 años que me cautibaron los Yndios a una hermanita unica llamada Marta Mujica.   —Selestino Mujica, from Río Cuarto

I certify that the R. F. Brother Marcos Donati, Franciscan Missionary, has paid to the Indians of the tribes of Chief Manuel Baigorria the amount of one hundred Bolivian pesos for liberating into his power the boy captured in San Rafael.

Certifico que el R. P. Fray Marcos Donati, Misionera Franciscano, ha pagado á los indios de las tribus del Cacique Manuel Baigorria la cantidad de cien pesos bolivianos por libertad de su poder al niño cautivado en San Rafael.

—Julio Ruiz Moreno, Commandant in Chief of the Southern Border of San Luis

We have ordered dresses to be sewn which will serve when it becomes necessary to cover the nakedness of our rescued ones.

Se han mandado coser trages que servirán para el momento que sea necesario cubrir la desnudez de nuestro redimidos

—Cruz Álvarez de González and Pastora S. de Hernández, President and Secretary of the Beneficence Society of Río Cuarto

[D]o not let my poor captives fall into oblivion.

[N]o eche en olbido de mis pobres cautivos.

—Mercedes González, "mother of Rita of the captive" [*sic*]

[A]nd send me notice, I assure you what I desire is my daughter's freedom.

[Y] pasamela cuenta q'yo le abonare Us. que yo deseo es la libertad de
mi hija. — Rosario de Torres, from Río Cuarto

— Fragments of *Cartas de frontera,* by Marcela Tamagnini, compiler

The inhabitants of the frontier: Do they think in different ways according to their different ethnic cultures? Missionaries and soldiers of the last
century used to affirm, in the best Enlightenment style, that the minds
of Indians — also called "savages" — were so primitive that they were
incapable of realizing certain discursive operations in thought. Anthropologists have claimed, in our own century, that such an incapacity is due
not to an innate defect in comprehension, but to a different method of
thought.[1] Cultural disparities also occur with regard to collective memory:
"savages" and minorities don't have the same methods of memory, even if
it is not because illiterate peoples must limit themselves to oral tales, songs,
and the preservation of objects and places that evoke and reproduce traditions. The question of which elements of reality are particularly relevant
for each social group is more determinant for molding the different modes
of thinking and preserving collective memory and identity. It is significant,
for example, that the civilized marvel at the memory of "primitives" (as
in Sarmiento's amazement in *Facundo* at the ability of the tracker or the
gaucho pathfinder to identify each horse of the pampa, to follow hoof
prints, or to recognize terrain), when the technique in question is really a
habit of survival. Memory, culture, identity, and knowledge: an equation
with proper names. In the end, social thought "is essentially memory";
its content is based on collective memory, and this, in turn, depends on
cultural identities.[2]

Human associations are subject to particular modes of thinking about
social practices and their relation to the world, modes that can easily differ
from the Manichaean logic of the hegemonic culture. Each group has its
own *ethics of representation,* its moral rhetoric, its symbolic logic, its justifications of the social dynamic and the reproduction of what is understood
as reality. That which we call "social reality" is an ethical construction supported by what Zizek calls a certain "as if" (we act *as if* we believed in
the omnipotence of the bureaucracy, *as if* the president embodied the will
of the people, *as if* truth could be found in laws); in the end, ideology
is an "illusion" or a group of discourses that structure, mask, order, and
simplify our social relations *as if* they were effective and real.[3]

To affirm that right is only on the side of the State machinery and Europeanizing, white civilization, while other systems of life — like nomadism — are symptoms of an almost animal barbarism, is an ideological operation of simplification and polarization typical of the Western world of the nineteenth century. Pascal said it: our reason is wrapped in the nets of a symbolic machine.[4] Therefore the vastness of the so-called desert [*desierto*] — a geographically inaccurate name, given that the territory it describes contains areas of notable fertility — alludes more precisely to the vastness of the space that from the city is imagined as empty or deserted, even if it is populated by a society that has norms of its own. It is for that reason that the desert must be filled with words, the words of "white" reason. The wilderness must be charted; the desert must be (re)populated with inhabitants different from the original ones.

THE BODY AS VEHICLE

This chapter considers the ethics of representation, this time addressing culture's residual material (letters, memoirs), that residue that never materialized as a visible part of the national ideological network, remaining within almost private domains of knowledge. Its authors are former captives, Indians, relatives of the disappeared or kidnapped. They are the little-known voices of those who cohabited with *the other side of the frontier;* they sketch a social reality with matrices and densities different from the one the literary canon has left to us. In light of the lack of available material from the captives themselves and in search of modes of thinking different from the logic of the State, I will use letters from the frontier and focus, in the following chapter, on the *Memorias del ex cautivo Santiago Avendaño* (Memoirs of the former captive Santiago Avendaño).[5]

There are many ways to think of the frontier. It is a place of encounter, of confrontation, exchange, contagion; of ambiguity, expansion, traffic. Everything depends on the eyes that look, on the pen that writes the frontier. As the voices cited as the chapter's epigraph — voices registered between 1868 and 1880 by individuals who were themselves for the most part historically secondary — are read, the frontier appears as the space of emotional pain, of the good intentions and misery of white colonization. But, above all, as the space of commercial exchange.

The few letters of Argentine Indians that have been preserved show a commercial logic as convincing as that of any white citizen: the two groups involved in the barter mobilize in the same way, differing only in the specifics of the discourse, which depend to a large extent on the long-range intentions and the resources and necessities of each. In this way, we see in the letters that the Indians request and complain; the whites inform, request, or establish. But business remains business. From both sides of the frontier — or from both sides of "race" — bodies are spoken of as raw material: salable goods whose possession determines economic well-being. The traffic in women is supported by different logics: the logic of necessity (in the words of the poor man who has no other negotiable goods to sustain him), of good habits and morality (of those who seek servants or souls to save for God), of productivity (work-hands) or reproduction (woman as baby-machine), or of mother-love (the vast majority of the letters in search of captives are signed by the mothers, as in the case of the mothers of the disappeared in Argentina during the 1970s).

With the exception of the love of those looking to recover a lost relative, the rest are fairly similar: a woman is essentially a vehicle, a trade good whose use-value depends on youth, beauty, color, and social origin. The logic of commercial exchange levels the groups, which are undifferentiated even in the dominion of Culture and Literacy, since most of the frontier letters belie the lack of education of their writers from either side.

Dozens of quotations speak of the frontier as a space of (human) commerce. Father Bentivoglio, for example, explains how he resolved the conflict General Roca had created by forbidding their "Indian friends" to have more than one woman:

> It seemed to me that the best way to come out of that on top was the following. The Indians wanted women, claiming to need them to wash clothes and prepare food. I, taking their claims literally, *did not give them* but *old women and the ugliest ones;* demanding from one and all the promise to have only the relations of *masters* and *servants* with them.

> A mi parecióme que el modo mas al caso de salir bien de aquello era el siguiente. Los indios pedian mujeres, protestando necesitarlas para la limpieza de la ropa y preparacion de la comida. Yo tomando sus palabras al pié de la letra *no les daba* sino *mujeres ya ancianas y de las mas feas;* exigiendo de unos y de otros la promesa de no tener entre si mas relaciones que la de *amos* y *sirvientes.* [sic] (Tamagnini, 284)

The difference between the "modes of thought" or the ethical rhetoric of Indians and whites, then, is not in the way of treating white and Indian captives, since in all of these cases — except in the language of emotion — women are measured by their use-value. Old and ugly women are secondhand or dispensable goods; the priest tries to avoid libidinal regressions and satisfies himself with the master/slave dynamic. This is possible because the ugly ones are worth so little in his society that, although white, they occupy the lowest of all possible ranks: that of the savage's servants.

As Gayle Rubin says in her critique of Marx's and Freud's theories, feminine surplus-value (read: the domesticated woman as a product) depends on race, class, and the value of the woman's work: someone must cook, do the housework, wash clothing, procreate, and so on.[6] Projects of economic development, racial conflicts, commercial systems, sexual and cultural norms are all inscribed on the body of the captive.

The body of the captive was like a living map revealing tensions and war practices between racial groups. Even more than the space of the frontier — if such is possible — the body of the captive is the place of encounter, of contagion, of confrontation and defeat, of racial mixing, of questioning the official discourse about the "reality" of *the other side*. It can perhaps be described, applying Derridean logic to the strange game of cultural memory and colonial desire, as the space/object/body that invokes the confusion between opposites and at the same time erects itself in the space between them: distance and nondistance, the speakable exteriority of the different or of their opposed poles.[7] It is curious (and perhaps questionable) that the term Derrida uses is *hymen* — which for him is, within the terms of the unspeakable, "the consummation of differends, the continuity and confusion of the coitus," but which, in social practice, disappears with the loss of virginity (an idea whose cultural weight Derrida has strangely omitted). The body of the captive, the tangible bodies of hundreds of women — the "hymen" of the frontier — summarize and evince what official history wants to erase: if virginity is also an allegory of innocence (understood as a singular vision of the world), its loss must be inadmissible. The captive is a threat to epistemological stability: her existence questions, among other things, the simplification offered by the discourse of the State in its habit of dividing reality between the two opposite poles that form the lineages in national epics.

The only text written by a captive woman in the excellent compilation *Cartas de la frontera* is a letter of a few lines that does not modify the essential logic of the commercial/sexual interpellation, perhaps because its author had already returned to "civilization" or because her captivity was not long enough to modify her vision of the world.[8] Dated September 12, 1875, in Mendoza, and addressed to the priest Marcos Donati, it says:

Reverend Brother Marcos:

I hope this letter finds you without news as I would like though I do not have the pleasure to know you. Reverend Father I know that you go often to rescue captive women from the wilderness with this motive I beg you to do me the kindness of getting me a little servant that was taken from me when I and Daniel were captured I have not been able to inquire after her because I did not know in what place she was but Daniel tells me that Camargo has told him that she is in Mariano's tents so it is I pray that it will be very easy for you to get her out for the rescue the Chinita is called María; they may have sent the name because the men are coming for her; I was ten months but I considered them ten centuries since I suffered so I fear she will suffer the same so it is I beg you to do me this kindness excusing the liberty I take with this motive I have the pleasure to address you with the respect your office deserves, your humble servant

Reberendo Fray Marcos:

Deseo se alle sin nobedad como yo le decea aun que no tengo el gusto de conoserle. Reberendo padre se que su paternidad ba siempre á sacar cautibas, del decierto en este notibo le suplico me haga la carida de sacarme una sirbientita que me yebaron cuando me cautivaron á mi y á daniel yo no he podido acer diligencia por eya por que no sabia en que lugar estaba pero Daniel me dice que Camargo lea dicho que esta en los toldos de Mariano asies que yo reso que á su paternidad le sera muy facil sacarla por lo que esta tan rescate la Chinita se yama maria; puede ser que la ayan mandado el nombre por quer los hombres bienen por ella; yo estube dies meses pero los considere como dies siglos y como sufre tanto me fiuro que ella sufrira lo mismo asies que poreso le suplico me aga esta carida dispensando la cofianza que me tomo con este motibo tengo el gusto de saludarlo con el debido respeto que su paternidad merece, su S.S.

(Jisdela de Amparan, in Tamagnini, 199)

What do we read in this letter? Except for the novelty of having been written by an ex-captive, nothing very different from what the logic of the State prescribes: the Church as mediator, indigenous space as diffuse and indeterminate, the conventional but revealing implication that the Indian will be happier as a servant of the whites than among Indians. Other details: handwriting indicative of the modest origins and scant education of the author, the whole experience of her own captivity summarized in a temporal hyperbole (ten months lived as ten centuries), no concrete details about the experience, not even in the form of gratitude toward whoever liberated her from captivity, save that the author was kidnapped with a relative (Daniel). There is no reason to doubt either her suffering or the good intentions that accompany this letter. What is notable is that the victim for whom she claims salvation is referred to first as a "little servant" (a diminutive that may be affectionate but is, ultimately, diminutive), later as *china* (a term used at that time with reference to Indian women, mestizas, and the wives of ranch hands), and that only her Christian name, María, is used after all those appellatives and the invocation of a long chain of masculine names: first reverend brother, addressee of the letter; then Daniel, an ex-captive who as such retains only his first name, like women and children; then Camargo, probably a bilingual/intermediary; and, immediately after, the chief Mariano Rosas, a figure of power *from the other side* (Rosas's political demise, according to the date of the letter, was imminent at the time it was written).

The letter of Jiselda de Amparan, who uses the possessive preposition to indicate her status as a married woman ("de" Amparan), denotes a certain resignation before the naturalness of the order of things. The emphasis is not on the extraordinary quality of her experience (she had been a captive for ten months, a fact that seems almost quotidian, since she grants it so little space); instead she has chosen as her persuasive strategy humility and submission to the priest as both intermediary and religious authority. We can infer that the author of the letter had little sense of the value of the word, especially given that its spontaneity and innocence make the letter all the more revealing.[9] Suffering and captivity do not seem to have modified substantially either the ex-captive's habits, or her values, or her way of understanding feminine relationships. Even after having shared the experience of captivity with her, the author does not introduce María as a woman subjected to the same Calgary, but as, above all, a little servant to recover (and to help).

The inhabitants of the frontier, then: Do they think in different ways according to their different ethnic cultures? Race and social origin are so determinant that the ideological structure is modified ("contaminated") in a significant way only by prolonged cohabitation with the *Other*; only if the exposed individuals see the attributes of their earlier subjectivity displaced by their new position within the social group, as in the case of those whites who sought refuge among the Indians — in the manner of Manuel Baigorria — and for that reason lived a peculiar form of captivity, as we will see. Some of those individuals recover their frame of reference if they manage to recover their position in the society to which they originally pertained. As Pascal said, reflecting upon the automatism of human beings: habits have much more sway on the system of beliefs than the most solid proof.[10] This is the phenomenon that has been explained, in good measure, through the term "interpellation."[11]

I will conclude these reflections on the chorus of epistolary voices of the frontier and the ethics of representation with a return to the beginning: the representation of the social is but a moral exercise, loaded with values, interests, and desires to a large extent "gridded" by ideological nets. Minds are not "primitive" or developed: each culture has its own logic. The only difference is that the dominant rhetoric attributes to itself the value of reason and buries the dominated in the miasma of impulse, intuition, improvisation, without noticing that the dominated demonstrates similar commercial interests, at least in what refers to the goods and the bodies of the frontier.

Chapter 7

THE STORY OF A JOURNEY
WITH NO RETURN

Why are the streets and squares emptying so rapidly,
everyone going home so lost in thought?
> *Because night has fallen and the barbarians have not come.*
> *And some who have just returned from the border say*
> *there are no barbarians any longer.*
And now, what's going to happen to us without the barbarians?
They were, those people, a kind of solution.

—C. P. Cavafy, "Waiting for the Barbarians,"
translated by Edmund Keeley and Philip Sherrard

This section of this chapter about different voices of the frontier is dedicated to a narrative of *desire to return*. The majority of nineteenth-century travel narratives register only the vicissitudes of the journey out, the astonishment, the discoveries, the unexpected landscapes and cultures on the other side, in the realm of the Other or others. The *return journey,* in contrast, implies a way of seeing different from that of someone who simply visits: it is the vision of someone who has *understood* so much that it has changed his language, the parameters of his understanding, and even the comfort he takes in his possessions. The example here is Santiago Avendaño, a nineteenth-century Argentine who was kidnapped by the Indians and remained among them so long that after his escape he could not with any degree of naturalness rejoin the white society he had left, and so spent the rest of his days attempting to mediate between the two spaces. Thus, while the conventional traveler attempts to illuminate a world for us (in his perpetual outward movement, journeying forth, losing nothing, always certain that he will return home), the former captive Santiago Avendaño is another kind of traveler, one who is making a *return* journey, or more precisely who is *trying to return*. But the journey has "contaminated" him. Avendaño's narrative vainly attempts to recuperate a sense of home: this type of traveler is incapable of freeing himself from the knowledge acquired during the journey.

What matters in the narrative of a *journey out* is power over the world visited. A *journey out* is a voyage of conquest and reveals the attitude of the visitor: interested in what is different, without allowing him or herself to become contaminated. William Henry Hudson's famous book *Idle Days in Patagonia* is a perfect illustration of what I call the journey out. What is notable is that, as Mónica Szurmuk has noted, the Anglo-Argentine Hudson never crossed Patagonia, having accidentally shot himself just as he was about to set out, and wrote the narrative in England twenty-three years after the frustrated trip.[1] Nevertheless, dozens of important books on Patagonia have been founded on Hudson's account, even those produced by Argentine authors like Jorge Luis Borges and Ezequiel Martínez Estrada.

The writing of the *journey out* relies as much on knowledge of the real as on the author's figuration of the real and capacity to insert it into the framework of the believable, into readers' horizon of expectation. In contrast, what matters most in writing of the *desire to return* is power: not the entomologist's gaze but the survivor's. So what do they look for, those who are trying to return? In general, to know and become known, to identify a place on the human and cultural map for the subject who writes, and at the same time to ask readers to allow themselves to be permeated by the experience, or rather by the traversal itself. Writing that longs to return is not on the lookout for unexpected scenes like the tourist with his photographic machine, nor does it stop to describe nature like someone who has never seen it before or to collect exotic details like an anthropologist. Unlike the writing of an individual just passing through, the textualization of the desire to return is preoccupied with belonging, with giving the lie to established prejudices about the culture visited, with inserting the author with some legitimacy in or among the places inhabited. This is the source of a preoccupation with genealogies, pacts, political alliances, power.

In an era in which the voyage was widely represented as revelation, at the moment of the great explorations of the hearts of Africa and Latin America, at the time of Livingstone's voyage and scarcely a decade after the appearance of Sarmiento's *Facundo,* a voice of undistinguished appearance arises. It commits an exaggeration of culture: the desire to return. The text is the *Memorias del ex cautivo Santiago Avendaño,* an account of the narrator's experiences after his kidnapping in the south of the Province of Santa Fe, Argentina, by a Ranquel raiding party in 1842.[2]

Avendaño lived as a captive between the ages of seven and fifteen.

His memoirs, begun in 1854 and written over almost a decade, were left unedited for more than a century. They were held in archives, first in the hands of Indians (can one speak of Indian "archives"?),[3] then in the archives of the soldier Estanislao Zeballos, watched over by Zeballos's heirs, and finally in the archives of the Museum of Luján. They were published for the first time in April 1999, 125 years after Avendaño's death, thanks to the efforts of Jorge Rojas Lagarde, who found and photocopied them, and Father Meinrado Hux, who corrected Avendaño's original spelling "to achieve better comprehensibility," set the text in chronological order, and added, in the form of a third chapter, "a page that was a sort of autobiography" enriched "by a few facts culled from his other pages."

Avendaño spent much of his adult life as an interpreter between cultures, ultimately occupying the official position of Intendente de los Indios, a kind of representative of the law who intervened in disputes between whites and Indians. But Avendaño's efforts as intermediary could have no effect within a policy of national development that did not want mediations, a policy that would continue to subjugate with violence and oblivion a reality that by sheer force of will would become white and European.

MAPS AND KNOWLEDGE

The *Memorias del ex cautivo* must be incomplete, since the prologue announces that a final section describing the customs of the Arauca Indians "will be published shortly." The book contains a map inserted between the prologue and the text itself but does not indicate whether it was Avendaño's idea to depict the itinerary of his flight or an addition of the editor. Every map is an act and at the same time an object of order and appropriation;[4] in this case Avendaño's text has been ordered as much as the territory itself, and it was appropriated when Zeballos borrowed heavily from Avendaño in writing *Painé*. Maps usually appear at the end of books, as in A. Guinnard's *Tres años de esclavitud entre los patagones (Relato de mi cautiverio)* (Three years of slavery among the Patagonians: The story of my captivity) or Lucio V. Mansilla's *Una excursión a los indios ranqueles;* there are few resources so efficient for constructing the concept of *place.*[5] *Memorias del ex cautivo* establishes itself as a tale/itinerary of an unstable zone that, at the time of the narrated events, was considered empty and not yet clearly inscribed within the topography of the nation.

Avendaño's description of his flight — despite following the indications of the path traced by Manuel Baigorria with references to places with

"Christian" names — is in fact limited to a rhetoric that is not civilized (as the Christian names would suggest) but rather nomadic: he speaks of rivers, lagoons, stars, and cows and determines distances covered in terms of days and nights of riding. The map, in contrast, is charged with normalizing the route by identifying places with their Christian names, neutralizing the protagonist's immersion in another culture, and inclining the tale more toward the logic of the whites than toward that of an ex-captive who never wished to rid himself of what he had learned among the Indians. In reality, the nomenclature of white topography surrounds the indigenous topography on the map, which uses Indian names (whose translation is utilitarian, given that it tends to refer to concrete facts about the place) to refer to the places of his flight.

The pulchritude of the map reinscribes the text. Notice the difference between Avendaño's logic and that of another former captive, Guinnard, whom I cite at length because his words are enormously interesting:

On the map that appears at the end of this tale I have traced an itinerary of the places I lived during so much time. This work could not be, and *is not, of mathematical certitude,* because I have lived in a state of almost complete deprivation and *I have not had at my disposal adequate instruments* to determine the diverse positions of the places I have been. Nonetheless, thanks to my *faithful memory* and to the care I always took to note the different directions that I followed with the Indians, my friends, and thanks also to the habit I acquired of calculating distances covered by the incomparable horses of those distant regions, which easily gallop from dawn to the setting of the sun, I obtained as measurement, after discounting what was due to the difficulties of the terrain, twenty-five leagues per day. However approximate this measure may be, it is not far from the truth.

En el mapa que figura al fin de este relato he trazado un itinerario de los parajes en que he vivido durante tanto tiempo. Este trabajo no podrá ser, y *no es, de una exactitud matemática,* porque como he vivido en el más completo estado de denudez, *no he tenido a mi disposición los instrumentos adecuados* para determinar las diversas posiciones de los sitios que he recorrido. Sin embargo, gracias a mi *memoria fiel* y al cuidado que siempre tuve de notar las diferentes direcciones que he seguido con los indios, mis amigos, y gracias también a la costumbre que adquirí de calcular las distancias recorridas con los incomparables caballos de esas regiones lejanas, que galopan fácilmente desde la aurora hasta la tardía puesta del sol, obtuve como media, después de descontar lo debido a las dificultades del terreno, veinticinco leguas por día. Por aproximada que sea esta medida, no está muy alejada de la verdad. (*Tres años,* 10)

Like Avendaño, Guinnard does not use the instruments of "white" science. In an exceptional example of respect toward the knowledge of the Other, Guinnard explains that the language used to designate places is also significant:

The reader will no doubt ask himself why the map is written in an *unknown language.* It is because, knowing the language of these nomads, I have arrived at the certainty that until now not only have the names of the tribes been truncated, but a very small number of them are even known. The spelling of those names differs from that generally used because I think not only that it is necessary to make those diverse denominations known, but that it is useful, at least, to preserve their true indigenous pronunciation.

[P]reguntará, sin duda, el lector, por qué ese mapa está escrito en *idioma desconocido.* Es porque, conociendo el idioma de esos nómadas, he llegado a la certeza de que hasta ahora no solamente se ha truncado el nombre de sus tribus, sino también que sólo se conoce un número pequeño de ellas. La ortografía de esos nombres difiere de la generalmente adoptada porque pienso que no solamene es necesario hacer conocer esas denominaciones diversas, sino que es útil, por lo menos, conservar su verdadera pronunciación indígena. (*Tres años,* 10)

Neither Guinnard (*Tres años,* 10–11) nor Avendaño (*Memorias,* 233) could preserve a single memory-object from his captivity or his journey, "so that many people refuse to believe in the possibility of my return after such trials" (*Tres años,* 11). Although Avendaño's writing strategy tends to cover this "fault" with an abundance of attention-getting dates and names, a large portion of the text is impregnated with nomadic logic, as we will see shortly. The first paragraph of "Una página autobiográfica de Santiago Avendaño" (An autobiographical page by Santiago Avendaño) demonstrates this abundance:

I, Santiago Avendaño, was captured by an invasion of Ranquilche Indians at a rural establishment in the South of the Province of Santa Fe on March 15, 1842. I was then exactly seven years, seven months, and 21 days old, when I was torn from my parents. Papá was named Domingo Avendaño and Mamá, Felipa Lefebre. We were five brothers: Juan José, Andrés, Pepe, Fausto, and I. The older ones taught me to read because there was no school in the neighborhood. I was the youngest of the children. I was born on July 24, 1834. On March 16 of that year, 1842, the Ranquilche Indians took me with them to their tents. I later learned that the invasion had been led by the chiefs Coliqueo, Painé, Nahuelcheo, Güenu-vil, Güenu-cal, and others, whose names I have forgotten.

Yo, Santiago Avendaño, fui raptado por una invasión de indios ranquilches en un establecimiento rural al Sur de la Provincia de Santa Fe, el 15 de marzo de 1842. Tenía entonces exactamente 7 años, 7 meses y 21 días, cuando fui arrancado de mis padres. Papá se llamaba Domingo Avendaño y mamá, Felipa Lebefre. Eramos cinco hermanos: Juan José, Andrés, Pepe, Fausto y yo. Los mayores me enseñaron a leer porque no había escuela en el vecindario. Yo era el menor de los hijos. Había nacido el 24 de julio de 1834. El 16 de marzo de ese 1842 los indios ranquilches me arrastraron consigo hacia sus toldos. Luego supe que la invasión había sido encabezada por los caciques Coliqueo, Painé, Nahuelcheo, Calfuqueo, Güenu-vil, Güenu-Cal y otros, cuyos nombres olvidé. (*Memorias,* 90)

The attention to such concrete fact — better yet, the deluge of facts in some parts of the text — seems to compensate for the writer's insecurity and need to prove something to the reader, who figures explicitly in the text. When the narrative addresses the reader, it is usually to announce a correction of historical facts or to assert that Avendaño knows this information well because it was personally related to him: the text wants to *prove something* to the whites and to *rectify* the deformations and abuses committed by false "experts" on the frontier.[6]

The writing style of the most famous white soldier to live extensively among the Indians, Manuel Baigorria, has little in common with Avendaño's. His *Memorias* are written in the third person and present syntactical difficulties so enormous that they affect the reader's comprehension.[7] He spent decades living among the Indians voluntarily, as a refugee from the Rosas government. It is a testimonial of great interest because it was written by a person of Baigorria's stature; nonetheless the text has little narrative or descriptive value since it avoids a personal tone at every moment and seems more like a list of activities.[8] In terms of its declared objective Baigorria's text is also very different from Avendaño's: Baigorria writes because he is bored — as he declares in the first paragraph of the book — whereas Avendaño writes to establish a truth (the indigenous one) and his knowledge of that truth or identity as a person capable of knowing that truth.

The uncertainty of his position and the need to prove himself an authority on the material lead Avendaño to produce a text that is a generic hybrid: instead of being simply autobiographical, *Memorias del ex cautivo* oscillates between a personal account and the outline of a history of the Indians. More than half the book consists of the reconstruction of deeds that he did not witness personally, but that his access to direct sources enables him to rectify or tell for the first time. In fact, the book assembles the origin of Cafulcurá's hegemony on the pampa, the history of the Ranquel, the death of Chief Painé, and anecdotes concerning the behavior of other chiefs along with the story of Avendaño's personal captivity, flight, return to civilization, imprisonment in Palermo, and conscription by order of dictator Juan Manuel de Rosas. Of all these, Avendaño managed to publish only "Fuga de un cautivo de los indios, narrado por él" (A captive's flight from the Indians, narrated by himself [1867]) and "La muerte del cacique Painé por testigo ocular" (The death of Chief Painé, by an eye-witness [1868]) during his lifetime, in the *Revista Buenos Aires*. These two are only testimonial fragments; what is interesting is that the book itself begins with a historical reconstruction rather than a rehearsal of its own lineage, as usually occurs in literary memoirs like Sarmiento's *Recuerdos de provincia*.

EDITING

The editor's corrections of the text are not as grave as those of another testimonial that was re-edited a century later, the Cuban Juan Francisco Manzano's *Autobiografía de un esclavo* (Autobiography of a slave). Manzano's text resulted from a rather different situation. It was originally written at the direction of a white man and was to be *used* for political purposes that included the author's liberation from slavery: in consequence Manzano's *Autobiografía* was modified by various mediators from the time it was written. The Cuban slave had to enter into "white" space in order to be heard; Avendaño, in contrast, was a white who had lived as a captive among Indians and wrote for a white audience, from white civilization, many years after the event: Avendaño traveled in the desire to return. Though both describe captivity, the problematization of the subject is very different in each text.[9] Much more serious, in terms of appropriations and manipulations of knowledge, is what soldier Estanislao Zeballos did as the temporary proprietor of Avendaño's manuscripts: he excerpted parts of the text, practically without citing them, to include in his book *Painé: La dinastía de los zorros*. Zeballos's *Painé*, in contrast to its source, is a paradigmatic text of what I have been calling the *journey out*. Reading *Memorias del ex cautivo* forces one to qualify the term "barbarism" that was so often ascribed to the Indians in order to differentiate them from the whites and justify the actions of the self-declared "civilization." Zeballos's text, in contrast, contains the topoi of other *journeys out*: from violence to the invasive eroticism of the Indians, martyrology of the Christian mothers in captivity, hostile nature, shame for the white victims' "outraged virginity," nostalgia for a lost order, horror at the atrocious cruelty of the savages, a strong textualization of bodies (absent from almost all nineteenth-century literature), and Hispanization of the white women (conceived essentially as mothers). The narrative voice of Zeballos's and other conventional texts is white and projects the values of urbanization and domesticity; it is inclined toward commercial development and private property. And it is directed toward a reading public that expects to find exactly these images, images that confirm its understanding of the world of the frontier.

President Avellaneda had charged Estanislao Zeballos to write in order to sway public opinion toward the Conquista del Desierto that would complete the extermination of the Indians. The writing of *Painé* shows the machine of the State appropriating and manipulating even the ambivalent memories of a former captive.

THE ANTIMODEL: *EL CAUTIVITO*

Against (or in the interval between) the appearance of two national texts as weighty as Domingo F. Sarmiento's *Facundo: Civilización o barbarie* and Lucio V. Mansilla's *Una excursión a los indios ranqueles,* another narrative was begun. It is the work of a provincial author whose project was to be nothing but that, whose only desire was to remain close to his family, to read, practice his religious traditions, and serve the country in a government position. But the tensions that divide the map (civilization/barbarism) threaten the text as well. The text is hidden as if within a crease that will not be opened again for a century and a half. The *Memorias* remain within the crease, even though the schema Avendaño proposed could have served as an alternative to the metropolitan models of commerce and progress that Europhile Argentina preferred to pursue.

The model that Avendaño's text shows is, simply, that of a nation established on notions of family, province, religion, work, and cooperation among the ethnic groups that inhabit the same territory. Avendaño's personal history demonstrates that his project was not admissible. On the one hand, he was not completely unhappy among the Indians. On the other — and much more revealing of the inadmissibility of the project embodied by his life as an intermediary — is the fact that Santiago Avendaño fell victim to the Mitrist Revolution.[10] He was murdered by the white army, killed with Chief Cipriano Catriel while he was trying to act as interpreter and secretary. Avendaño died as one Indian more.

Avendaño's inaugural text establishes an indigenous genealogy that refers to the myths of origin: it describes the almost mythical foundation of a people, but with a tricky and manipulative hero — Cafulcurá — capable of political operations so Machiavellian, so carefully calculated to consolidate his power that they immediately give the lie to the stereotype that Indians are not rational. The organization of the text is extremely important, and its editor, Meinrado Hux, insists that he followed Avendaño's indications regarding the organization of the material very closely. The account takes place between two poles that frame it, two powers that determine its content: Cafulcurá and Rosas, in the first and last chapters, respectively.

Michel de Certeau has said that "every narrative is the narrative of a journey — a spacial practice," that narratives cross and organize places, select and relate them.[11] In the case of *Memorias del ex cautivo* the traversal is produced throughout a clear territorial space but is framed — at least in the structure of the only edition to which we have access today — by the figure of the "strongman." The life narrated is generated between these two poles of strong, wicked men on either side of the frontier: mothers who lose their children to the arbitrariness of men who kidnap or imprison them, tribes that relate and negotiate with each other, families that live on one side of the frontier or the other. The landscape, which one could certainly suppose was important in the description of the space of the frontier, occupies only a secondary place: it is described only with regard to its effect on human beings, who suffer from the lack of food and the aridity of the environment, search for signs that indicate whether or not they are on the correct trail, and remember certain sites for what has occurred there — murders, flights, burials. Only once is the landscape described as a place of beauty and pleasure, inhabited by birds and flowers (*Memorias,* 185): but the "beauty" of the scene is determined by the presence of water, horses, and cows.

The figure of the "strongman," embodied most often by Rosas, was fundamental to the establishment of the subject and the writer's location before diverse forms of barbarism in *Facundo: Civilización y barbarie,* the texts of Esteban Echeverría, and José Marmol's *Amalia*. The great works of nineteenth-century Argentina are figurations of citizenship, an interpretative key that can be applied to the *Memorias,* even though Avendaño was not "lettered" in the conventional sense and his concept of "citizenship" includes understanding indigenous life. The presence of the strongman in Avendaño's text is indicative of the enormous extent to which support or rejection of Rosas, the Restorer, tended to polarize identity in Argentina at midcentury.

It warrants saying, in passing, that if this text has no pretensions to literary greatness, the quality of Avendaño's writing is an agreeable surprise. There are passages that for style and force are worthy of the best of the era, such as the unforgettable account of a group of Indians who challenge the laws of the jungle by spending the night there and fall victim to a tiger who quarters the most obstinate among them. The role of religion is much more active in *Memorias del ex cautivo* than in the texts of the literary canon: the captive boy maintains his identity thanks to the preservation of a few Catholic rituals and his identification of filial love and loyalty with love of the Virgin and "civilization." Associations of this kind are common among children of little formal education; and it is important to note that *Memorias del ex cautivo* stops short of the religiosity of North American captivity narratives, many of which are imbued with a profound Puritan morality.

In terms of attitude toward captive women the *Memorias del ex cautivo* diverges little from the white masculine gaze of the era. The 1999 edition, excluding the prologue, numbers 330 pages: in all these there are only two mentions of the white woman who shared Avendaño's captivity in the same indigenous family. He names "Rosa" (with no surname) only three times to demonstrate how much the family from which he was to escape loved him: nothing more is said of her throughout the account. Curiously, Avendaño sees captive women much as the others of his era do: as objects of exchange and negotiation that deserve first and last names only to indicate their value.[12]

Avendaño is not totally unhappy among the Indians, as I have said, contradicting the few narratives that exist about captivity in Argentina — written, with the exception of Mansilla's, by authors who had never traveled to the frontier — in which the emphasis is generally on the savagery of the raid (the moment of the kidnapping) and the cruelty of the Indians, as in the case of Echeverría's poem *La cautiva*. Avendaño's real complaints against captivity are that he misses his parents and — even more strongly — he fears that he will lose his religious faith by continuing to live among the

Indians. Out of loyalty to his faith, out of fear of losing it in prolonged contact with other customs and ways of seeing the world, he decides to attempt an escape. Curiously, as he makes his flight Avendaño feels terribly guilty for having betrayed the Indian he had called "father" and for having stolen a pair of horses. In more conventional captivity narratives the space of the Indian is represented as infernal: the fleeing captive would represent his or her escape as redemption or salvation rather than betrayal. Avendaño is reassured by the conviction that he acts in the service of his God and the Virgin of Mercies, protector of captives. The episode of the flight is certainly the only one in which nature is really present, but it is present because the protagonist's survival depends upon it. Before and after the episode the traveler ignores the landscape, ignorant of the fact that nature is one of the principal ingredients of nineteenth-century travel narrative.

When the young fugitive finally reaches a civilized area, he spends a few days recovering. He is finally sent to Buenos Aires for an interview with Rosas: the dictator interrogates him in detail about the Indians' movements and gives him permission to visit his parents, as he has so long desired. But if the text could be read as the narrative of a return to the maternal bosom, in truth Avendaño spends scarcely two days with his parents, and then a brother. By Rosas's order he returns to Buenos Aires, where he begins to study for the priesthood, because he feels that he should dedicate his life to the Church in thanks for his return to "civilization," or — to put it in terms more faithful to Avendaño's values — for his return to the world of his elders. Nonetheless, things do not go according to his plan: Rosas conscripts him for a project that the former captive describes as hell itself. If *Una excursión a los indios ranqueles* is Mansilla's Oedipal journey from Fort Sarmiento to the huts of Chief Mariano Rosas — a metaphor for the lettered author's conflict between his relationship with Sarmiento and his uncle, the former dictator Rosas[13] — then *Memorias del ex cautivo* is the traversal of a humble worker of the lower middle class who travels from point to point in the space dominated by the great chiefs. Indians on one side, Rosas on the other — Avendaño has no way to choose between them. The tragedy of his fate is unbecoming to Argentina's genealogical traditions, in which the conventions of community and citizenship were established with far from common accord among the inhabitants. A small, provincial citizen, he is a captive on either side: there is no place on the map where he can feel the liberating return home.

Avendaño's text does not inform in the way of travel narratives, which approach the space of the Other with eyes predisposed for awe, conditioned to be amazed by exotic nature, exotic animals, exotic humans and their exotic customs. For Avendaño the only thing that really matters is constituting a subject with some power of arbitration or, in more contemporary terms, with some power to arbitrate and to recover the genealogies (of the local powers, not of the lineages the nation has chosen as its origin). His writing reconstructs the guile of the indigenous pacts, pacts between Indians and whites, pacts between friends and enemies. His logic is not that of civilization and barbarism, as could be expected from what we know of the epistemology of the era; his logic is that of the traitor or the friend—those are the values that matter for survival, those are the values that the narrator will construct again and again. It is probably for that reason that he does not pause to describe the Indians' foods or how they marry or celebrate; the raids themselves he describes without detail, and the only thing that matters is the success or failure of each attack, since survival depends upon it. But to hope that Avendaño will describe customs among the Indians would be like hoping that he will also describe them after his return to Buenos Aires: he is a traveler in both spaces, a traveler who does not pertain to any group, who will remain in that unstable traversal until the moment he dies as Intendente de los Indios, appointed by the whites, murdered by the whites as if he were an Indian. His description of Buenos Aires must be as utilitarian as his description of the pampas.

In *Memorias de ex cautivo* the only episode Avendaño describes with the amazement and detail of a typical traveler is the arrival in San Luis after his arduous flight: in those days of transition he looks at the whites as cautiously as if he were trying to recognize his own true identity in them. In reality the one being looked at is Avendaño, in his new identity as "el cautivito." The boy Avendaño has returned among the whites to become a local attraction: the entire population takes turns to come look at *el cautivito*, who cannot withstand the weight of their gazes. During a dinner in which his new identity has been on display, *el cautivito* bursts out:

> After much insistence I confessed that the twenty-two gazes that were directed at me at the same time seemed to find there a being unlike the others and that, being the same as everyone else, I could not suffer them to do to me what I did not do to anyone.

> Yo después de mucha instancia confesé que las 22 miradas que se dirigían a mí a un mismo tiempo parecía que encontraban allí un ser extraño a los demás y que, siendo igual a todos, no podía sufrir que hiciesen conmigo lo que yo no hacía con nadie. (246)

Avendaño's protest is the note of someone who journeys with the desire to return: no one is strange to him, and he cannot bear to be considered strange himself. What is more, the boy has just survived a terrible adventure to escape from captivity and return to his own kind: a terrible paradox, given that he has lost the privilege of being the adored son of a powerful Indian to become — with all the weight of that identity — *el cautivito,* a stranger, forever. Among the Indians he could have remained the favorite, nurturing the hope of recovering another "full" (if utopian) identity: among the Indians he could have become a citizen as if he had never been captured by a raid. But now, social reality falls upon him with all its weight: unlike the tourist or the conventional traveler, this young white man has been "touched" by the experience — according to the eyes of those who look at him — and for that reason he is no longer from here or there, he is a half-citizen, he is a "touched" stranger. Although in the text Avendaño assures us that his dinner companions understood his discomfort at being the object of so many curious gazes, after that night *el cautivito* is passed from one person to another, like an exhibition.

THE INTERMEDIARY

The *Memorias del ex cautivo* participate in the rhetoric of power in the sense that they construct a subject who aspires to a position within that power: Avendaño seeks to legitimate himself as a mediator. As he does so, he introduces a subject that differs from the one the men of letters were establishing but that reproduces canonical values with regard to captive women.[14] If Sarmiento's *Facundo: Civilización y barbarie* (1845) and *Recuerdos de provincia* (1850) can be read as constructions of a writer who mediates between European culture ("high" culture) and Argentine reality (gauchos, Rosas, nature, politics, the countryside, the provinces, and the city), then *Memorias del ex cautivo* can be read as the construction of a different type of mediator, one who intervenes between the logic of the State and the logic of the Indians. The objective of the text is clear: to convince readers that not just anyone can opine about the frontier, nor much less be authorized to intercede in the establishment of peace treaties.[15]

Avendaño reiterates his legitimacy in different ways. He says, "I do not think like that, because what I affirm *I have experienced personally*. And I have collected among the Indians all that I recount of past years" (Yo no pienso así porque lo que afirmo *lo he palpado personalmente*. Y he recogido

entre los indios cuanto refiero de años atrás) (75). The end of his autobiographical page declares that although he "cries tears upon remembering
the past" among the Indians,

> now I like to remember that time, those people and their customs. I
> have read some writing, a few articles that speak of the history and
> the customs of the Indians without having known them up close,
> expressing themselves in a way that is incomplete, insufficient, and
> adulterated. I hope to express myself better here.

> ahora me gusta recordar aquel tiempo, aquella gente y sus costum-
> bres. He leído algunos escritos, algunos artículos que hablan de la
> historia y de las costumbres de los indios sin haberlos conocido
> de cerca, expresándose de una manera incompleta, insuficiente y
> adulterada. Espero expresarme aquí mejor. (90)

In the construction of the subject/mediator, direct knowledge of the
Other alone is insufficient: *savoir dire* is also indispensable. Avendaño,
though of humble origins and kidnapped too early to have received a
formal education, continually emphasizes the value of his autodidactic
knowledge in a play of (displaced) mirrors with the Sarmiento of *Recuerdos
de provincia*. The last paragraph of *Memorias del ex cautivo* insists:

> To the government, I would report many advantages in employing
> in these matters persons who combine good instruction, honesty,
> good judgment, and practical sense, and are versed in the knowledge
> of uses and customs and especially of the language of the Indians.
> The agent must indispensably possess such qualities. Without them
> one could only do what has been done up to now and would be at
> the mercy of the roguish interpreters, who are usually those villains
> that have lived many years among the Indians and have a genius for
> disturbing things more than improving them.

> Al gobierno le reportaría muchas ventajas emplear en estos asun-
> tos a personas que reúnan buena instrucción, honradez, buen juicio
> y sentido práctico, y estén versadas en el conocimiento de usos y
> costumbres y especialmente de la lengua de los indios. El empleado
> deberá indispensablemente poseer tales cualidades. Sin ellas sólo se
> haría lo que hasta aquí se ha hecho y tendría que estar a merced de
> los pillastres intérpretes, que por lo regular son de esos malvados que
> han vivido muchos años entre los indios y que por su genio se afanan
> en descomponer las cosas más que en mejorarlas. (359)

In contrast to other captives too poor to have had any education (160), Avendaño was taught to read by his older brothers "to keep me from getting into mischief," an accomplishment that will win him the admiration of the Indians. "They believed they saw a prodigy when they saw me read with such facility. For my age, according to the Indians, this was a lot of knowledge" (Ellos creían ver un prodigio cuando me veían leer con tanta soltura, pues para mi edad, según los indios, esto era mucho saber) (160).

Avendaño comes to be considered the favorite son of his master Caniú. In one notable passage he puts into the mouth of the Indian the wisdom the narrator aspires to produce in his white readers: the belief that he is an amphibian, extraordinarily capable of moving between two worlds. "Son," Caniú tells him, "you are going to be a great man. When you are mature, you will have us in the palm of your hand. Our fortune will depend on you. *You know how to speak our language as if you were an Indian and you speak with the paper as if you were speaking with someone*" (Hijo, vos vas a ser un gran hombre. Cuando seas maduro, nos vas a tener en la palma de tu mano. Nuestra suerte va a depender de vos. Sabés hablar en la lengua nuestra como si fueras indio y hablas con el papel como si hablaras con alguien) (156). The Indian compares him to other whites living among the Indians (Baigorria, the Chileans Zúñiga and Valdebenito, the mulatto Iturra) and predicts that his future will be much more brilliant because he *knows the language better than they do*. In a gesture unusual in the owner of a captive, Caniú tells him, during the same dialogue: "I do not charge you with more than my sons, your brothers, with whom you are growing up. That you look after them and give them a slice of bread if destiny carries you to your land and if, as I hope, you make yourself a son of this free land and you are married in it" (Yo no te encargo más que a mis hijos, tus hermanos, con quienes te vas criando. Que los mires bien y arrojes una rebanada de pan si el destino te llevara a tu tierra y si, como lo espero, te hacés hijo de esta tierra libre y te casas en ella). What is more, the sense of the entire text is summarized in the words of Caniú, which follow the logic of Avendaño, who remains "civilized" thanks to the filial love he has learned from Christian devotion: "Who knows to what end God tore you from your land so that you would come to these lands? Perhaps so that with time the Indians would have someone to do something for them?" (¿Quién sabe con qué fin Dios te arrancó de tu tierra para que vinieras a estas tierras? ¿Tal vez para que con el tiempo los indios tuvieran quien haga por ellos?) (157).

Every memoir, like all autobiography, is a gesture of self-representation. Avendaño presents himself as a chosen one who can save one side and the other without putting either lineage at risk. In fact, unlike more traditional captives, Avendaño never runs the risk of having a mestizo ("contaminated") progeny, since his master intends for him to marry a white like himself, even if he continues to live among the Indians. Even his high value among the Ranquel — his master refuses to include him in a shipment of ten captives being sent to Buenos Aires to show good will in the peace negotiations — is rooted in the fact that, despite having learned what was necessary to serve the indigenous (as in the care of horses), he continues to be a "white": he has not forgotten his language, he knows how to read and write, he serves as mediator when necessary, he has a "Christian" book of prayers that Baigorria has given him, and, upon reaching adulthood, he will return to "white" civilization and power over the Indians. The relative power attributed to the young Avendaño was certainly never shared by the women or girls in captivity.[16]

Setting aside the enormous distances between their beliefs about the world and, even more importantly, what each represented as a figure in the society of his time, we can see that Avendaño as much as Sarmiento was one of the "chosen." One will ascend from the provinces and a not-too-illustrious lineage to become president of the republic, an ascent that was laboriously built with political activity and autobiographical texts like *Mi defensa* (My defense) and *Recuerdos de provincia*. The other, also provincial but of rural origins,[17] would have been one the great figures of Argentine history, as a negotiator who allowed civilization to advance in a direction that also included the Indians. Lacking Sarmiento's zeal for the civilizing mission, Avendaño (his text) remained sepulchered among the sand dunes with the Indians (in fact he dies murdered by whites as an Indian, beside an Indian). He remains a very marginal character, author of a text that was until now practically a secret despite its merits. *Facundo* helps to figure the destiny and the identity of the nation, while *Memorias del ex cautivo* could not have been more peripheral to Argentine culture: the comparison illuminates the process of canon formation as an ethics of representation and collective memory.

NOMADIC LOGIC

In "Treatise on Nomadology: The War-Machine,"[18] Gilles Deleuze and Félix Guattari reflect on the logic of nomads and the logic of the State. They compare the logic of the State to chess, since everything in the game is already codified with properties that determine the movements of the pieces. One of the reasons that *Memorias del ex cautivo* is such a fascinating text to read is that it reflects a logic different from that of chess. Avendaño, as has been said, writes from within the white culture, remembering his experience of many years ago. Although he has returned and is arguing for his own position in civilized society, his logic differs from that of the State machine and resembles instead the logic Deleuze and Guattari describe with regard to the nomadic war machine. I will summarize their theoretical proposal because it is extremely useful for understanding the richness of the former captive's writing. This perspective is especially rich for comparing Avendaño's writing to *Facundo,* since Sarmiento's work was and continues to be extraordinarily important in Argentine and Latin American culture.

The law of the State divides the representation of reality between interior and exterior; nomads see space as something undivided, while the State sees it as divided (metered). In one case, space is occupied without being measured; in the other, it is measured so that it may be occupied. The State needs to subordinate hydraulic force to conduits, canals, and dikes that impede its turbulence, that oblige the flow to move from one point to another. Nomadic science, on the other hand, consists in expanding itself through turbulence in an undivided space, in producing movement that occupies the space and affects all points simultaneously: in the case that concerns us, it is the logic of the raid.

Neither is better or worse: the nomad, unlike the migrant who goes from one point to another, only passes through the points as stages in a course that distributes human beings and animals in an open, undivided, and growing space. The logic of the State, in contrast, includes men in its conception of space, as well as forests, gardens, goods, and modes of communication.

It is clear that at the time of writing *Facundo,* Sarmiento occupied a marginal position in Argentine society: he was exiled in Chile. Nonetheless, his writing perpetuates the logic of the State, dependent not on a moment of privilege but rather on a textual will to develop a project and obtain legislative primacy. This is not, therefore, the analysis of a particular moment, but rather of modes of understanding reality: *Facundo* sustains a divisive and stately knowledge, while *Memorias del ex cautivo* is, if not entirely nomadic, much more ambiguous. The brilliant Sarmiento writes a way of thinking that could be mistaken for a public minister's, not only in the last chapter's discussion of his concrete plans for government but in his entire binary conceptualization of reality.

Of course the separation between the civilized and the savages in the nineteenth century came accompanied by a pseudoscientific discourse that created hierarchies among racial species. The idea of barbarism was part of the exercise of cultural distancing and a mode of projecting onto a foreign group the fears that had to be controlled at home.[19] The communitarian social form of the Indians, with its *caciquismo* and lack of productivity, seemed monstrous and had to be mutilated to avoid projective identification with the savages, the antimodel for self-control and progress. Indigenous nomadism was seen as an enemy because its relationship to space was repudiated. That repudiation implied ignoring a reality as evident as the fact that the Indians were productive in their way, that they had agriculture and had developed their own technology and instruments for cultivation. But every child learns the opposite in school: "nomadic peoples do not plant anything." The particularity of those cultivating instruments, made of algarrobo, is described by Avendaño in his *Memorias* during an interrogation by the dictator Juan Manuel de Rosas, after his return from captivity to civilization.

If *Facundo* organizes social logic between the poles of civilization and barbarism, in *Memorias* survival depends upon negotiation and relations among human beings, and these terms therefore become fundamental: betrayal/loyalty, honor/offense, hospitality/ingratitude, well-being/poverty. Even Avendaño's position before the civilization/barbarism paradigm lacks the condemnatory charge it usually took in the nineteenth century. The former captive writes, shifting the discussion to a new locus of enunciation and articulating what others found unspeakable, oscillating from one side of the frontier to the other (*us*/the *Others*), or maintaining his equilibrium on the line between hegemonic reason and the reason of the indigenous minority. On this point the *cautivito* is as informed as he is unfortunate:

> According to [the governments], they have no duties toward the Indians other than to keep them in a state of degradation until they can exterminate them. They do not offer civilization, they do nothing to attract them [to Christianity]. Brutes they were born, to die even more brutal and degraded by vices. They have neither gold nor silver, nor anything else to attract those who attack them; they are assaulted only to take away their land and then to kill them.

> Según [los gobiernos] ellos no tienen más deberes para con los indios que mantenerlos en el estado de embrutecimiento, hasta poder exterminarlos. No les ofrecen civilización, nada hacen para atraerlos (al cristianismo). Brutos han nacido para morir más brutos y degradados por los vicios. No tienen oro ni plata, ni otro atractivo para los

que los atacan, son agredidos únicamente para quitarles sus terrenos
y matarlos luego. (93)

For Santiago Avendaño the Indians are not vile, but poor and neglected.
His locus of enunciation is that of a white whose understanding of
"civilization" includes well-being and Christianity (family, reading, home,
Virgin). He wants the society of the whites to approve of his Indian
part and tries to open a breach in the machinery of white reason so that
nomadic logic will be understood, but he never renounces civilization.
Translator and intermediary, but *from the other side.* His ambivalence breaks
the hegemonic, binary colonizing logic that simplifies reality by dividing
it between two poles. The *Memorias* aspire, like *Recuerdos de provincia* or
Facundo, to gain respectability by comprehending the national reality (or
partially national, since each one has a different idea of what "national"
means), but unlike Sarmiento, Avendaño does not speak from a position
of "cultured" culture.

What emerges from this material is a displacement of traditional du-
alities.[20] For example: Indians are not represented as the "good" side in
the partitioning of opposites. Avendaño's worldview is not Manichaean
even with regard to racism, whose social effects exploit "Others" in various directions. Thus Cafulcurá incites the tribe by insisting that captive
Indian women are so badly treated by the whites that their lost wives and
daughters must be sleeping with blacks — information, as the tone of the
narration suggests (and the historical background supports), that would
imply extreme humiliation for the Indians.

Avendaño's gaze contradicts the Manichaeanism of the logic of the
State. The central government (Rosas) originally pursues Baigorria because he is a Unitario; later he is "wanted" because he is deemed
responsible for the entire raiding party, as if the Indians were incapable of
planning efficient actions without the leadership of a Great White Chief.
In *Memorias del ex cautivo* Baigorria is shown to be arbitrary, often violent
and authoritative, but Avendaño also explains that this behavior is what the
Indians expect from Baigorria and that he must continually demonstrate
his loyalty to them. Since peace treaties are in effect between the Indians
and the government of Rosas, who wants Baigorria's head, Baigorria is
in a dangerous position: for that reason he must be, to put it one way,
more Indian than the most Indian among them. As often as he can he se-
cretly helps captives to escape from the tribe, a breach for which he must
respond to the Indians' growing (and justified) mistrust of him. Neither
good nor bad in Avendaño's text, Baigorria helps the young Santiago to

escape. Each time the price of these actions is paid with better political advice, initiatives and acts in favor of the indigenous tribe (to prove his "loyalty"), benefiting the nomadic war machine in a way that is much more complex and perhaps valuable than the master/slave binomial.

STRATEGIES OF MEMORY AND OBLIVION

Memorias de un ex cautivo uses two systems of memory and narration: Judeo-Christian scientism (dates, proper names, refutation of documents, genealogies, the written word, magazine testimonials) and indigenous orality as a mnemotechnical system. The nomads supposedly have no history, only geography. But Avendaño, giving the lie to the affirmations of false experts on the indigenous past, explains another mechanism: the Indians' "machine" whose function is to transmit the account of past events. The transmission may be oral, but it is very careful to preserve history/ collective memory: "No Indian who reaches the age of reason is ignorant of the events of the past, because they are with the masters who teach them. And the word of an old man, among the Indians, is the word of God for his people. They respect the elders very much and the elders are exact in the relation of past events" (Ningún indio que llega al uso de razón ignora los sucesos del pasado, porque están con sus maestros, que se lo enseñan. Y la palabra de un viejo, entre los indios, es palabra de Dios para su pueblo. Respetan mucho al anciano y éstos son exactos en la relación de acontecimientos pasados) (73).

Avendaño uses the same recourse of memory: he respects what the Indians have told him as a way of establishing true history, correcting the reason/version of the whites. In his texts, many of the white captive women prefer to remain among the Indians with their mestizo children rather than return to civilization. He recounts only one case of real cruelty that ends with the death of a captive (171), and — in another departure from the usual binarisms — describes the abuse of indigenous women by enemy tribes. The white women (and men) who wish to return do so because they miss their former way of life. Avendaño himself can hardly complain of mistreatment but fears degradation and wishes to return to see his parents. There are scenes demonstrating whites' extreme ferocity against Indians, especially Indian women:

> Unbridled soldiers collided with the *chinas,* who trembled with terror. Throwing a foot to the ground, they tore off whatever the women wore over their bodies and committed every kind of rape

and brutal excess. All the women were conducted to the camp, where they suffered double abuses because they were seen to pass from hand to hand in the power of the most dishonest, brutal, and obscene "Christian" men they could have known.

Los soldados desenfrenados atropellaron a las chinas que temblaban de terror. Echando pie a tierra, les quitaron cuanto tenían sobre el cuerpo y cometieron toda clase de violaciones y de excesos brutales. Todas fueron conducidas al campamento, donde sufrieron el doble de vejámenes, porque se vieron pasar de mano en mano y en poder de los hombres "cristianos," más deshonestos, más brutos y más obscenos que podían haber conocido. (130)

Two unforgettable narratives in *Memorias de un ex cautivo* illustrate by counterpoint the Manichaeanism of the conventional narratives that represent the national territory through the classic simplification civilization/ barbarism. *Memorias* does not fit into that logic: on the contrary, the ethics of its representation must have been intolerable for the times. The first of the episodes describes the burial of Chief Painé. When the great chief dies, his son Calvaiñ decides to kill as many witches as he can find along the funeral cortege's route to the burial site. How does he decide who the witches are? Does he choose the old and frightening women? No. Calvaiñ "determined that every man . . . [who] had two women would be allowed to kill one, and he who had three would kill two, and he who had only one would lose her" (determinó que todo hombre . . . [que] tuviese dos [mujeres] dejaría de matar una, y el que tuviera tres dejaría matar dos, y el que tuviese una, la perdería) (94). The account of the desperation of the women is impressive: they accuse one another, trying to escape this horrific end. Worse still is the clamor of Painé's youngest wife, a new mother, who cries for her life, arguing that she has scarcely had time to be a wife to the dead chief. They let her nurse her child and, while she does so, shoot her, once, in the head. The episode, despite the vividness of the narrative, could not have been witnessed by Avendaño. Avendaño may himself give in to the temptations of exoticism, exaggerating a few notes in describing the scene. If this narrative is unforgettable, it is obviously not because it breaks any white or urban schema about the life of the savages. It is memorable instead for precisely the intensity of the savagery described.

There is another space that the narrator has suffered himself, a place he describes as "the earthly hell" where "it would have been necessary to be reborn to be able to accustom oneself to bearing that world swollen with smoke; that hell of shouts, of frenetic obscurities; of blasphemies

against God; some singing; others shouting; the rest fighting to the bone"
(el infierno terrenal . . . habría sido necesario nacer de nuevo para poder
acostumbrarse a soportar aquel globo henchido de humo; aquel infierno
de gritos, de frenéticas oscuridades; de blasfemias contra Dios; cantando
unos; gritando otros; peleando a huesazos los demás) (275–76). It is not
a raid, as could be inferred after reading Echeverría, but a journey through
Rosas's jails. Under Rosas is applied "a human butchery that has no orthography in any sister language" (una carnicería [humana] que no tiene
ortografía en ninguna lengua hermana) (282). This is the space of Buenos
Aires for the narrator, the hell of Rosas, the savagery that life in the capital
was for him.

Can we speak, then, of civilization and barbarism as opposed spaces?
From the position of one who only goes away, from the position of a
simple provincial who has experienced a *journey of no return* — Can we? It
seems not.

Memoirs, as a genre, are a peculiar form of public history that erects a
monument for future generations.[21] If the symbolic system that ultimately
imposed itself in Argentina had been satisfied with overthrowing Rosas's
political machine, Avendaño's text would have been rescued and consecrated as a monument: few tales are as effective as his in showing Rosas's
savage cruelty, and it should be said that in *Memorias del ex cautivo* Rosas
is far more savage and cruel than the worst of the Indians. Nonetheless,
the logic of the literate governors did not allow for the legitimization of
Avendaño's social position and the ethics of representation that he and
others like him proposed. To allow the interpreter to speak, to allow him
to speak seriously, would have implied cohabiting with the Other, *sharing*
territory and modifying the white, civilized system of morals and values.

Chapter 8

NEWS OF A DISAPPEARING WORLD

> *He is silent, since he is the bearer of a letter that threatens the foundations of the pact. He is the bearer of a threat of a profound, unrecognized, repressed disorder, and he is silent.*
>
> *Il se tait, alors qu'il est porteur d'une lettre qui menace le fondement du pacte. Il est porteur de la menace d'un désordre profond, méconnu, refoulé, et il se tait.* —Jacques Lacan

What do I recall from my readings of *Una excursión a los indios ranqueles?* I know that this is the first text of nineteenth-century Argentine literature that dared include the voices of the Indians, that it is a text of limits, a representation of a world, of territorial and linguistic expansion: a journey to the internal frontier by a soldier-dandy who advances into barbarian territory wearing a red cloak and kid gloves, delighting in gastronomic descriptions while his soldier's eye takes in locations and goods, assesses risks, projects maps. Soldier and tourist, the narrator journeys into the past — filling postcards with accounts of primitive customs, descriptions of a world in the process of extinction — and toward the future, since his descriptions and the map Mansilla ultimately produces will expand the frontiers of the white city.

Outside of these vague, impressionistic, and entirely personal memories, *Una excursión a los indios ranqueles* has become a canonical text and archetypal narrative of journeys to the frontier and encounters with Argentine Indians.[1] Its stature in the canon is monumental, in the sense that the text has become what Pierre Nora defines as a *site of collective memory:* a space reproducing a narrative of national identity.[2] Despite what Mansilla called his "coquettish marginality" (his posture of rebellion) — playing the role of oppositional politician, making outspoken remarks, wearing extravagant clothing, dabbling in disobedience *pour épater le bourgeois* like the dandy he was — Lucio Víctor Mansilla was in the perfect position to become the builder of public monuments. As author/narrator, that position obliges him to be constantly aware of his readers. The "I" constructed in *Una excursión a los indios ranqueles* is not that of a circumstantial narrator looking only to legitimate the voice of the witness of events. On the contrary, it is the hinge between two eras, two worlds, two systems of government: the city and the country, Europe and the interior, civilization and barbarism. Nephew of Juan Manuel de Rosas, incurable cosmopolitan, self-appointed mediator between Indians and the urban whites, irresistibly sophisticated and humorous writer and soldier, Mansilla is the model of the Generation of 1880 that will soon consolidate the national State. Perhaps most important of all, the textual "I" of *Una excursión a los indios ranqueles* is the true *monument* of an Argentina entering modernity.[3] In other words, it is the construction and combination of images for collective identity, it is the construction of the memory of modernity.

I recall the "Santiago amigo" to whom the author/narrator Lucio V. Mansilla directs the tales of his journey into Ranquel territory, when not directly to the public, which he calls a "monster with a thousand heads" (monstruo de mil cabezas). I remember very clearly the description of the Indian Linconao's attack of smallpox. Mansilla suppresses his disgust and carries the victim away so that Linconao will be cured and Mansilla himself will continue to fill his paternalistic role before the Indians. I recall the rituals of their meetings. (The first is a sort of Indian acrobatics on horseback; later come unforgettable episodes with hundreds of embraces, celebrations, and inebriation.) I recall, of course, the interlaced stories of gauchos running from the law and unhappy love affairs, especially the stories of Miguelito and Corporal Gómez. I remember formal negotiations with Indian chiefs bearing Christian names,[4] and that the only important figure with an indigenous name — Epumer — is a drunkard inspiring mistrust and fear. There is also the black accordionist (a sort of runny-nosed demon), the priests who accompany Mansilla, and the daughter of a chief dressed for her baptism with garments stolen from a church Virgin. I recall Mansilla imagining himself emperor of the Ranquel and a sentence that is repeated throughout the text, *"Vivan* the Argentine Indians" (Vivan los indios argentinos). And that the narrative ends with a rough map of the region.

As I have argued throughout this book, what is chosen for representation in culture and in memory reveals the identity of individuals, social groups, and nations.[5] Imaginaries are narratives constituted by sequences of actions, including some and excluding others, with a beginning, middle, and end, with protagonists who act and others who recover, remake, and repeat these narratives through tales and newspaper articles.[6] *Una excursión a los indios ranqueles* is — besides the narrative of an eighteen-day excursion into Ranquel territory told through sixty-four letters the author wrote after his return and published serially in a newspaper — an emblematic text of identity and the poetics of collective memory. The letters are received with such enthusiasm that in that same year, 1870, they appear in book form with four additional letters and an epilogue. In 1875 the book receives a prize from the Geographic Congress of Paris and is declared "a book to be read by children and adolescents" and, more to the point, "a paradigmatic narrative on the Indians."[7] As a *macronarrative, Una excursión a los indios ranqueles* goes beyond the encounter with the Indians to construct a monument of Argentina as the place of Western culture, Europeanized, infused with the spirit of progress, property, and good living, disposed toward commerce, and more or less tolerant and paternalistic in its attitude toward the exotic inhabitants of the internal frontier, inhabitants who in any event will soon disappear through assimilation or war.

Una excursión can be read as a letter from the author/narrator to his social equals. The text re-creates an immediate experience, almost diary-style, but is directed from the interior to the public of the city of Buenos Aires.[8] The narrative stresses the author's abilities as a qualified witness and simultaneously inaugurates and closes a way of seeing: inaugurates, because Argentine literature offered no precedents on the subject of similar quality, and closes, because in just a few years the Conquista del Desierto will eliminate "the problem of the frontier."

This is not to say that Mansilla was aware that the disappearance of the Indian was imminent and was only buying time while the government prepared to expand the "pacified" territories; at the time of the book's writing the Conquista del Desierto had not even been planned in its final form.[9] Nonetheless, the adventure in Ranquel territory functions like the purloined letter of the epigraph: rather than a negotiator and emissary of peace, Mansilla is the harbinger of the destruction of a world. Mansilla declares his desire to sign a treaty (with no authority to do so), but the real "pact" between Indians and whites will ensure the extinction of the indigenous. After the colonel-dandy will come the railroad and a new social/industrial alliance promoted by the so-called Generation of 1880, a plan to assimilate the gaucho into the productive system as a peon or laborer, exterminate the Indians, and populate the country with European immigrants. If Mansilla as narrator expresses his opposition to the plan of exterminating the Indians, he does not seem to appreciate that the assimilation or adaptation of the Indians into the civilizing program is also tantamount to their disappearance. He writes:

Is no one arguing that it is better to exterminate them, instead of *Christianizing and using their arms for industry, work, and the common defense,* since so many shout that we are threatened by excessive spontaneous immigration?

¿No hay quien sostiene que es mejor exterminarlos, en vez de *cristianizarlos y utilizar sus brazos para la industria, el trabajo y la defensa común,* ya que tanto se grita de que estamos amenazados por el exceso de inmigración espontánea? (52)

Also:

Great and generous thoughts lead me, noble and elevated ideas dominate me, my mission is worthy of a soldier, of a man, of a Christian—I told myself, and I have already seen the hour in which *those barbarians, subjected and Christianized, their arms utilized for labor, surrendered a pledge of loyalty to civilization* because of the effort of its most humble servants.

Grandes y generosos pensamientos me traen, nobles y elevadas ideas me dominan, mi misión es digna de un soldado, de un hombre, de un cristiano—me decía, y veía ya la hora en que *reducidos y cristianizados aquellos bárbaros, utilizados sus brazos para el trabajo, rendían pleito homenaje a la civilización* por el esfuerzo del más humilde de sus servidores. (109)

As in Edgar Allan Poe's story, the "letter" is in sight. Mansilla, who declares himself the first white to enter these territories ("I will penetrate, in the end, the protected region" [Voy a penetrar, al fin, en el recinto vedado] [109]), is its symbolic bearer. If he falls silent about its latent content it is probably because he himself cannot see it.

THE FRONTIER AS TEXT

Lucio Mansilla, author and narrator, is self-constructed as the great translator of "Europe to America, America to Europe, barbarism to civilization and vice-versa" (Europa a América, América a Europa, la barbarie a la civilización y vice versa). On the one hand, Mansilla takes the risk of including and carrying to the limit indigenous reasoning, and has the additional merit of being the first writer to represent it along with the arguments of the white civilization.[10] On the other, Mansilla also embodies the discourse of Power, which always proceeds by annexation; its procedure is a sleight of hand that eliminates the central critical elements and, at the same time, enacts the "exaltation of the picturesque anecdotal ingredients."[11] We will return later in the chapter to this vanishing act; for the moment we will examine the position of the text and its author. In the meantime it can be said that Mansilla tries to conciliate the extremes of the civilization/barbarism schema posited by Domingo F. Sarmiento, and, although he does not entirely achieve his goal, he does neutralize the extremes of the schema.[12]

Mansilla is, of course, the epitome of the Generation of 1880. Noé Jitrik's description of this generation is perfectly appropriate for Mansilla's strategy as a writer:

> Distinction became a cult from which one could not diverge without falling into the no-man's land of marginality; the antidote is extravagance and even originality. . . . Distinction in dress . . . in manners . . . in artistic tastes . . . in residence and in foods . . . in reading, and in the extreme care with which authors are cited, in sentiments.[13]

Mansilla's textual "I" is a monument to Argentina as it enters modernity. As such it must resolve the uncomfortable presence of the prehistoric and primitive that the nation pursued at the end of the nineteenth century and that defined its memory.[14] Thus in *Una excursión a los indios ranqueles* the voyage from Fort Sarmiento to the territory of Chief Mariano Rosas is almost an allegorical passage from the locus of civilization (represented by then-president Domingo Faustino Sarmiento) to the space of barbarism (embodied in turn by the Indian "adopted" by former dictator Juan Manuel de Rosas, uncle of the narrator).[15] It is also a textual voyage to knowledge of the space and the culture of the Other, a construction of the narrator as a character with knowledge of Western reason, facing the attractions of orality and a foreign language, belonging to indigenous culture as well as to the Argentine, French, English, or Latin cultures.[16]

Una excursión is a frontier text par excellence.[17] Text and frontier as theory of the nation: as in all such theories, a machine of memory is produced, in this case structured by "white" logic or the logic of the State. This machine of memory determines what we apprehend and recognize during the stream of experience.[18] *Una excursión* is a theory that, like subsequent theories of the Generation of 1880, confuses the nation with the social class that proposes it.[19] Theories organize what we notice and, in consequence, what we remember; by determining the interpretative framework, the theory inevitably functions as a pattern for memory.[20] *Una excursión* became part of that framework to such a degree that it is an unavoidable reference for other authors of the frontier, be they writers of fiction, historians, soldiers, or other specialists.

The frontier is by definition a place of limits, and authentic limits are never neutral: they are antagonistic designations that presuppose exclusions. Thus as much as Mansilla incorporates the voice of the Other, he clearly does so *from* the space of the city, using even the voice of the Other to create his own social position, to build a pattern for the memory of the nation, and to introduce criticism of some of his contemporaries' customs.[21]

In this sense, to speak of the Indians when they will so soon be exterminated is not unlike the gesture performed by gauchesque literature in its nostalgic odes to banditry as the rebellion of idealized rural societies that refuse to submit to national authority. The machinery of the State was able to tolerate the gauchesque because at the time the real gauchos had all but disappeared from the pampa.[22] Indigenous ways of life, especially family structures and styles of government, allow Mansilla to write his own ode. It praises not the Indians but the intermediaries: Mansilla himself, as a frontier colonel and author, the gauchos and priests who accompany them, Indians already so "civilized" that they bear Christian names and are apt to be incorporated into the workforce, like the industrious Chief Ramón.

Even if he falls silent, Lucio V. Mansilla is the bearer of *the threat of profound disorder,* a threat that will put an end to a pact. This does not mean that he prophesies the extermination of the Indian, or that *Una excursión* manages to introduce the reason of the Other in such a way as to open true fissures in Argentine culture. It means instead that the text, although useful for visualizing the Ranquel, is much more useful for facilitating the modernization of Argentina because it enables its author and its readers, finally, to rationalize cohabitation with the primitive. The apparent contradiction between the two truths of *Una excursión* (the text gives voice to the *Other*/the text appropriates the voice of the *Other*) ultimately finds a space of resolution because, in the larger view, the objective of the lettered elite is not to represent the Indians, but rather to define the modern, urban, Argentine *us.* The lettered, after all, were simultaneously plagued by the idea that their nation was insufficiently European and driven by a desire to determine the country's distinctive qualities.[23]

It is worth remembering that after 1879 indigenous resistance was eliminated and nearly nine million hectares of "freed" land came into the hands of the less than four hundred individuals who financed Roca's expedition. Indigenous culture was left to oblivion by the population in general and studied only by professional anthropologists.[24] Industrialization, commerce, urbanization, and development are the windows through which this text should be read: it should be interpreted through a framework of what will become vague nostalgia for a space that was once uncivilized.

THE OTHER, THE SELF

A paradigmatic narrative of the *Other:* everything depends upon how we read the identity of that Other. Is it the Indian, the object of the textual representation? Or is the Other a part of the Self, the source of the desire to define one's own identity? In other words, for whom does the narrative perform? Which gaze is examined when the narrating subject (who bears the same name as the author) identifies himself with determined images? When Mansilla identifies with or distances himself from civilized customs, his uncle Juan Manuel de Rosas, the plans of the National Congress, or Ranquel rites, to whom is he speaking? When he imagines himself as emperor or all the figures of the frontier at once, from what position does he speak? What place does he occupy?

The first temptation is to answer that he occupies the locus of enunciation of the conquistador; this response, doubtless, is not untrue. Nevertheless, if I follow Zizek's logic,[25] I must then ask, What is it that the Other wants? Seen this way, *Una excursión a los indios ranqueles* is organized to construct a character or a discourse not in opposition to the Indian, but in opposition to its readers. These readers, after all, are so important that they are expressly invoked as narratees: on one hand is the "Santiago amigo" (Mansilla refers to Santiago Arcos)[26] to whom the narrative is frequently directed in the second person and — also a paradoxically indefinite and ubiquitous organizing presence — the public, "this monster with multiple heads, [who] knows many things that it should not know and is ignorant of many others which it ought to know" (este monstruo de múltiple cabeza, [que] sabe muchas cosas que debiera ignorar e ignora muchas otras que debiera saber) (18). The text works very hard not to bore its reader. But, we must ask, what is it the Other wants to read? We must try to think like Mansilla, using that conjecture to make a journey that will define and defend his own conflictive situation within society, acting his role, describing what he sees.[27]

If the logic of exclusions and antagonisms is considered from the assumption that the *reader* is the Other, the apparent contradictions of *Una excursión* disappear. In the text Mansilla sermonizes against the idea of exterminating the Indians rather than assimilating them into civilization. But like a good tourist who plays the understanding connoisseur during his immersion in the exotic and does not give up his well-shined boots or prolong his journey by one day, in his subsequent extratextual existence Mansilla returns to the center of political life and actually supports the killing led by General Julio Argentino Roca, the project euphemistically called the Conquista del Desierto. The same man who, as a politician and diplomat, will help President Avellaneda to implement Argentina's plan of *blanqueamiento* (whitening) with the importation of European immigrants is the one who writes that "[if] all Americans have Indian blood in our veins, then why that constant cry of exterminating the barbarians?" (todos los americanos tenemos sangre de indio en las venas, ¿por qué ese grito constante de exterminio contra los bárbaros?) (392). Some years later, Mansilla's military trial — conducted in absentia during the expedition — already half-forgotten, he will leave these gestures aside and write, remembering his experiences in Río Cuarto but not his dreams of being emperor of the Ranquel: "And what was sadder still, to show how baneful anarchy is, there was no lack of persons who felt some affinity for the barbarians, so audacious they actually boasted of it" (Y lo que era más triste aún, para que se vea cuán funesta es la anarquía, no faltaba quien tuviera afinidades con los bárbaros, llegando la audacia hasta el colmo de jactarse de ello).[28]

The movement attempted by *Una excursión,* seen as a symbolic order and chain of meanings, or as textual space that also becomes a model of the structure of the social space, is a complex game of simulations and representations that ends in silence. First, the narrator must pretend both that he understands the adversary and that he has come to share with him the arguments for civilization; later, to proceed toward annihilation it is necessary to feign an armistice; that annihilation must finally be turned into silence, into oblivion.[29] The Indians will remain in the collective memory only as something exotic that *was,* something to be described by remote, entertaining anecdotes, a part of the vague and, above all, sterile and vanished past. A past, that is, that did not engender the present; a past that was not the root of contemporary civilization but an illustration of civilization's progress and triumph over barbarism.

As a text of the frontier, *Una excursión* contains the characteristics of that space: hybridity, breaches and opposing discourses, subversions, antagonisms, contradictions. Multiple languages, charged encounters. And tricks. In chapter 40, practically the midpoint of the narrative, Mansilla describes one of his great conversations with Chief Mariano Rosas about the advantages of civilization and the projects of the government. This time the subject is land ownership, and Mansilla, as always, shows off his rhetorical abilities until the chief says to him, "Look, brother, *why don't you tell me the truth?*" (Mire, hermano, ¿por qué no me habla la verdad?) (222). Then the chief pulls out an *archive*.

Here the narrative performs an eclosion, revealing its inglorious self like a larva emerging from its egg. The text has been spun under the sign of "authenticity" ("this is how the Indians are"), but in this scene it reveals itself as another act of discursive violence against the Other: it inscribes the native or indigenous under the sign of the savage.[30] Civilizable or not, they are always savages. Eclosion is produced by the text's radical inconsistency: after presenting the reader with descriptions of so many drunken nights and absurd rituals, after so much folkloric information about the barbarians, the text is confronted with nothing less than an archive, the central sign of rationalization, of the organization of knowledge and, for that matter, of civilization.[31]

It is an archive that has been perfectly catalogued by the Ranquel chief, in which the same material that the bourgeois metropolitan readers of the fin de siècle desire — records of newspapers, letters, official notes — is very clearly organized. Mansilla writes:

> Each little bag contained official notes, letters, drafts, newspapers. He knew the paper perfectly.
>
> He could point out with a finger the paragraph to which he referred.
>
> He turned his archive over, took a little bag, drew back the covering, and took out of it a printed document so folded and wrinkled it must have been handled many times.
>
> It was the Buenos Aires *Tribuna*.[32]
>
> In it he had marked an article about the great interoceanic railway.

> Cada bolsita contenía notas oficiales, cartas, borradores, periódicos. Él conocía el papel perfectamente.
>
> Podía apuntar con el dedo al párrafo que quería referirse.
>
> Revolvió el archivo, tomó una bolsita, descorrió la jareta y sacó de ella un impreso muy doblado y arrugado, revelando que había sido manoseado muchas veces.
>
> Era *La Tribuna* de Buenos Aires.
>
> En ella había marcado un artículo sobre el gran ferrocarril interoceánico. (222)

Something does not correspond in this scene: previously, when he was poised to enter Rosas's village, Mansilla had declared, "I will penetrate, in the end, into the forbidden region. The echoes of civilization will resonate peacefully for the first time where a man of my stature has never before planted his foot" (Voy a penetrar, al fin, en el recinto vedado. Los ecos de la civilización van a resonar pacíficamente por primera vez, donde jamás asentara su planta un hombre del coturno mío) (109). Not only is the space of the frontier less isolated than Mansilla pretends, but the chief knows perfectly the government's true plans at that moment. Mariano Rosas accuses Mansilla of disingenuousness: "[Y]ou have not told me that they want to buy these lands from us so that a railway will pass by the Cuero [road]" ([U]sted no me ha dicho que nos quieren comprar las tierras para que pase por el [camino de] Cuero un ferrocarril) (222). He also knows that "the Christians say it is better to finish us off" ([los] cristianos dicen que es mejor acabar con nosotros) (223). Mansilla finds himself "extremely embarrassed" and discomposed, first struggling to offer promises, then falling silent, then digressing from the subject. He ends the chapter with one of his favorite strategies, escaping to the pleasures of chatter and wine. *Una excursión* repeatedly demonstrates that the poles of civilization vs. barbarism are less opposed than Sarmiento formulated, but while Mansilla's savory deviations and gratuitous descriptions enrich and nuance the terms, in the end they leave each pole fixed firmly in its place. Information and images that could unite or confuse them, like the archive in the hands of a barbarian, are diluted in the flood of anecdotes and campfire tales.

The author/narrator does not take responsibility for the farce that has been exposed. After all, he is a self-confessed dandy and a member of the all-powerful Generation of 1880. Neither Mansilla nor his readers experience much anguish before these voids in his field of representation: they are dazzled by the consolidation of institutions and laws, proud of belonging to their predestined and brilliant class.[33] The I/Other axis of symbolization in this text is Mansilla and the image by his side in the mirror, that of the Generation of 1880.

In the center is Lucio V. Mansilla, who enters territory never before trod by whites (an inexact statement), and whose real motive for the expedition may not be a philanthropic wish to help in the peace negotiations with the Indians, but rather an entirely personal desire to be granted a reprieve from the trial brought against him (for abuse of authority) and obtain the rank of general.[34]

What is more, Lucio V. Mansilla had used his friendship with the owners of *La Tribuna* to write between late 1869 and early 1870 a series of self-aggrandizing articles signed with indigenous pseudonyms like Atahualpa, Caupolicán, Wincarramanca, Quirquincho, and Manco Capac, but the maneuver was denounced by Sarmiento himself.[35] Mansilla appropriated indigenous names — obviously legendary names, intended perhaps as a clue for informed readers — to construct himself a heroic image as a great negotiator: in these articles the "Indian" signers attest that Mansilla is the only intermediary they trust. The capable dandy of the frontier later made his expedition into Ranquel territory to "give voice" to the Indians, but the disinterestedness of that impulse to "give voice" and Mansilla's defense of the Indians are thrown into doubt by the fact that Mansilla did all he could to impede or delay at least one mission of peace toward the frontier. Father Moysés Álvarez directed his complaints to the minister of justice in a letter of 1877:

> The F[ather Donati] was pleased, believing he had made a step toward his humanitarian idea and cherishing at the same time the hope of recovering from Satan so many lost souls, avoiding the horrible daily butchery of Indians and Christians, rescuing from captivity innumerable unhappy creatures who for so many years have dragged the heavy chain of indescribable misfortunes, and doing other good turns that will readily be seen by anyone who cares to observe. He arrives at Río Cuarto and speaks with Mansilla: *hoc opus, hic labor est;* Mansilla is disposed to invade the Indians, needing only to prepare what is necessary for their expedition. Occupied with carrying out his battle-plan, he refused to give the F. [Father] what he requested with a superior order.

> Contento se volvió el P[adre Donati], creyendo haber dado un paso en pro de su humanitaria idea y acariciando al mismo tiempo la esperanza de arrebatar a Satanás tantas almas perdidas, evitar la horrible carnicería diaria de indios y cristianos, sacar del cautiverio a innumerables criaturas desgraciadas que tantos años ha arrastraban una cadena pesada de infortunios indescriptibles y hacer muchos otros bienes que fácilmente se dejan ver por quien quiera observarlo. Llega al Río Cuarto y habla con Mansilla; *hoc opus, hic labor est;* éste se disponía para invadir a los indios, trataba precisamente de preparar lo necesario para su expedición. Ocupado de llevar su plan de guerra, no quiso dar al P. lo que con orden superior solicitaba.[36]

SLEIGHT OF HAND

As anecdotes, the figures of the frontier are the reflection thrown by a society fitfully constructing its image as civilized rather than barbaric. I have already said something of the fate of the Indians and the gauchos; Argentina's black population remains to be discussed. As was described in the second chapter of this book, in the early nineteenth century one in three Buenos Aires residents was black, while by the time *Una excursión a los indios ranqueles* was written blacks numbered no more than two or three per hundred. Nevertheless, the character most repugnant to the narrator is the black accordionist, the chief's buffoon. Mansilla ostentatiously degrades the accordionist: significantly, his first criticism of the black man is that he is a bad musician, even though Argentina's popular music had its origins in African traditions and the great *payadores* or minstrels were Afro-Argentines.[37]

Mansilla strips the black of the only social role he was permitted (performer of oral poetry) and limits him to being only a poor imitator of the white *payadores* (172). It is obvious that Mansilla's generation is troubled by the black minstrels: soon after the protagonist of José Hernández's famous *Martín Fierro* will fight and resoundingly defeat a *moreno*. The textual gesture is the same in the representation of the black and the Indians: if they are granted a voice it is never entirely their own or representative of their real pains and pleasures. In fact, much of the "Ranquel" discourse in this book is but a poor projection of the reader-Other, the white, urban consumer of newspapers. The Indians complain, for example, that the Christians have not taught them how to work (304).

But these are not the only groups who inhabit the frontier. In chapter 65 of *Una excursión a los indios ranqueles* a beautiful young woman, emaciated and ragged, presents herself to Colonel Lucio V. Mansilla and tells him of her martyrdom as the slave of an Indian whose desire for her is as intense as the physical punishments he inflicts when she resists his sexual demands. The unfortunate woman, Petrona Jofré, is one of very few white captive women whose history is registered with a first and last name in Argentine literature. Another is the resigned and perhaps even happy Doña Fermina Zárate, a lady of good family who was kidnapped decades ago by Chief Ramón and is now the mother of his children.

These moving stories occupy scarcely two and a half pages of the four hundred that comprise *Una excursión a los indios ranqueles,* that entertaining chronicle and first literary testimony of the reality of the internal frontier. In its sixty-eight chapters and epilogue, white captive women barely appear as a blurred backdrop, positioned as the last link of the social chain. Anonymous slaves of the Indians, they occupy the most marginal space possible in an Argentina that already looks toward the twentieth century. They occupy the margin of the margin of civilization: as servants of the Indians, their tortured bodies full of scars, scorned by jealous Indian women, mothers of mestizo children they would have to abandon if they ever managed to return to civilization.

The captive woman questions the precarious possessions of the fathers of the nation: if a woman was an extension of the family, how could a white male face these women who were potential vehicles of the foundation of new mestizo hegemonies? This is not a purely rhetorical question, since in *Una excursión a los indios ranqueles* Mansilla reiterates again and again the presence of mestizo caudillos; in fact the majority of the chiefs he encounters are the sons of white women. Perhaps he describes them in such a way as to make the characters more sympathetic for his reading public, rendering them more similar, more white, drawing them closer to the familiar and comfortable world of Buenos Aires, but strategic or not, his characterizations of the chiefs reflect a real circumstance. Mansilla never explains who their white mothers are, but we know that they can only be captives.

In this text the chiefs are either mestizos or blond whites. As Sander Gilman has written, the more the Other resembles the Self, the more the power of the Self is affirmed.[38] While the captive woman has no place in this last attempt at creating a national pact, her mestizo son does.

She is not the only conflictive figure of the frontier; in the first chapters the chronicler must confront another unassimilable individual, an enemy called the White Indian. Mansilla writes:

> By its banks lived the White Indian, who is neither a chief, nor a captain, but rather what the Indians call a *gaucho Indian*. That is, an Indian with no law, subject to no one, to no greater chief, much less a captain; he is entirely on his own, sometimes allied with the others, sometimes an enemy. He sometimes rides a horse, other times draws close to the huts of a chief; he sometimes travels about the camps, raiding, invading, whole months together; other times he wanders to Chile trading, as has happened lately.

> A la orilla de ella vivía el indio Blanco, que no es ni cacique, ni capitanejo, sino lo que los indios llaman *indio gaucho*. Es decir, un indio sin ley ni sujeción a nadie, a ningún cacique mayor, ni menos a ningún capitanejo; que campea con sus respetos; que es aliado a veces

de los otros, otras enemigo; que unas veces anda a monte, que otras se arrima a la toldería de un cacique; que una anda por los campos maloqueando, invadiendo, meses enteros seguidos; otras por Chile comerciando, como ha sucedido últimamente. (55)

Notice the signification of the enemy's name: a white Indian who does not give in, as the chiefs do, to the possibility of ratifying a treaty with the government. To vanquish this circumstantial enemy, General Mansilla decides to attack him with his own tactics: by confronting him not with the army, but with thieves hired for the job. The leader of these villains is a mysterious person whom the text calls only the Cautivo (56–58). Mansilla's description of the thieves is terrible:

The Pharisees who crucified Christ could not have looked more thoroughly sinister.

Their garments were ragged, their faces fierce, all hunched up and dragging their feet in the dirt; only the spirit of the public good could move one to gather the resolve to deal with them.

Los fariseos que crucificaron a Cristo no podían tener una fachas de forajidos más completas.

Sus vestidos eran andrajosos, sus caras torvas, todos encogidos y con la pata en el suelo; necesitábase estar animado del sentimiento del bien público para resolverse a tratar con ellos. (56)

The Cautivo is nothing less that the head of this group, of which Mansilla says: "I confess that on sending those devils on such a risky mission, I reflected: if they are caught or killed little will be lost" (Confieso que al mandar aquellos diablos a una correría tan azarosa, me hice esta reflexión: si los pescan o los matan poco se pierde) (58). But the Cautivo does not have the persistence of the White Indian, who will reappear throughout the narrative as a symptom of those who plan to resist any treaty (91, 197).

Although the Cautivo is a very marginal character in the narrative, he allows Mansilla to close the great text that begins with the displacement of the captive Brián in Esteban Echeverría's poem *La cautiva,* that supposed hero of the Independence Wars who falls prisoner to an indigenous raid, whose role is limited to being rescued by his self-abnegating wife, María, before they both come to their tragic end. Now, in contrast, the raid is white and wears a uniform: behind it come the law, the railroad, white immigration, modernity, the disappearance of the frontier and its threatening irregularity.

WOMAN OR SYMPTOM

Even more than these rebellious individuals, the captive woman represents irregularity and the nonbourgeois. When the space of the female body (salvation, purity, protection) is trespassed by the uncivilized, the captive's body — like the prostitute's — becomes contaminated and threatens to contaminate others. What does the narrator do, faced with what the reader-Other wants from these figures, neither travelers nor bandits, who have crossed the frontier? In these passive beings, in their bodies, the threat of contagion is verified: unlike prostitutes, they are not simply "bad women" whose utility justifies their presence, the codifiable desire they incite. In their bodies, moreover, the captives carry the mestizo.

In order to distance the Other or ward off the fear of seeing him or her, the Other is always described according to attributes, in fragments. (The celebrating Indians of Echeverría's *La cautiva* are a clear example.) Mansilla wants to approach the Ranquel and dedicates himself to recording their physical details as well as their habits and domestic arrangements. The captives, however, are treated differently: their attributes are suffering, resignation, perdition, and obscurity. In general they appear as a backdrop, as part of the court of servants, differentiated from the Indian women or *chinas* because they are profoundly pleased if the priests who accompany Mansilla offer them a Mass or baptize their children. Except for the two previously mentioned women whose first names are given, the text pauses only three times to offer terse comments on the captives. All of them are part of a clichéd code: the captive as sufferer, the captive as a woman who has resisted the assault of the indigenous and lives as a martyr, the captive as a coquette who takes advantages of her situation. In every case the text counsels resignation: Mansilla proposes no change.[39]

A highly revealing episode occurs in chapter 41. Having explained that "humility and resignation is the only recourse that remains for them" [*sic*] (la humildad y la resignación es el único recurso que les queda) (226), Mansilla comes to speak of a heroic woman who refuses to "let herself be vilified" (dejarse envilecer) and whose body is full of scars. But there is no identification or recognition of the woman who is without a doubt as white as the narrator. He notes: "She was from San Luis, I have her name noted in Río Cuarto. *I don't remember it now.* The poor woman is no longer among the Indians. I had the good fortune to rescue her and I sent her to her land" (Era de San Luis, tengo su nombre apuntado en el Río Cuarto. *No lo recuerdo ahora.* La pobre no está ya entre los indios. Tuve la fortuna de rescatarla y la mandé a su tierra) (226). Is this the gesture of a "gentleman" who conceals the name to avoid aggravating the dishonor of the woman who has been a captive? Or is it that the captive matters so little that he has, in fact, forgotten her name? Very little time has passed since the expedition into Ranquel territory, and Mansilla has done something heroic in recovering a lost white woman, but the way he tells it — at least within the context of the book — reflects how unimportant the act was. In contrast, Mansilla remembers not only the names of the gauchos met by chance during his adventure, but also the names of the woman or women who long ago caused the trouble from which each one sought refuge on the frontier.

The narrator shows no more interest in the origin than in the fate of the captives: he does not tell how they were captured or in what terms their ransom is negotiated. He neglects to mention how they escaped (if they did), to what extent they were used as interpreters or *lenguaraces,* or what happened to them after they were reincorporated into society. He is uninterested even in the role they played in the upbringing of many chiefs and *lenguaraces,* a key element of the politics of the frontier.

It is not a question of asking the book to be other than what it is, but rather of pointing out that while representing itself as a book of knowledge and encounter, *Una excursión* omits part of what is sees: once again the *purloined letter* is so visible that no one sees it. Mansilla claims that one of the narrative's objectives is to "make known" to those who don't leave the elegant neighborhoods of Buenos Aires "what our beloved Nation is" (lo que es nuestra Patria amada) (52) and that he wants to correct the "errors of previous writers [made] out of ignorance of the Pampa" (errores de escritores previos por ignorancia de la Pampa) (55). Nonetheless, though their texts are neither abundant nor canonical, other soldier-writers and travelers of the era did recognize much of what Mansilla ignores, including the captive women who remained among the Indians of their own free will.[40] The problem is aggravated in the epilogue:

We were horrified that women are sold among the Ranquel, and that they bring us terrible raids to capture and appropriate our women.

And among the Hebrews, in the time of the Patriarchs, did a husband not pay the father the *moharo* price of the daughter? And among the Arabs did the widow not constitute part of the legacy or of the goods left behind by the deceased? And in Rome, didn't the *coemptio* exist, that is, the sale and the *usus,* or the possession of the woman? And in Germania, as Saxon Law shows, didn't the *mundium* and other analogous customs exist? And the Visigoths, did they not have *arras,* a sort of nuptial price that replaced the pure and simple purchase, recalling the old usage? And the Franks, did they not pay the value of the wives to their fathers, who divided it with the women?

Nos horrorizamos de que entre los Ranqueles se vendan las mujeres, y de que nos traigan terribles malones para cautivar y apropiarse las nuestras.

¿Y entre los hebreos, en tiempo de los Patriarcas, el esposo no le pagaba al padre el moharo precio de la hija? ¿Y entre los árabes la viuda no constituía parte de la herencia o de los bienes que dejaba el difunto? ¿Y en Roma, no existía el coemptio, es decir, la compra y el usus, o sea la posesión de la mujer? ¿Y en Germania, como lo muestra la Ley Sajona, no existían el mundium, y costumbres análogas? ¿Y los visigodos, no tenía las arras, especie de precio nupcial, que reemplazaba la compra pura y simple, recordando la vieja usanza? ¿Y los francos, no pagaban el valor de las esposas a los padres, que éstos dividían con aquéllas? (392)[41]

Here, as *Una excursión a los indios ranqueles* closes, the narrator legitimates the capture of women by making it analogous to the practices of ancient civilizations (392); he will correct these assertions in one of his *causeries* almost a decade later, when the Indians have been exterminated and the dandy-writer can voice his disgust without betraying the good manners appropriate to one who has been a guest in another's home.[42] But, beyond Mansilla's changes of opinion toward the indigenous population, in his text the female body is the vehicle of hatred among men; it is one contested masculine possession among others. The captive woman is the dramatization of desires and antipathies; her body, as throughout the culture of the nineteenth century, is only a symptom.

As author-narrator, Mansilla manipulates discourse. He lies when he promises the Indians what he cannot secure for their future: although he may not do it deliberately, he is aware of the difficulties of negotiating with the government. He lies again when he explains the motive of his trip: he explicitly says that the government has sent him to negotiate with the Ranquel, when in fact Congress ratified the treaty a month and a half earlier. He also conceals the judicial process that pursues him and will conclude after his return from the expedition with a demotion in rank. Perhaps the appropriate word is neither "manipulates" nor "lies," but "conceals," "occludes." What is notable in his description is the sense of indifference: Mansilla and the captive women look at each other more than once, but he avoids the subject of their captivity by saying only, "Who would not be moved by a woman's sad and tearful look?" (¿Quién no se conmueve con la mirada triste y llorosa de una mujer?) (193). Another example: "Various male and female captives enter — one of the women had been a servant of Rosas — bringing great concave plates of wood, made by the Indians themselves" (Entraron varios cautivos y cautivas — una de éstas había sido sirvienta de Rosas — trayendo grandes y cóncavos platos de madera, hechos por los mismos indios) (139). What Mansilla describes in detail is the ritual of the meal, an event that is much more important for the narrator (and perhaps for the reader) than what has happened to those individuals condemned to servitude.

Why would Mansilla, the writer who finally travels toward the Desert and now has the opportunity to make himself heard publicly, choose to omit or diminish the situation of the captive women, the individuals by all appearances most like him? The women of the frontier, especially those who live in captivity, but poorly serve the purposes of collective memory. The nation (even the noun *la nación* is feminine) is usually represented as a woman threatened by violation or domination, a woman whose plight inspires her sons to sacrifice themselves and battle for her honor. As I have argued throughout this book, eroticizing the nation as the beloved body of a woman leads to associating sexual danger with the transgression of limits and the necessity of defending those limits. As a female body the nation can be contaminated, possessed, or tainted by enemies from outside and, above all, by the enemies from within: those who could ruin the racialized and idealized image of the woman/nation. In order for the trope woman/nation to function, the image of the feminine must be chaste and obedient, a good daughter, wife, and mother, beautiful, domestic, apolitical, and dependent upon the activity of the men.[43] For a well-mannered gentleman like Mansilla to give more space, for example, to Carmen — the interpreter who on more than one occasion rescues him — would have been absurd, because as a single mother and a figure of the frontier Carmen was too knowledgeable about both worlds for someone who was not a man and a soldier.

The soldier, dandy, and chronicler advances into unknown territory but never loses sight of his explicit interlocutor — that "Santiago amigo," promoter of the extermination of the Indians — as if to keep hold of his own identity. He does not really journey to learn about the Other, to open himself to the Other. Nor does he write to please those who assisted him in his adventure. The true threat to the reader — a threat so extreme that it cannot be seen on the surface of the text, but only sensed — is the intuition that every cultural encounter implies that the world is shared with Others. But it is one thing to intuit that and another to be capable of developing an *epistēmē* and a social space common to the various groups that inhabited Argentina.[44]

I have spoken here of the threat Lucio V. Mansilla carries into indigenous territory: the imminence of its disappearance. But the dandy may also be the bearer of another profound, unknown, repressed disorder, and he falls silent for the sole reason that he cannot speak of it without profoundly altering *his own limit,* his own language, his own representation of the world. Or perhaps the textual performance does not even "repress" those other, obscure ways of life that he has scarcely glimpsed (white Indians, *lenguaraces,* Indians, captive women, mestizo chiefs, white refugees), since repression implies that something extant has been held back or silenced, just as negation requires a prior affirmation. The textual minimization or erasure of the captive women resembles instead what Lacan calls "foreclosure" or "preclusion": it expresses the abolition of what should be drawn out into the light of day, but has not arrived; its result is a void in the Symbolic Order.[45]

Una excursión a los indios ranqueles — as is traditional in Argentine literature of the nineteenth century — strips the Indians of all historicity and denies them a place in the foundation of the lineage that constitutes the nation. At the same time, the text disregards the existence of the captive women as completely insignificant. It creates a place of memory for modernity out of the campfire — that representation of a masculine space, site of camaraderie after the day's labors, of gauchos' tales describing more often than not the treachery of a woman — and the map, the army, the newspaper, the Buenos Aires reader: spaces or agents that exercise the power of language.

Seen this way, Sarmiento's imperative to fill the void of the country with words acquires a new meaning: the voids here are the empty spaces of identity. To avoid threatening the integrity of the I/Other, the female victims of the frontier are buried again and again among distractions and ingenious literate quotations, buried without sadness or glory, without mourning. Limits and words: the captives are killed again and again with oblivion, negation, and silence.

NOTES

Unless otherwise indicated, translations of texts cited in the Spanish edition of this book are original to the English-language edition. Emphasis in citations is the author's unless "emphasis in the original" is indicated. — Trans.

1. Against Oblivion

1. This information is from Frances Yates's erudite study *The Art of Memory* (Chicago: University of Chicago Press, 1966), 10–14; trans. Ignacio Gómez de Liaño as *El arte de la memoria* (Barcelona: Taurus, 1974).

2. Many factors entered into the struggle among accounts competing to recover the space that had been silenced, among them the invaluable activism of the Mothers of the Plaza de Mayo. There are many others, but I can cite here only two of the most central texts: *Nunca Más: Informe de la Comisión Nacional sobre la Desaparición de Personas* (Buenos Aires: Eudeba, 1984) and *El Diario del Juicio,* thirty-six weekly editions of a newspaper dedicated exclusively to the trial (Buenos Aires: Perfil, May 27, 1985, to January 28, 1986). With regard to the system of representation of this period, the impact of the activities of Teatro Abierto (Open Theater) has been influential. Among the books that examine it are Andrés Avellaneda, *Censura, autoritarismo y cultura: Argentina, 1960–1983* (Buenos Aires: Biblioteca Política Argentina, 1983); Saúl Sosnowski's anthology, *Represión y reconstrucción de una cultura: El caso argentino* (Buenos Aires: Eudeba, 1988); and Diana Taylor's study of public space as performance, *Disappearing Acts: Spectacles of Gender and Nationalism in Argentina's "Dirty War"* (Durham, N.C.: Duke University Press, 1997).

3. Videla's comment is from the television documentary *ESMA: El Diario del Juicio,* by Walter Goobar and Rolando Graña; produced by Magdalena Ruiz Guiñazú (Buenos Aires, 1998).

4. Michel Foucault, "Film and Popular Memory," in *Foucault Live (Interviews 1966–1984),* trans. Martin Jorgin, ed. Sylvere Kitrunger (New York: Semiotext[e], 1989), 92.

5. This story was proven to be untrue in the previously cited film, *ESMA: El Diario del Juicio,* which mentions more than five hundred hours of recorded material.

6. Despite the Argentine government's efforts to obliterate the past through national reconciliation, the subject of the torture, murders, and disappearances returns again and again, proving that the wounds cannot be erased by decree. So much insistence on forgetting has doubtless produced the judicial alternative to the pardon that the Alfonsín and Menem governments extended to the comman-

dants. As is known, the alternative has been to try them for crimes for which they were not tried earlier but allegedly committed during the same period: they are incarcerated now for having sequestered children. The phenomenon of unhealed memory can be seen in other latitudes also, as for example in Brazil, where, many years after the dictatorship, efforts are being made to revoke the license of doctors who collaborated in the torture (*New York Times,* March 11, 1999). Nicole Loraux reflects on the failed attempt to achieve amnesia through amnesty in "De la amnistía y su contrario," in *Usos del olvido,* ed. Y. Yerushalmi et al., trans. Irene Agoff (Buenos Aires: Nueva Visión, 1989), 27–52; in the same book Yerushalmi raises disquieting questions about the relationship between justice and oblivion ("Reflexiones sobre el olvido," 13–26).

7. Ernest Renan, *¿Qué es una nación? Cartas a Strauss,* trans. Andrés de Blas Guerrero (Madrid: Alianza, 1987), 65–66; the quotation of Anderson is from *Imagined Communities: Reflections on the Origin and Spread of Nationalism* (London: Verso, 1991 [1983]).

8. See Gérard Noiriel, "French and Foreigners," in *Realms of Memory: Rethinking the French Past,* vol. 1, ed. Pierre Nora, trans. Arthur Goldhammer (New York: Columbia University Press, 1996), 146–47.

9. I owe this information on the Constitution to Tomás Eloy Martínez, who developed the subject in "En defensa de los diferentes," in the Buenos Aires newspaper *La Nación,* February 27, 1999.

10. See David Viñas, *Indios, ejército y frontera* (Mexico City: Siglo XXI, 1983).

11. Nostalgic for Europe, Eduardo Mallea says, "Exiles, all of us Argentines are exiles. Exiled from the spirit, exiled from the civilization from which we came, from that ancestral trunk in which, unlike us, men produced art, thought, philosophy" (Desterrados, los argentinos lo somos todos. Desterrados del espíritu, desterrados de la civilización de que venimos, de aquel nudo ancestral en que, a diferencia nuestra, los hombres produjeron arte, pensamiento, filosofía) (in *Historia de una pasión argentina,* 4th ed. [Buenos Aires: Espasa-Calpe, 1945], 184; trans. and ed. Myron I. Lichtblau as *History of an Argentine Passion* [Pittsburgh: Latin American Literary Review Press, 1983]).

12. Marta B. Goldberg, "La mujer negra rioplatense (1750–1840)," in *La mitad del país: La mujer en la sociedad argentina,* comp. Lidia Knecher and Parta Panaia (Buenos Aires: Centro Editor de América Latina, 1994), 67–81.

13. Walter Benjamin speaks of memory in "Theses on the Philosophy of History," in *Illuminations,* ed. Hannah Arendt, trans. Harry Zohn (New York: Schocken Books, 1969), 255. See also Robin George Collingwood, *The Idea of History* (Oxford: Clarendon Press, 1967); Hayden White, *The Content of the Form: Narrative, Discourse, and Historical Representation* (Baltimore: Johns Hopkins University Press, 1987); and White, "The Value of Narrativity in the Representation of Reality," in *On Narrative,* ed. W. J. T. Mitchell (Chicago: University of Chicago Press, 1981), 1–23. The quotation of Nietzsche is from *The Use and Abuse of History,* trans. Adrian Colins (Indianapolis and New York: Liberal Arts Press and Bobbs-Merril, 1957), 40. My reading of Nietzsche corresponds with Gilles Deleuze's interpretation in *Nietzsche and Philosophy,* trans. Hugh Tomlinson (New York: Columbia University Press, 1983). The reference to Sande Cohen is to "Structuralism and the Writing of Intellectual History," *History and Theory* 17,

no. 2 (1978): 206. This chapter is indebted to Matt K. Matsuda's *The Memory of the Modern* (New York: Oxford University Press, 1996).

14. In *Tristes Tropiques* (New York: Atheneum, 1974), Lévi-Strauss studies the traffic in women and the establishment of kinship ties among primitive human groups and ascribes them a mythical value. His thesis was refuted from a feminist/ Marxist/psychoanalytical perspective in order to demonstrate that the kinship system produces not only the oppression of women but also definitions of gender different from the biological question of sex. See Gayle Rubin, "The Traffic in Women," in *Toward an Anthropology of Women,* ed. R. Reiter (New York: Monthly Review Press, 1975), 157–210; for a feminist analysis that opposes Rubin's, see Nancy C. M. Hartsock, *The Feminist Standpoint Revisited and Other Essays* (New York: Westview Press, 1998).

15. For a good iconographic study of the illustrations of Echeverría's work and other representations of captive women, see Laura Malosetti Costa, *Rapto de cautivas blancas: Un aspecto erótico de la barbarie en la plástica rioplatense del siglo XIX,* Hipótesis y Discusiones, 4 (Buenos Aires: Facultad de Filosofía y Letras, UBA, 1994).

16. See Maurice Halbwachs, *The Collective Memory* (New York: Harper and Row, 1980 [1928]). See also Patrick Hutton, "Collective Memory and Collective Mentalities: The Halbwachs-Aries Connection," *Historical Reflections/Reflections Historiques* 15, no. 2 (1988): 314. Other studies I have found helpful in this chapter include Andreas Huyssen, *Twilight Memories: Marking Time in a Culture of Amnesia* (New York: Routledge, 1995), and, to a different degree, John Cowper Powys, *The Art of Forgetting the Unpleasant* (London: Village Press, 1974); Barbie Zelizer, *Remembering to Forget: Holocaust Memory through the Camera's Eye* (Chicago: University of Chicago Press, 1998); Geoffrey Hartman, introduction to *Holocaust Remembrance: The Shapes of Memory,* ed. Hartman (Oxford: Basil Blackwell, 1994); John Gillis, "Memory and Identity: The History of a Relationship," in *Commemorations: The Politics of National Identity* (Princeton, N.J.: Princeton University Press, 1994); James Fentress and Chris Wickham, *Social Memory* (Oxford: Basil Blackwell, 1992); Amritjit Singh, Joseph T. Skerret Jr., and Robert E. Hogan, *Memory and Cultural Politics: New Approaches to American Ethnic Literatures* (Boston: Northeastern University Press, 1996); Marc Augé, *Las formas del olvido,* trans. Mercedes Tricás Precler and Gemma Andújar (Barcelona: Gedisa, 1998). My most profound debt of gratitude is, without a doubt, to Pierre Nora, for *Realms of Memory,* an extraordinary multivolume collection of many scholars' work.

17. Father Meinrado Hux, *Memorias del ex cautivo Santiago Avedaño* (Buenos Aires: Elefante Blanco, 1999).

18. See Nicolas Shumway, *The Invention of Argentina* (Berkeley: University of California Press, 1991).

19. [Sarmiento's best-known work was originally published in 1845 with the title *Facundo: Civilización o barbarie: Vida de Juan Facundo Quiroga y aspecto físico, costumbres y hábitos de la República Argentina;* or, *Facundo: Civilization or Barbarism: Life of Juan Facundo Quiroga and the Physical Features, Customs, and Habits of the Argentine Republic.* Sarmiento wrote and published the book while in exile in Chile, having fled Argentina to escape persecution by dictator Juan Manuel de Rosas. A hybrid of genres and literary styles, *Facundo* is at once a biography of the

gaucho-soldier Facundo Quiroga, a physical and human geography of the pampas, a political diatribe against Rosas, and a exposition of Sarmiento's plan to modernize Argentina by settling the pampa and liberalizing the nation's economy. Sarmiento was president of Argentina from 1868 to 1874. — Trans.]

20. Reification is like memory: an account that appears "given" and hides the fact that it is the result of a process, an interpretation, or a theory. See George Lukács, "Reification and the Consciousness of the Proletariat," in *History and Class Consciousness,* trans. Rodney Livingstone (Cambridge: MIT Press, 1971); Roland Barthes, *Mythologies,* selected and trans. Annette Lavers (New York: Hill and Wang, 1972).

21. Matsuda, *Memory,* 13.

22. Jorge Luis Borges, *Obras completas, 1952–1972* (Buenos Aires: Emecé, 1993), 2:166.

23. Martínez Estrada adds the following in a footnote: "The dogs fled from the houses and became ferocious enemies of herds and of men. The abundance of meat, abandoned in the countryside, where cattle remained after the hides, horns, and fat had been removed, made them wild. They formed, against the herds, intense packs: they were no longer dogs, but jackals. It was necessary to organize military expeditions against them. In a few years they regressed hundreds of centuries" (Los perros huían de las casas y se hacían enemigos feroces de los rebaños y los hombres. La abundancia de carne, abandonada en los campos, donde las reses quedaban luego de quitárseles el cuero, las astas y el sebo, los embraveció. Formaban, contra los rebaños, manadas intensas; ya no eran perros, sino chacales. Fue preciso organizar expediciones militares para combatirlos. En pocos años retrogradaron centenares de siglos) (*Radiografía de la pampa* [Buenos Aires: Losada, 1953], 20).

24. The citations from "Historia del guerrero y la cautiva" are in Borges, *Obras,* 1:556–60. For an analysis of the story see Beatriz Sarlo, *Borges, un escritor en las orillas* (Buenos Aires: Ariel, 1995).

25. Borges notices savagery only in the customs of the indigenous, ignoring the cruelty of the whites on the frontier. Alfred Ebelot, for example, describes the technique by which cows or calves were slaughtered: "Sometimes in order to prevent an offensive turn, the hooves are cut off first. Then it drags along on the stumps, pain forcing out terrible cries. It is a cruel spectacle, but this necessity pleases the soldiers, in whom it contributes more than a little to the development of those sanguinary tastes all too frequently revealed in battle" (A veces para prevenir una vuelta ofensiva, se le cortan ante todo los garrones. Entonces se arrastra sobre los muñones y el dolor le arranca gritos penosos. Es un espectáculo cruel, pero esta necesidad place a los soldados en los que contribuye no poco a desarrollar los gustos sanguinarios que revelan con demasiada frecuencia en las batallas) (*Recuerdos y relatos de la guerra de fronteras* [Buenos Aires: Plus Ultra, 1961], 91).

26. Unless otherwise indicated, quotations from *Facundo* are from the edition with the prologue by Noé Jitrik, notes by Nora Dottori and Susana Zanetti (Caracas: Biblioteca Ayacucho, 1997), 191–92.

27. See Deleuze, *Nietzsche and Philosophy,* 188.

28. William Henry Hudson, *Tales of the Pampas* (New York: Alfred A. Knopf, 1939), 190; trans. Luis Justo as "Marta Riquelme (Del manuscrito de Sepúlveda),"

in *El ombú y otros cuentos* (Buenos Aires: Belgrano, 1981), 125–62; successive page references in the text are to the English version. This is one of the few nineteenth-century stories that deals with the subject of captive women; its author, as is well known, was of North American parentage.

29. Yates, *Art of Memory*, 12.

30. Nora, *Realms of Memory*, 1:xxii, 16–20.

2. In Conquest of a White Nation

Portions of this chapter appeared as "La literatura del silencio: Próspero en la pampa," *Latin American Literary Review* 25, no. 50, special twenty-fifth anniversary issue (July–December 1997): 139–58; and in "La mirada de Próspero," in *Cautivas argentinas: A la conquista de una nación blanca*, Latin American Program Working Paper Series, Woodrow Wilson International Center for Scholars, 233 (December 1997), 1–32.

1. See Y. Yerushalmi et al., eds., *Usos del olvido*, trans. Irene Agoff, 2d ed. (Buenos Aires: Nueva Visión, 1998).

2. In general, Latin American liberal historiography of the nineteenth century tore out the indigenous past because of what it contained of the pre-Hispanic; the past was canceled as a way of negating the importance of the Spanish colony and reaffirming the nation's independence. The difference is that other countries of the continent eventually re-created the indigenous origin, when it became seen — at least on the level of discourse — as an essential ingredient for pride in Latin Americanness and cultural hybridity. David Viñas explains: "if in other countries of Latin American the 'voice of the conquered Indians' has been put in evidence, why not in Argentina? Argentina has nothing to do with Indians? And with Indian women? Or nothing to do with Latin America? I continue to ask: Was no one conquered? No one raped? Or were there neither male nor female Indians? Or the Indians were conquered by the pious exhortations of liberal-bourgeois civilization that convinced them to submit and integrate peacefully? And what does it mean to "integrate"? But, I am encouraged to insist: Why does no one speak of Indians in Argentina? And of their sexuality? What are the implications of their displacement toward the fringe of ethnology, of folklore, and, more injuriously, of tourism or the newspaper sections dedicated to *faits divers*? For all of this I stubbornly continue to ask: Didn't the Indians have voices? Or was their sexuality a disease? And the disease of silence? Is it, paradoxically, the discourse of silence?" (*Indios, ejército y frontera* [Mexico: Siglo XXI, 1983], 12).

3. [The Conquista del Desierto, also referred to as the Campaña del Desierto, was a military operation undertaken by the government of Argentina in 1879–80 to end definitively the threat of Indian attack on the southern pampas by killing most of the indigenous inhabitants and displacing those who survived. Some 390,000 square kilometers of land were opened to settlement by whites. The English word "desert" is only a loose cognate for the Spanish *desierto*, which was often used with reference to the Argentine pampa in the nineteenth century. The term may refer to a geographical region with the extremely arid and sandy conditions of the English "desert," but it refers more generally, as in the case of the

pampa, to an unpopulated region in which vegetation and physical features remain in their natural state. Unlike the term "wilderness," its closest English equivalent, *desierto* adds the literal, adjectival sense of "empty" or "deserted." This last connotation, as Rotker explains, was a crucial part of the official discourse of writers like Sarmiento and Juan Bautista Alberdi. — Trans.]

4. On the Conquista del Desierto and Roca, see, among others, John Lynch, *Argentina Dictator: Juan Manuel de Rosas 1829–1852* (Oxford: Clarendon Press, 1981); José Arcé, *Roca 1843–1914* (Buenos Aires: Real Academia de la Historia, 1960); Alfred Terzaga, *Historia de Roca: De soldado federal a Presidente de la República* (Buenos Aires: Pena Lillo, 1976). In the compilation entitled *Congreso Nacional sobre la Conquista del Desierto* (Buenos Aires: Academia Nacional de la Historia, 1981), see especially Silvia Leonor Belenky et al., "El pensamiento de los conquistadores del desierto (A propósito del general Lorenzo Vintter)," 4:269–350; Olga Noemí Bordi de Ragucci, "Las bases dadas por Roca a la Campaña del Desierto a juicio de sus opositores porteños," 3:41–55; Silvia Paz Illobre, "Algunas consideraciones geoeconómicas y geopolíticas acerca de la Conquista del Desierto," 1:347–58.

5. Domingo Faustino Sarmiento, in chapter 14 of *Facundo: Civilización y barbarie,* prologue by Noé Jitrik; notes and chronology by Nora Dottori and Silvia Zanetti (Caracas: Biblioteca Ayacucho, 1977), 218. The original spelling has been respected in the Spanish text cited.

6. George Reid Andrews's study is indispensable: see *The Afro-Argentines of Buenos Aires: 1800–1900* (Madison: University of Wisconsin Press, 1980); published in Argentina as *Los afro-argentinos de Buenos Aires,* trans. Antonio Bonanno (Buenos Aires: La Flor, 1989 [1980]). About the relationship between castes and racial groups during the independence era, see Tulio Halperín Donghi, *Revolución y guerra: Formación de una élite dirigente en la Argentina criolla* (Mexico: Siglo XXI, 1972). Among recent studies on the strong black presence in Argentine culture in the nineteenth century is Marvin Lewis's *Afro-Argentine Discourse: Another Dimension of the Black Diaspora* (Columbia: University of Missouri Press, 1996), which coincides with the interpretation that blacks were decimated by the wars in the Andes, in Paraguay, and against the Indians, in addition to the apathy of official policy, miscegenation, and the destruction caused by the epidemic of 1871. See also John Garganigo, "El perfil del negro en la narrativa rioplatense," *Historiografía y Bibliografía Americanistas* 21 (1977): 71–109.

7. Laura Fejerman has shown that 4.8 percent of the inhabitants of the city of Buenos Aires today have African ancestors. Fejerman performed a genetic analysis of the population based on molecular data for her master's thesis at Oxford University, England (1999). Her data corroborate the thesis that racial mixing was much more prevalent than is generally recognized. Moreover, Fejerman's thesis maintains that the 1887 census diminished the real proportion of Afro-Argentines, registering them as only 1.8 percent of the population, as Reid also noted. According to Fejerman's study of DNA, at that time and even at the turn of the century, the proportion of blacks among residents of Buenos Aires was 10 percent.

Fejerman has worked with the support of Dr. R. F. Carnese, biological anthropologist and dean of the School of Philosophy and Letters of the University of Buenos Aires at the time of the investigation. Carnese also directed another graduate thesis, Sergio Avena's "Análisis de participación del componente indígena" (1998), which proves that racial mixing between whites and indigenous persons, in samples taken from Gran Buenos Aires and Capital Federal, reaches 22 percent for Gran Buenos Aires and 14 percent for Capital. This means the capital of the discursively white nation of the Americas would have a miscegenation index around 25–30 percent, even more than a century after the whitening campaigns. (Information provided to the author by Laura Fejerman via electronic correspondence, with authorization to cite, September 1999.)

8. See Nicolás Sánchez Albornoz and José Luis Moreno, *La población de América Latina: Bosquejo histórico* (Buenos Aires: Paidós, 1968).

9. The very concept of citizenship (participation and equality) is, in and of itself, the negation of its existence: false homogeneity and the subordination of second-class citizens according to social class, race, gender, and sexual orientation. As Renato Rosaldo has seen, national identity should not be understood as a collective fiction ("where the line between something made and a falsehood can be difficult to draw") but instead as an area of negotiation, disputes, and conflicts that in the long run resist silencing. See Rosaldo, "Social Justice and the Crisis of National Communities," in *Colonial Discourse/Post-colonial Theory,* ed. F. Barkers, P. Hulme, and M. Iversoned (Manchester: Manchester University Press, 1994), 239–52.

10. Ivy Schweitzer, *The Work of Self-Representation: Lyric Poetry in Colonial New England* (Chapel Hill: University of North Carolina Press, 1991), 7–13.

11. Edward Said, *Orientalism* (New York: Vintage, 1978).

12. Lacanian psychoanalysis recognizes this mechanism as "foreclusion," or the blind spot over which the false being is constructed and related with the law of the father. What is negated is in the very base of identity. See Jacques Lacan, *Seminario 3* (Barcelona: Paidós, 1984), 24–25; and Lacan, *Escritos 2* (Buenos Aires: Siglo XXI, 1975), 540 and 556–58. I owe this information to Susana Balán and Cristina Horstein. See also, from another discipline, Jacques Le Goff, *Histoire and mémoire* (Paris: Gallimard, 1988), 204.

13. "Postcolonial" theorists such as Edward Said, Homi K. Bhabha, and Gayatri Spivak have made extraordinary advances in theorizing ways in which the Power of the central countries thinks (and appropriates or deforms) the culture of the countries of their Periphery. But what is of interest here is to revise the tension Power/Periphery within each specific country, in this case the Latin American countries and Argentina in particular.

14. Letter from Brother Pío Bentivoglio, chaplain of the Third Division, cited by Marcela Tamagnini in *Cartas de frontera: Los documentos del conflicto inter-étnico* (Río Cuarto: Universidad Nacional de Río Cuarto, 1994), 267.

15. José Enrique Rodó, *Ariel* (San Juan: Editorial del Departamento de Instrucción Pública, 1968), 1–2; trans. Margaret Sayers Peden as *Ariel* (Austin: University of Texas Press, 1988).

16. Roberto Fernández Retamar, "Caliban," in *Caliban and Other Essays,* trans. Edward Baker (Minneapolis: University of Minnesota Press, 1989), 7, 14; original: *Calibán y otros ensayos: Nuestra América en el mundo* (Havana: Editorial Arte y Literatura, 1979).

17. The intellectual's complicity with Power is amply studied. It is sufficient to

cite a classic of the entire continent: Angel Rama's *La ciudad letrada* (Hanover, N.H.: El Norte, 1984); trans. and ed. John Charles Chasteen as *The Lettered City* (Durham, N.C.: Duke University Press, 1996).

18. The power of Prospero has been emphasized in readings from the late twentieth century. In fact, cinematographer Peter Greenaway made his own version of *The Tempest* in the film *Prospero's Books* (1991) with John Gielgud in the title role, where the hallucinatory settings and movement of the characters practically unhinge the mind of Prospero, his books, and his writing. I owe the information on this film to Kate and Joseph Tulchin. Prospero's supposed cultural superiority has also been studied as one of the methods of imposing colonialist power; see, for example, Gauri Viswanathan, "English Literary Study in British India," in *"Race," Culture, and Difference,* ed. James Donald and Ali Rattansi (London: Sage, 1992); also of interest is Allen Carey-Webb, "Imagi/Native Nation: The Tempest and the Modernization of Political Authority," in *Making Subject(s): Literature and the Emergence of National Identity* (New York: Garland, 1998), 57–92.

19. Dominique O. Mannoni, *Prospero and Caliban: The Psychology of Colonization* (New York: Praeger, 1964 [1950]), 108, 110.

20. Frantz Fanon, *Black Skin, White Masks* (New York: Grove Press, 1967 [1952]).

21. *The Riverside Shakespeare,* ed. G. Blakemore Evans et al. (Boston: Houghton Mifflin, 1974), 1616.

22. In Ruy Díaz de Guzmán, *Anales del descubrimiento, población y conquista de las provincias del Río de la Plata* (Asunción: Ediciones Comuneros, 1980), chap. 7. The coincidence between the names was noted by Montserrat Ordóñez during a conversation at Bogotá's Universidad de los Andes.

23. [Godofredo Daireaux (1849–1916) was born in Paris and immigrated to Argentina in 1868. He first worked in agriculture and ranching but later dedicated himself to teaching and journalism. His narratives, which include *Tipos y paisajes criollos* (1903), *Las veladas de un tropero* (1905), and *Los milagros de la Argentina* (1910), convey the foreigner's amazement at the pampa. —Trans.]

24. Godofredo Daireaux, *El fortín* (Buenos Aires: Agro, 1945), 55–56.

25. Homi Bhabha develops the idea of "the gaze and colonial discourse" as the site of enunciation of the colonizer. The gaze is projected onto the Other from the point of view that defines "the lack of the Other" as colonized or barbarian according to the references of the hegemonic culture. See Bhabha, "The Other Question — the Stereotype and Colonial Discourse," *Screen* 24, no. 6 (November–December 1983): 18–36.

26. In *Nationalist Thought in the Colonial World: A Derivative Discourse* (Minneapolis: University of Minnesota Press 1986), Partha Chatterjee analyzes how the new nations incorporated the foreign parameters of the nation to define their self-identity through France and England (education, level of industrialization and development, etc.). To do this implies self-deprecation, since the countries — in this case Latin American — faced completely different conditions. Mannoni and Fanon had written with particular lucidity on colonial relations toward supposedly inferior races long before the advent of the vogue of so-called postcoloniality.

27. In *Sistema económico y rentístico;* cited in David Viñas, ed., *Historia de la literatura Argentina* (Buenos Aires: Centro Editor de América Latina, 1986), 1:358.

[Juan Bautista Alberdi (1810–74) was a crucial statesman of Argentina's early national period whose influence was perhaps most directly felt in the Constitution of 1853. Like Sarmiento, Alberdi advocated a liberal program based on European immigration, education, and modernization. See John Lynch, "From Independence to National Organization," in *Argentina since Independence*, ed. Leslie Bethell (Cambridge: Cambridge University Press, 1991), 38. — Trans.]

28. This definition, as we have seen, arose not only from the necessity of regimenting an educational system that "civilized" the native population, but also from a desire to discard the original racial diversity. According to Abdul JanMohammed, the neocolonial leaders of the nineteenth century (the Fathers of the Nations) acted as reproducers of the social pathology of the colonizer. This means maintaining the terms of domination and race based on the rationalization of white superiority, whites' mission of civilizing the rest of the world, and the incapacity of the "natives" to govern themselves. In fact, the literary mode of reproducing the nonurban/noncultured (Europeanizing) world tends toward the Manichaean absolutism of colonial narrative. See Abdul JanMohammed, *Manichean Aesthetics: The Politics of Literature in Colonial Africa* (Amherst: University of Massachusetts Press, 1983); and JanMohammed, "The Economy of Manichean Allegory: The Function of Racial Difference in Colonialist Literature," *Critical Inquiry* 12 (fall 1985): 59–86.

29. Sarmiento, *Obras completas* (Buenos Aires: Luz del Día, 1948–56), 26:312; hereafter referred to as *OC*.

30. Alberdi's *Cartas quillotanas* will certainly contest Sarmiento's formulation of the relationship between city and country as a bipolar opposition, asserting that it is "an historical and empirical error, and a source of artificial antipathy between sectors that need and complement one another" (un error histórico y empírico, y una fuente de antipatía artificial entre sectores que se necesitan y complementan uno al otro).

31. See Juan Bautista Alberdi, *Obras completas* (Buenos Aires: Luz del Día, 1948–56), vol. 26.

32. Ricardo Rojas himself has echoed this type of affirmation of Argentine identity(ies): "The white nucleus of our origins was so small that, if not for its proven intellectual superiority, it would have disappeared, entirely assimilated into the extremely numerous pre-Columbian population.... In the native crucible of initial fusion a third element later came to join: the black, considered less noble by white anthropologists and without a doubt historically inferior, for his retarded type of culture" (El núcleo blanco de nuestros orígenes fue tan pequeño que, a no ser su probada superioridad intelectual, hubiera desaparecido asimilado del todo por la numerosísima población precolombina.... En el crisol nativo de la fusión inicial vino a unirse más tarde un tercer elemento, el negro, considerado menos noble por los antropólogos blancos y sin duda alguna históricamente inferior, por su retardado tipo de cultura) (*Historia de la literatura argentina: Ensayo filosófico sobre la evolución de la cultura en la Plata*, 4th ed. [Buenos Aires: G. Kraft, 1957]: 1:119).

33. Pierre Chaunu, *L'héritage: Au risque de la hain* (France: Aubier, 1995).

34. The negative definition of space (to describe it by what it lacks: for example, it has no mountains, no rivers, no visible limits) is a traditional rhetorical

recourse of those who write on "inferior" countries or places, as has been the case of Darwin, Marlowe, Gide, and Conrad. The subject is well analyzed in the chapter "Negation" by Richard Spurr in *The Rhetoric of Empire: Colonial Discourse in Journalism, Travel Writing, and Imperial Administration* (Durham, N.C.: Duke University Press, 1994), 92–108.

35. Homi K. Bhabha, "A Question of Survival: Nations and Psychic States," in *Psychoanalysis and Cultural Theory: Thresholds,* ed. James Donald (New York: St. Martin's Press, 1991), 94.

36. Domingo F. Sarmiento, *Facundo: Civilización y barbarie,* ed. and intro. Raimundo Lazo (Mexico City: Porrúa, 1998), 36–37.

37. Sarmiento, *Conflicto y armonía de las razas en América* (Buenos Aires: La Cultura Argentina, 1915), 68.

38. Academia Nacional de Historia, *Historia argentina contemporánea, 1862–1930* (Buenos Aires: El Ateneo, 1963), 1:271; hereafter referred to as *HAC.*

39. [Estanislao S. Zeballos (1854–1923) was an journalist, politician, and diplomat in his native Argentina. During Zeballos's undistinguished term as minister of foreign relations, his awkward diplomacy resulted in Argentina's loss of thousands of kilometers of land in the Misiones region, which were ceded to Brazil. In 1878 the government ordered Zeballos to write *La conquista de las quince mil leguas* to influence public opinion in favor of the extermination of the Indians. He ultimately wrote two trilogies describing the Desert Campaign, including *Callvucurá y la dinastía de los Piedra* (1884). — Trans.]

40. Zeballos, *Callvucurá y la dinastía de los Piedra,* 3d ed. (Buenos Aires: J. Pesuer, 1890), 114.

41. Manuel Olascoaga, *Estudio topográfico de la Pampa y Río Negro* (Buenos Aires, 1939), 50. The National Academy of History confirms: "The problem of the Indian had been predominant for all the successive governments since independence. All the same, they could not free themselves from the savage, who with his forays limited the terrain of agricultural and cattle-raising labors of the inhabitants of the country. Large ranches and small were established within the limits of territory scarcely advancing beyond cities or towns like San Luis, Mercedes, Junín, and even Buenos Aires; they periodically suffered raids, with the cost of loss of valuable lives, the degrading captivity of the women, the looting of the settlements, and the robbery of ranches" (El problema del Indio había sido dominante para todos los gobiernos que se sucedieron desde la Independencia. Aún no podían librarse del salvaje, que con sus correrías limitaba el campo de las labores agrícolas y ganaderas de los habitantes del país. Las estancias y los puestos que se establecían en las avanzadas de un límite apenas alejado de ciudades o pueblos como San Luis, Mercedes, Junín y hasta Buenos Aires, sufrían periódicamente los malones, con su secuela de pérdidas de valiosas vidas, el cautiverio degradante de las mujeres, el saqueo de las poblaciones y el robo de las haciendas) (*HAC* 1:271).

42. Richard Slatta, *Gauchos and the Vanishing Frontier* (Lincoln: University of Nebraska Press, 1983), 72; translated by Rafael Urbino as *Los gauchos y el ocaso de la frontera* (Buenos Aires: Sudamericana, 1985). See also Ricardo E. Rodríguez Molas, *Historia social del gaucho* (Buenos Aires: Centro Editor de América Latina, 1982); Carlos Astrada, *El mito gaucho* (Buenos Aires: Cruz del Sur, 1964).

43. Slatta, *Gauchos,* 138.

44. Ibid., 94.

45. The engineer contracted for the construction of the ditch, Alfred Ebelot, wrote *Relatos de la frontera* (Buenos Aires: Solar/Hachette, 1968).

46. In *The Origins of Totalitarianism,* 2d ed. (New York: Schocken, 1958), Hannah Arendt suggests that the prolonged encounter between "advanced" and "primitive" peoples has been a determining factor in the origin of totalitarianism. Michael Paul Rogin in *Fathers and Children: Andrew Jackson and the Subjugation of the American Indian* (New Brunswick, N.J.: Transaction Publishers, 1991) explains how the idea of savagery was a force of cultural distancing. In the mid-nineteenth century, the division between civilized and barbarian created racial hierarchies; the division replaced Christian and Enlightenment discourses of equality among human beings.

47. Viñas, *Indios,* 12.

48. Examples of episodes silenced by official history, in addition to the thousands who disappeared during the dictatorship of Videla, include the murder of workers in Patagonia between 1921 and 1923, the shootings at José León Suárez in the Peronist uprising of 1956, and the Trelew massacre. The last two episodes were recounted, one by Rodolfo Walsh in *Operación masacre* and the other by Tomás Eloy Martínez in *La pasión según Trelew.* The former paid for the denunciations in his "Carta a Juana" with his life; the latter published his at the cost of exile.

49. Michael Paul Rogin applies this line of thought to North American Indian policy in *Fathers and Children.*

50. See Sigmund Freud, *Totem and Taboo: Resemblances between the Psychic Lives of Savages and Neurotics,* trans. A. A. Brill (New York: Vintage, 1946 [1918]).

51. Stuart Hall, "New Ethnicities," in Donald and Rattansi *"Race," Culture, and Difference,* 255.

52. Sonia Montecino, "La conquista de las mujeres: Las cautivas, símbolo de lo femenino en América Latina," in *500 años de patriarcado en el Nuevo Mundo,* ed. Asunción Lavrin (Santo Domingo: CIPAF, 1992), 73–74.

53. Mary Louise Pratt, *Imperial Eyes: Travel Writing and Transculturation* (New York: Routledge, 1992).

54. [The terms *fortinera* and *cuartelera* are derived from *fortín,* a small fort, and *cuartera,* barracks. — Trans.]

55. Alfredo Ebelot, *La pampa* (Buenos Aires: A. V. Editor, 1943), 113; Ebelot, *Recuerdos y relatos de la guerra de fronteras* (Buenos Aires: Plus Ultra, 1961), 91. The quotation is from Norma Mabel Buffa and Mabel Cernada, "Aspectos de la vida en la frontera," in *Congreso Nacional de Historia sobre la Conquista del Desierto* (Buenos Aires: Academia Nacional de la Historia, 1981), 8:304, 307; hereafter the compilation will be referred to as *CNH.*

Buffa and Cernada maintain that the inhabitants of the frontier were not racist (*CNH* 306–7). About the *cuarteleras,* they add: "These women who attached themselves to the troop arrived there through different circumstances. Some united their life to that of an errant soldier out of love. Others, for their irregular conduct, were destined to the frontier instead of a correctional institute. And finally there was the indigenous woman who, taken prisoner, was sent to the soldiers as soon as her attributes were known" (*CNH* 8:304).

56. Ana Teresa Zigón, "La conciencia territorial en dos momentos del pensamiento argentino (1837–1880)," in *CNH* 3:232.

57. See James Clifford, "Traveling Cultures," in *Cultural Studies,* ed. L. Grossberg, C. Nelson, and P. Treichler (New York: Routledge, 1992), 96–116; Peter Stallybrass and Allon White, *The Politics and Poetics of Transgression* (Ithaca, N.Y.: Cornell University Press, 1986); Rob Shields, *Places on the Margin: Alternative Geographies of Modernity* (London and New York: Routledge, 1991). A basic anthology of ways of understanding different uses of the term "frontier" is David J. Weber and Jane Rausch, eds., *Where Cultures Meet: Frontiers in Latin American History* (Wilmington, Del.: SR Jaguar Books on Latin America, 1994).

58. Alvaro Barros, *Fronteras y territorios federales de las Pampas del Sur* (Buenos Aires: Hachette, 1957 [1872]), 116. These "shudders of fear" were emphasized in writing allied with a project of national expansion and conquest that found in them a justification for the extermination of the indigenous. According to recent studies, despite the raids, the coexistence of settlers and indigenous on the frontier was more harmonious than the literature allows. About the social extraction of the captives, see Carlos A. Mayo, *Fuentes para la historia de la frontera: Declaraciones de cautivos* (Mar del Plata: Universidad de Mar del Plata, 1985).

59. Mayo, *Fuentes,* 6, 77–78.

60. See Father Meinrado Hux, ed., *Memorias de ex cautivo Santiago Avendaño* (Buenos Aires: Elefante Blanco, 1999). A reference on the number of captive women: in the 1832 campaign with the Chilean army against the Pehuenche Indians of the mountain area, the Chilean division "returned repatriating more than 2,000 captive women; but they did not leave in their legitimate country the 40,000 head of cattle that the irregular armies stole away to the ranches of Mendoza" (regresó repatriando más de 2,000 mujeres cautivas; pero no dejó en su legítima patria las 40,000 cabezas de ganado que los montoneros traían arrebatadas en las estancias de Mendoza) (cited by Walther, *La Conquista del Desierto,* 4th ed. [Buenos Aires: Eudeba, 1980], 184).

61. Viñas, *Indios,* 19.

62. Ezequiel Martínez Estrada maintains in *Muerte y transfiguración del Martín Fierro* (Mexico City: Fondo de Cultura Económica, 1958), 1:286, that the motifs of conquest and captives were already present in *El Cid,* and were simply transferred with the conquest of America: instead of Moorish women, the Spanish cohabited with Indian women. The establishment of the rules of the game during the colonial era is one of the central theses of Cristina Iglesia and Julio Schvartzman in *Cautivas y misioneros: Mitos blancos de la conquista* (Buenos Aires: Catálogos, 1987).

63. See Janet L. Beizer, *Family Plots: Balzac's Narrative Generations* (New Haven: Yale University Press, 1986); A. Parker et al., eds., *Nationalisms and Sexualities* (New York: Routledge, 1992); Eve Kosofsky Sedgwick, *Tendencies* (Durham, N.C.: Duke University Press, 1993), especially the chapter "Nationalisms and Sexualities" (143–53); George L. Mosse, *Nationalism and Sexuality: Respectability and Abnormal Sexuality in Modern Europe* (New York: Howard Fertig, 1985). For a reflection on the role of women, men, and the family in Latin American literature, see Doris Sommer, *Foundational Fictions: The National Romances of Latin America* (Berkeley: University of California Press, 1991); Francine Masiello, *Between Civi-*

lization and Barbarism: Women, Nation, and Literary Culture in Modern Argentina (Lincoln: University of Nebraska Press, 1992). For the specific case of the norms stabilizing the family and their role in Argentine modernity, see Mark Szuchman, *Order, Family, and Community in Buenos Aires: 1810–1860* (Stanford, Calif.: Stanford University Press, 1988); Ricardo Ciccerchia, "Familia: La historia de una idea: Los desórdenes domésticos de la plebe urbana porteña, Buenos Aires 1776–1850," in *Vivir en familia,* ed. Catalina Wainerman (Buenos Aires: Unicef/Losada, 1994), 49–72; J. C. Garavaglia and J. Moreno, eds., *Población, familia y migraciones en el espacio rioplatense: Siglos XVIII y XIX* (Buenos Aires: Cantaro, 1993).

64. Ebelot, *Relatos,* 118–19.

65. Ibid., 113.

66. Slatta, *Gauchos,* 93. The "vagrants" to be recruited were "(1) All the lazy men without occupation in farming or other useful exercise, (2) Those who on workdays and frequently are found in gambling houses, taverns, tracks, and similar diversions, (3) The sons of families resistant to obeying their parents, (4) Those who for the use of the knife, blade, and slight wounds are destined by law to prison" ([1] Todos los ociosos sin ocupación en la labranza y otro ejercicio útil, [2] Los que en días de labor y con frecuencia se encuentran en casas de juego, tabernas, carreras y diversiones de igual clase, [3] Los hijos de familia substraídos de la obediencia de sus padres, [4] Los que por uso de cuchillo, arma blanca y heridas leves son destinados por ley a presidio). In 1853 an additional definition of vagrancy is added: "those who run like ostriches in the field" (los que corren como avestruces en la campaña) (Pascual Paesa, "Milicios y fortines," *Revista de la Junta de Estudios Históricos de Bahía Blanca* 2 [1970]: 28).

67. Daza, *Episodios militares,* 89.

68. Cited by Félix Weinberg, "Sarmiento y el problema de la frontera (1845–1858)," in *CNH* 1:501. The justice of the peace is quoted on page 503 of that study.

69. Barros, *Fronteras,* 116–17.

70. Luis Campoy, "Conquista del Desierto y desaparición del gaucho: Una perspectiva histórica-sociológica," in *CNH* 3:315–22.

71. Daireaux, *El fortín,* n.p.

72. See Elizabeth Garrles, "Sobre indios, afroamericanos y los racismos de Sarmiento," *Revista Iberoamericana, Siglo XIX: Fundación y Fronteras de la Ciudadanía* 178–79 (January–June 1997): 99–114.

73. Ezequiel Martínez Estrada, *Muerte y transfiguración en Martín Fierro,* 1:234–5; Jorge Luis Borges and Bioy Casares, *Poesía gauchesca* (Mexico City: Fondo de Cultura Económica, 1955), 1:viii.

74. If *gauchesca* poetry begins with the poems of Barmolomé Hidalgo in 1811, it acquires legitimacy when Leopoldo Lugones elevates José Hernández's popular *Martín Fierro* to the category of national poem.

75. Juana Manso, *Compendio de la Historia de las provincias unidas del Río de la Plata: Desde su descubrimiento hasta el año de 1871,* 5th ed. (Buenos Aires: Pablo E. Com, 1872), 7, 9.

76. The problem of the captive mothers of Indians appears from very early on. For example, among the first pacts that were attempted in the nineteenth century is that of 1825 in the laguna of Huanaco, signed by thirty-nine chiefs and fifty

indigenous representatives, in which they recognize the Argentine government and promise to impede invasions of the provinces of Buenos Aires, Santa Fe, and Córdoba by other Indians; Article 4 reads: "The captives will be exchanged for each other, since to deliver them all as is solicited would not be possible, *because the majority are married and have children:* but they will be ransomed equitably" (Que las cautivas serán canjeadas una por otra, pues entregarlas todas como se solicitaba no era posible, *por estar la mayor parte casadas y con hijos:* solo sí que serán rescatadas equitativamente) (Documents 241, 242, and 249, archived in the División de Historia del Estado Mayor General del Ejército; cited by Juan Carlos Walther, *La Conquista del Desierto,* 4th ed. [Buenos Aires: Eudeba, 1980], 171).

77. On identity, see L. Appignanesi, ed., *Identity: The Real Me,* ICA Documents, 6 (London: Institute of Contemporary Art, 1987), especially the article "Interrogating Identity" by Bhabha.

3. No One Mourns for Captives

Parts of this chapter appeared as "Silenciar el olvido" in *Cautivas argentinas: A la conquista de una nación blanca,* Latin American Program Working Paper Series, Woodrow Wilson International Center for Scholars, 233 (December 1997): 33–67. Emphasis in quotations is mine unless otherwise indicated.

1. If the figure of the captive is mentioned in poems by Juan Cruz Varela, Ascasubi, or José Hernández, she is never the main subject of those texts. In the only cases in which captives are central — including Echeverría's poem of the same name — they are dealt with as archetypes rather than literary characters. The captive of reality appears in writing more forcefully when captives and Indians no longer exist; meanwhile, other subjects concern the national literature being founded, which is understood to be a system of alliances and political reading-pacts that establish "*topos* (the countryside, the city, the neighborhood, the plaza, sexuality, etc.) and *rhetorics* . . . [that] are reproduced through generations and lineages" (Nicolás Rosa, *El arte del olvido* [Buenos Aires: Puntosur, 1990], 88–89).

2. In his re-creation of life among the Ranquel Indians, Estanislao Zeballos quotes Vicente Fidel López: "Three hundred families have been sacrificed in the province; the girls have been violated, the men have had their throats cut even at the foot of altars, the children have been captured and the soil soaked with torrents of innocent blood in the town of Salto. Everything has been sacked: houses and haciendas; and what yesterday was a town and a flourishing district is today prisoner of fire and wasteland, in which all has been destroyed and trampled underfoot by the voracious passage of the tribes and the ponies of the pampa" (*Painé y la dinastía de los zorros, I. Relmu, reina de los pinares, II* [two works published in one volume] [Buenos Aires: Biblioteca del suboficial, 1928], 84; subsequent quotations are from this edition).

3. The subject has been amply studied with regard to Latin American literature by critics such as Angel Rama, Josefina Ludmer, Julio Ramos, Arcadio Díaz Quiñones, Francine Masiello, Beatriz Sarlo, and Jean Franco, to name only a few.

4. This use of "the Real" is based on Slavoj Zizek's reading of Lacan in *The Sublime Object of Ideology* (London: Verso, 1989). On memory I refer to Roger

Bastide, "Problems of the Collective Memory," in *The African Religions of Brazil: Toward a Sociology of the Interpenetration of Civilizations,* trans. Jelen Sebba (Baltimore: Johns Hopkins University Press, 1978), 240–59; also Maurice Halbachs, *Les cadres sociaux de la memoire* (Paris: Presses Universitaires de France, 1952), 249–50.

5. Mitchell Robert Breitwieser, *American Puritanism and the Defense of Mourning: Religion, Grief, and Ethnology in Mary White Rowlandson's Captivity Narrative* (Madison: University of Wisconsin Press, 1990), 40.

6. The title is *A True History of the Captivity and Restoration of Mrs. Mary Rowlandson* (1682, four editions). In the decades to follow the literary genre of captivity narratives produced testimonies as well as fiction; these sometimes represented captivity as an idyllic existence among the Indians; other times the captivity was characterized by torture and rape; but it was always presented as either a threat to civilization or the emblem of noble savagery. The Puritans initially saw these experiences as a text through which believers would be redeemed, but toward the eighteenth and nineteenth centuries the writings became more political. Other works of interest include "A Brief History of the War with the Indians in New England," by Increase Mather, which contains Rowlandson's story. There are also captive men like Captain John Smith, who was saved by Pocahontas; the protagonist of "The Narrative of Colonel Ethan Allen's Captivity" (1779, twenty editions in two years); and Charles Broden Brown. A diary that served as the justification for the killing of Indians was "An Affecting Narrative of the Captivity and Sufferings of Mrs. Mary Smith" (1815). Colonel Daniel Boone was the first to boast of his adoption by the Indians, in *The Adventures of Col. Daniel Boone, One of the First Settlers,* supposedly dictated to John Filson. Other accounts include Lydia Maria Child's novel *Homobok: A Tale of Early Times,* and Sarah Wakefield's "A Narrative of Indian Captivity."

7. See Christopher Castiglia, *Bound and Determined: Captivity, Culture-Crossing, and White Womanhood from Mary Rowlandson to Patty Hearst* (Chicago: University of Chicago Press, 1996), and Annette Kolodny, *The Land before Her: Fantasy and Experience of the American Frontiers, 1630–1860* (Chapel Hill: University of North Carolina Press, 1984).

8. The full title is *A Narrative of the Life of Mrs. Who Was Taken by the Indians in the Year 1755 When Only about Twelve Years of Age and Has Continued to Reside amongst Them to the Present* (1824).

9. Doris Sommer has written an excellent study of Cooper's influence on nineteenth-century Argentine literature, especially Sarmiento's *Facundo,* in *Foundational Fictions: The National Romances of Latin America* (Berkeley: University of California Press, 1991).

10. Mary Louise Pratt, *Imperial Eyes: Travel Writing and Transculturation* (New York: Routledge, 1992), chap. 2.

11. The quotation is from Annette Kolodny's "Among the Indians: The Uses of Captivity," book review, *New York Times,* January 31, 1993, 27. Kolodny lists titles of studies and reeditions of the 1990s, confirming the persistence in the United States of interest in the subject: *Captured by the Indians: 15 Firsthand Accounts, 1750–1870,* ed. Frederick Drimmer; *Indian Captivities, or Life in the Wigwam,* by Samuel G. Drake; *The Indians and Their Captives,* ed. James Levernier and

Hennig Cohen; *Journeys in New Worlds: Early American Women's Narratives,* ed. William L. Andres; *A Narrative of the Life of Mrs. Mary Jemison,* by James E. Seaver; *North Country Captives: Selected Narratives of Indian Captivity from Vermont and New Hampshire,* ed. Colin G. Calloway; *Puritans among the Indians: Accounts of Captivity and Redemption, 1676–1724,* ed. Alten T. Vaughan and Edward W. Clark; *Six Months among Indians,* by Darius B. Cook; *Six Weeks in the Sioux Tepees,* by Sarah F. Wakefield; *True Stories of New England Captives: Carried to Canada during the Old French and Indian Wars,* by C. Alice Baker.

12. Bonnie Frederick, "Reading the Warning: The Reader and the Image of the Captive Woman," *Chasqui* 18, no. 2 (November 1989): 10. The previous chapter also considers the social classes most affected by indigenous attacks.

13. Susan Migden Socolow, "Los cautivos españoles en las sociedades indígenas: El contacto cultural a través de la frontera argentina," trans. G. Malgesini, *Anuario del IEHS* 2 (1987): 136.

14. Shoshana Feldman, "Education and Crisis, or the Vicissitudes of Teaching," in Shoshana Feldman and Dori Laub, *Testimony: Crises of Witnessing in Literature, Psychoanalysis, and History* (New York: Routledge, 1992), 5.

15. See Eric J. Hobsbawm, *Nations and Nationalism since 1780: Program, Myth, Reality* (Cambridge: Cambridge University Press, 1983).

16. *Relación* (Chacabo: Imprenta del Estado, 1835). The Academia Nacional de Historia published a facsimile edition under the title *Juan Manuel de Rosas y la redención de cautivos en su campaña del desierto (1833–34)* (Buenos Aires: Academia Nacional de Historia, 1979).

17. Silence contaminates Argentine historiography, which only obliquely takes into account a problem that lasted from the colony to the end of the nineteenth century. This does not mean that the subject has absolutely not been studied, but rather that — despite having generated a number of serious investigations — it has not been *diffused* enough. Without attempting to be exhaustive, the following lists some of the most outstanding of the studies documented by Carlos A. Mayo in *Fuentes para la historia de la frontera: Declaraciones de cautivos* (Mar del Plata: University of Mar del Plata, 1985); Mayo, "El cautiverio y sus funciones en una sociedad de frontera: El caso de Buenos Aires (1750–1810)," *Revista de Indias* 45, no. 175 (1985); Mayo and Amalia Latrubesse, *Terratenientes, soldados y cautivos: La frontera (1737–1815)* (Mar del Plata: University of Mar del Plata, 1986); see also Socolow, "Los cautivos." Kristine Jones addresses the subject in "La Cautiva: An Argentine Solution to Labor Shortage in the Pampas," in *Brazil and the Río de la Plata: Challenge and Response: An Anthology of Papers Presented at the Sixth Annual Conference of Icllas,* ed. Luis Clay Méndez and Laurence Bates (Charleston, Ill., 1983), 91–94; Jones, "Conflict and Adaptation in the Argentine Pampas, 1750–1880" (Ph.D. diss., University of Chicago, 1984); Jones, "Nineteenth-Century British Travel Accounts of Argentina," *Ethnohistory* 33, no. 2 (1986); Jones, "Indian Creole Negotiations," in *Revolution and Restoration,* ed. J. C. Brown and M. Szuchman (Lincoln: University of Nebraska Press, 1994). This list is only a sampling; other studies have been and will be mentioned throughout the present work.

18. The austerity of detail is such that the introduction to the facsimile edition states that: "The book does not contain the cries of *viva* and *muera* that came

into use during that era. The pain, the anguish, the martyrdom, the desolation, the affliction in the case of every man or woman who lived in the villages, quiet the dictator's political passion; [the report] expresses simply the terrible years those other human beings spent as slaves in their own country (*Relación*, 20). It is known that Rosas to a large extent erected his first political platform on the achievements of this incursion into the wilderness; the instability of the country was such that in 1829 he was declared governor, in the spirit of compensating for "the utter failure of all attempts to institutionalize power," as Jorge Myers explains in *Orden y virtud: El discurso republicano en el régimen rosista* (Buenos Aires: Universidad Nacional de Quilmes, 1995), 19; see Juan Carlos Walther, *La Conquista del Desierto* (Buenos Aires: Eudeba, 1970).

19. Socolow, "Los cautivos," 135. The introduction to the facsimile edition confirms that "From 1834 to '35 the justices of the peace delivered former captives to their families, when they could be found, and the Beneficent Society took charge of the children and helpless women" (20).

20. Memoirs of the time as well as anthologies of texts compiled a posteriori perform a sleight of hand where the Argentine captives are concerned. See *Memorias del General Gregorio Araoz de la Madrid*, vols. 1–2 (Buenos Aires: Eudeba, 1969); Francisco P. Moreno, *Viaje a la Patagonia Austral (1876–1877)* (Buenos Aires: Solar/Hachette, 1969); José M. Paz, *Memorias de la prisión: Buenos Aires en la época de Rosas* (Buenos Aires: Eudeba, 1960); Manuel Baigorria, *Memorias* (Buenos Aires: Solar/Hachette, 1970); José Luis Busaniche, ed., *Estampas del pasado: Lecturas de la historia argentina* (Buenos Aires: Hachette, 1959); Alfred Ebelot, *Relatos de la frontera* (Buenos Aires: Solar/Hachette, 1968). The same occurs in basic texts like Adolfo Saldías's *Historia de la Confederación Argentina* (Buenos Aires: Juan Carlos Granda, 1967). On the other hand, a very useful book for this subject is Marcela Tamagnini's compilation, *Cartas de la frontera: Los documentos del conflicto inter-étnico* (Río Cuarto: Universidad Nacional de Río Cuarto, 1994), analyzed in chapter 6 of the present work.

21. [The dictionary published by the Real Academia Española defines *chino* and *china* as terms used in Argentina, Chile, Paraguay, Uruguay, and Venezuela to describe individuals of indigenous appearance or descent. Despite the obvious homonym (*chino* and *china* also mean "Chinese"), the South American term is derived from the Quechua *china*, which means "woman," or "female." — Trans.]

22. Cited by Santiago Luis Copello, *Gestiones del Arzobispo Aneiros en favor de los indios hasta la Conquista del Desierto* (Buenos Aires: Coni, 1945), 227–28.

23. José Daza, *Episodios militares,* corrected and expanded edition (Buenos Aires: Librería La Facultad de Juan Roldán, 1912), 229; in subsequent references, page numbers will be given in the text.

24. Zeballos, *Painé,* 66–68; subsequent references are from these pages.

25. Sander Gilman has studied the cultural representation of female sexuality as abnormality, hysteria, or illness in "Black Bodies, White Bodies: Toward an Iconography of Female Sexuality in Late Nineteenth-Century Art, Medicine, and Literature," *Critical Inquiry* (fall 1985): 204–42; Gilman, *Disease and Representation: Images of Illness from Madness to AIDS* (Ithaca, N.Y.: Cornell University Press, 1988); Gilman, *Sexuality: An Illustrated History Representing the Sexual in Medicine and Culture from the Middle Ages to the Age of AIDS* (New York: Wiley, ca. 1989).

See also Michel Foucault, *The History of Sexuality,* vol. 1, trans. Robert Hurley (New York: Vintage, 1980); following Foucault's theories about sexual repression in nineteenth-century culture, according to which the asylum and the brothel were the only places of tolerance, it is not surprising that the frontier region was also imagined and/or visualized as an uncontrolled space. On the other hand, there is also the tension between sensuality and the civilizing desire: reading Sarmiento, Rosa calls these the "Oriental ethos" and the "Roman ethos" (106).

26. George L. Mosse, *Nationalism and Sexuality: Respectability and Abnormal Sexuality in Modern Europe* (New York: Howard Fertig, 1985).

27. Michael Taussig, *Mimesis and Alterity: A Particular History of the Senses* (New York: Routledge, 1993), 64.

28. See *Enciclopedia de la literatura argentina,* ed. Pedro Orgambide and Roberto Yahni (Buenos Aires: Sudamerica, 1970), 638–39.

29. See chapter 7 in the present volume.

30. *Relación,* 20. During the colonial era many tribes found the captives a source of commerce with the Spanish. The Spanish, for their part, also took Indian prisoners to use as slaves. See the abundant documentation cited by Mayo and Socolow.

31. Cited by Walther, *La Conquista del Desierto,* 220. For other captives' prices see the examples collected by Mayo, *Fuentes,* 78ff.

32. Michel de Certeau, *Heterologies: Discourse on the Other,* trans. Brian Massumi (Minneapolis: University of Minnesota Press, 1986).

33. Renato Rosaldo, "Social Justice and the Crisis of National Communities," in *Colonial Discourse/Postcolonial Theory,* ed. F. Barkers, P. Hulme, and M. Iverson (Manchester: Manchester University Press, 1994), 245.

34. José Arce's investigations are less categorical on this point. He remarks that "Regarding the captive men: [the Indians] made use of them to obtain more money, demanding ransom for them; those who were not ransomed served for diverse tasks and were instructed in some useful activities. By utilizing the women as concubines of the chiefs and the principal warriors, they procured very valuable assistants in the gentle life they led in their distant Andean villages" (*Roca: Su vida–su obra* [Buenos Aires: Academia de la Historia, 1960], 97–98).

35. See Zygmunt Bauman, *Modernity and Ambivalence* (Ithaca, N.Y.: Cornell University Press, 1991).

36. [Hilario Ascasubi (1807–75): soldier, journalist, and one of the earliest authors of gauchesque verse, including the narrative poem *Santos Vega* (1851). Ascasubi's poetry often campaigns directly against the Rosas regime; like Sarmiento he wrote much of his best-known work in exile. — Trans.]

37. A study of interest is Adriana Rodríguez Pérsico's "Modelos de estado: Figuras utópicas y contrautópicas," *Filología* 23, no. 2 (1988): 89–11; indispensable for understanding gauchesque poetry is Josefina Ludmer's *El género gauchesco: Un tratado sobre la patria* (Buenos Aires: Sudamérica, 1988).

38. J. P. Robertson and W. P. Robertson, *Letters of South America* (London: John Murray, 1843), 3:161–62.

39. Taussig, *Mimesis and Alterity,* 66.

40. Silvia Paz Illobre, "Algunas consideraciones geoeconómicas y geopolíticas acerca de la Conquista del Desierto: Las ideas de la época," *Congreso Nacional de*

Historia sobre la Conquista del Desierto (Buenos Aires: Academia Nacional de la Historia, 1981), 1:348.

41. Robertson, *Letters,* 179–84.

42. Alvaro Barros, *Fronteras y territorio federales de las Pampas del Sur* (Buenos Aires: Hachette, 1957 [1872]), 120.

43. R. B. Cunninghame Graham, "Los Indios," in *The South American Sketches,* ed. John Walker (Norman: University of Oklahoma Press, 1978), 71. See Luis Busaniche, ed., *Estampas del pasado: Lecturas de historia argentina* (Buenos Aires: Hachette, 1959), 543.

44. Alcide D'Orbigny, *Voyage dans "Amérique Meridionale"* (1835–38), 1:634.

45. Socolow, "Los cautivos," 124.

46. Ibid., 134–35.

47. Reproduced in *Revista de la Junta de Estudios Históricos de Mendoza* 9, no. 2 (1980): 367.

48. Mistrust toward the former captive resounds through the texts. The idea that she has become an Indian is constant. In *De los tiempos de antes,* for example, in the twentieth century, Carlos Molina Massey re-creates the kidnapping of two well-to-do women. The mother manages to escape, but the beautiful daughter, Rosarito, remains for years in captivity among the Boroga Indians. I will not enter here into the subject of the desiring gazes that cross between chiefs and white women before the kidnapping since I discuss a similar instance in the chapter on Lucía Miranda. The episode is ambiguous, given that there is no way of knowing whether Rosarito's flight is the happy journey of one returning home after years of martyrdom or the desperate act of a woman who has nowhere to go after the murder of her Indian husband. The chain of transformations is perturbing: the child Rosarito of the beginning, delicate and well-bred, as fearful of the Indians as she is modest, suddenly acts in the world as if she were a man, has ceased to speak like an educated person, shares the point of view of the Indians, and is disposed to return home, free in her body, with two mestizo children as well. At the historical level it is nonetheless clear that this "güena cría," a bastard and mestiza with altered gender traits, has no place within the social project. Carlos Molina Massey, *De los tiempos de antes (Narraciones gauchas)* (Buenos Aires: Agro, 1946), 165–88.

49. Cristina Iglesia, "La mujer cautiva: Cuerpo, mito y frontera," in *Historia de las mujeres: Del renacimiento a la edad moderna,* ed. Georges Duby and Michelle Perrot (Madrid: Taurus, 1992), 3:558. The theory of the abject appears in Julia Kristeva's *Powers of Horror: An Essay on Abjection,* trans. Leon S. Roudiez (New York: Columbia University Press, 1982).

50. Laura Malosetti Costa, *Rapto de cautivas blancas: Un aspecto erótico de la barbarie en la plástica rioplatense del siglo XIX,* Hipótesis y Discusiones, 4 (Buenos Aires: Facultad de Filosofía y Letras, UBA, 1994), 22.

51. Godofredo Daireaux, *Tipos y paisajes criollos* (Buenos Aires: Agro, 1945), 50–51.

52. R. B. Cunninghame Graham, "The Captive," in *South American Sketches,* 82.

53. R. B. Cunninghame Graham, "La cautiva," from *El Río de la Plata;* cited by Ezequiel Martínez Estrada, *Muerte y transfiguración de Martín Fierro* (Mexico City: Fondo de Cultura Económica, 1958), 1:290. Another captive, registered in

Mariano Vedia's biography of Roca, refuses to return to her Christian children in the city, preferring to flee back to the tent of the chief and their mestizo children. This does not necessarily signify a value judgment on urban/white vs. indigenous life; a similar phenomenon appears among captive Indian women who became accustomed to their new lives among the whites. See Vera Pichel, *Las cuarteleras: Cuatro mil mujeres en la Conquista del Desierto* (Buenos Aires: Planeta, 1994), 65–67.

54. Manuel Baigorria, *Memorias* (Buenos Aires: Solar/Hachette, 1975 [1868]), 74.

55. Ciro Bayo, *La América desconocida* (Buenos Aires: Caro Raggio, 1927), 29.

56. Walther, *La Conquista del Desierto*, 610.

57. Bauman, *Modernity and Ambivalence*.

58. Viñas, *Indios*, 49–50.

4. Frontier Bodies

1. See *Obras completas de Esteban Echeverría*, ed. Juan María Gutiérrez, 2d ed. (Buenos Aires: Antonio Zamora, 1972); hereafter referred to as *EOC*.

2. Peter Berger and Thomas Luckmann, *The Social Construction of Reality: A Treatise in the Sociology of Knowledge* (New York: Irvington Publishers, 1966).

3. Adolfo Prieto, *La literatura autobiográfica argentina* (Buenos Aires: Centro Editor de América Latina, 1982).

4. See Fermín Chávez, *La cultura en la época de Rosas: Aportes a la descolonización mental de la Argentina* (Buenos Aires: Theoria, 1973). Jorge Myers exhaustively studies Rosist propaganda, which, he writes, "would manifest a sharp awareness of the great importance of producing propaganda in favor of his activities and of controlling the political messages that circulated in the local media" (*Orden y virtud: El discurso republicano en el régimen rosista* [Buenos Aires: National University of Quilmes, 1995], 22ff.).

5. Domingo F. Sarmiento writes the phrase in *Recuerdos de provincia*: "We, on the day after the revolution, had to turn our eyes in all directions *seeking to fill the void* that was left by the destroyed Inquisition, by vanquished absolutism, by broadened religious exclusion" (Nosotros, al día siguiente de la revolución debíamos volver los ojos a todas partes, buscando con qué llenar el vacío que debían dejar la inquisición destruida, el poder absoluto vencido, la exclusión religiosa ensanchada) (*Recuerdos de provincia* [Buenos Aires: Sopena, 1966 (1843)], 92). On the role of the lettered elites, see Angel Rama, *The Lettered City*, trans. and ed. John Charles Chasteen (Durham, N.C.: Duke University Press, 1996); Josefina Ludmer, "Quién educa," *Filología* 20, no. 1 (1985): 105–16; Ludmer, *El género gauchesco: Un tratado sobre la patria* (Buenos Aires: Sudamericana, 1988); Julio Ramos, *Desencuentros de la modernidad en América Latina* (Mexico City: Fondo de Cultura Económica, 1986); and Ramos, *Paradojas de la letra* (Caracas: Excultura, 1996).

6. I cite John W. Kronik's definition in "Editor's Note," *PMLA* 107 (1992): 425. See Michel de Certeau, *The Practice of Everyday Life*, trans. Steven Randall (Berkeley: University of California Press, 1988); and Andrew Parker and Eve

Kosofky Sedgwick, eds., *Performativity and Performance* (New York: Routledge, 1995).

7. See Myers's *Orden y virtud;* also Ana María Amar Sánchez, "La gauchesca durante el rosismo: Una disputa por el espacio del enemigo," *Revista de Crítica Literaria Latinoamericana* 28, no. 35 (first semester 1992): 7–19.

8. Cited by José Luis Romero, *Las ideas políticas en Argentina,* 10th ed. (Buenos Aires: Fondo de Cultura Económica, 1987), 143.

9. The gesture is, of course, totally different in 1981 when César Aira publishes his novel *Ema, la cautiva,* a sort of fantastical diversion that takes as its point of departure the villages, forts, and raids of the nineteenth century. The novel's protagonist is a heroine (in the traditional sense, the opposite of a hero) who changes (or is made to change) husbands with all naturalness, becomes a concubine in an indigenous court resembling those of Arabian tales, takes charge of a business that uses a delirious process to reproduce quantities of pheasants, and ends up living in a cave. Entertaining and overflowing with imagination, *Ema, la cautiva* (Buenos Aires: Belgrano, 1981), is a parody that does not endeavor to fill the voids that Culture left regarding the captives of reality. As a fiction about indifference and letting go, it takes the space of the desert and the frontier between civilization and barbarism as a scene of emptiness.

10. In his classic study *Orientalism* (New York: Vintage, 1979), Edward Said writes that in the eighteenth century European identity was formed as a negation of the Orient; see also Walter Mignolo, "Putting the Americas on the Map: Cartography and the Colonization of Space," *Colonial Latin America Review* 1 (1992): 25–63. A good summary of this debate is found in Beatriz Dolores Urraca, "The Literary Construction of National Identities in the Western Hemisphere: Argentina and the United States, 1845–1898" (Ph.D. diss., University of Michigan, 1993).

11. This document, "An Account of the Christians Saved from Slavery by the Left Division of the Expeditionary Army against the Barbarians, under the Command of Brigadier General D. Juan Manuel de Rosas," is analyzed in the previous chapter.

12. Tulio Halperín Donghi, *Guerra y finanzas en los orígenes del Estado argentino (1791–1850)* (Buenos Aires: Belgrano, 1982), 172.

13. Discrediting the success of Rosas's desert expedition seems to have been constant in the discourse of his lettered enemies. Sarmiento affirmed that Rosas's only achievement was knocking over a few Indian huts and taking some of the rabble prisoner. He admitted, in the second edition of *Facundo* (1851), that geography had made important conquests, discovering territories, and that, thanks to the expedition that distanced and subjugated many tribes, settlement could extend into the south. Despite this affirmation, Sarmiento always insisted — since he believed in the necessity of establishing agricultural colonies on the frontier — that the results obtained by Rosas were ephemeral, since the Indians continued their sporadic invasions and the territory remained largely unpopulated. See Féliz Weinberg, "Sarmiento y el problema de la frontera (1845–1858)," in *Congreso Nacional de Historia sobre la Conquista del Desierto* (Buenos Aires: Academia Nacional de la Historia, 1981), 1:497; in subsequent citations this compilation will be identified as *CNH.*

14. The poem *La cautiva* resuscitates the subject of the raid in order to question Rosas's effectiveness. But to do history justice, it should be mentioned that Rosas had the virtue of negotiating with the chiefs: his government ruled during the only period of relative peace on the frontier in the better part of the nineteenth century; see Juan Carlos Walther, *La Conquista del Desierto* (Buenos Aires: Eudeba, 1970), 235–40. But the enemy is never given the benefit of the doubt.

15. Francine Masiello, *Between Civilization and Barbarism: Women, Nation, and Literary Culture in Modern Argentina* (Lincoln: University of Nebraska Press, 1992), 21–28.

16. See Cornelius Castoriadis, "The Imaginary: Creation in the Social-Historical Domain"; cited by L. Appignanesi, *Identity: The Real Me,* ICA Documents (London: Institute of Contemporary Art, 1987), 40.

17. The poem inaugurated Argentine romanticism because narrative verse was itself a novelty and because Echeverría gave an epic tone to anonymous heroes, mixing styles and allowing "individuals of the popular classes to speak in elevated language." Its innovative versification that "seeks the Spanish popular style" varies between octosyllables and hexasyllables, grouped in ten-line stanzas, sestinas, and romances. See Noé Jitrik, *Esteban Echeverría* (Buenos Aires: Centro Editor de América Latina, 1967), 26. Other studies include David Lagmanovich, "Tres cautivas: Echeverría, Ascasubi, Hernández," *Chasqui* 8, no. 3 (May 1979): 24–33; Juan Carlos Mercado, *Building a Nation: The Case of Echeverría* (Lanham, Md.: University Press of America, 1996); Eduardo de Agüero, "El paisaje como adversario en *La cautiva,*" *Cuadernos de Aldeen/Asociación de Licenciados y Doctores Españoles en EE.UU.* 1, nos. 2–3 (May–October 1983): 157–74; Edgar C. Knowlton, *Esteban Echeverría* (Bryn Mawr, Pa.: Dorrance and Company, 1986); Knowlton, "The Epigraphs in Esteban Echeverría's 'La cautiva,'" *Hispania* 44, no. 2 (May 1961): 212–17; David Viñas, *Literatura argentina y realidad política* (Buenos Aires: Centro Editor de América Latina, 1982).

18. I cite the edition of *Facundo: Civilización y barbarie* introduced by Noé Jitrik (Caracas: Biblioteca Ayacucho, 1997), 39–40.

19. Carlos Altamirano and Beatriz Sarlo, *Ensayos argentinos: De Sarmiento a la vanguardia* (Buenos Aires: Ariel/Espasa-Calpe, 1997 [1987]), 39–40.

20. Homi K. Bhabha, "DissemiNation...," in *Nation and Narration* (London: Routledge, 1990), 295.

21. See Rob Shields, *Places on the Margin: Alternative Geographies of Modernity* (London: Routledge, 1991).

22. Mary Louise Pratt, *Imperial Eyes: Travel Writing and Transculturation* (New York: Routledge, 1992). James Clifford writes that the frontier is a specific place of hybridity and struggle, vigilance and transgression, an experience that produces political visions so powerful that they subvert binarisms; see "Traveling Cultures," in *Cultural Studies,* ed. L. Grossberg, C. Nelson, and P. Treichler (New York: Routledge, 1992), 96–116.

23. *La cautiva* reflects a common feeling toward the Rosas government; coincidences in language can be observed between Echeverría's poem and a text published in *El Nacional* in December 1838: "[G]iven the attacks of the savage hordes, of thieves on the desolate roads, in effect, who are more truly children of Buenos Aires than an unfortunate family upon which has fallen a merciless, faithless plague of

bandits?" ([B]ajo los ataques de las hordas salvajes, de los ladrones en los caminos desamparados y en efecto, ¿qué más son los hijos de Buenos Aires que una familia infeliz sobre la cual ha caído sin piedad, sin religión, una plaga de bandidos?) (cited by Helene Tzitsikas, *Los exiliados argentinos en Montevideo durante la época de Rosas* [Montevideo: Ediciones de la Plaza, 1991], 31).

24. Mary Louise Pratt explains that when the poem was written, Argentina was in a long-standing state of civil war between the progressives, the traditional centers of power, and the emergent transatlantic commercial alliances. According to her thesis, Echeverría establishes not a utopian vision like Bello's but a "moral and civic dystopia" (*Imperial Eyes,* 182–83) in the void of the American landscape.

25. Graciela Montaldo writes: "Since the romantics of '37, [writers] name the space of the desert, the void that must be filled. With the desert political-cultural programs are constructed, discourses to form the base of the nation. The term they use does not fix only a place, it also fixes a relationship with the territory and stamps it for the national literature." Also: "The desert is one of the forms of naming the chaos that is experienced in public life, resistant in those incommensurable expanses" (*De pronto, el campo: Literatura argentina y tradición rural* [Rosario: Beatriz Viterbo Editora, 1993], 34).

26. Ana Teresa Zigón, "La conciencia territorial en dos momentos del pensamiento argentino (1837–1880)," *CNH* 3:232.

27. Referring to the gauchesque, Ezequiel Martínez Estrada notes that "when Ascasubi and Hernández take up the subject, surpassing Echeverría successively, they will enrich it with a less rhetorical language, greater narrative vivacity, and an art more certain of describing and telling. But they will add nothing to alter the canon of Echeverría, in which the savage justifies the renewed atrocities of the whites with his excessive cruelty, a point of view that is unalterable in our history of the Spanish conquest of the desert" (*Muerte y transfiguración del Martín Fierro* [Mexico City: Fondo de Cultura Económica, 1958], 1:287).

28. As with everything, there were exceptions. A notable one is the former captive, "Señor don Francisco Barlai," who wrote a grammar during his captivity among the Indians of Calfucurá. After his return to Buenos Aires, Barlai sent the text to be published, as he explains in a letter to Fray Moysés Álvarez published in *Cartas de la frontera: Los documentos del conflicto inter-étnico,* ed. Marcela Tamagnini (Río Cuarto: Universidad Nacional de Río Cuarto, 1995), 100.

29. A. Guinnard, *Tres años de esclavitud entre los patagones (Relato de mi cautiverio)* (Buenos Aires: Espasa-Calpe, n.d.), 63.

30. Cited by Estanislao Zeballos in *Painé y la dinastía de los zorros, I. Relmú, reina de los pinares, II.* (Buenos Aires: Biblioteca del Suboficial, 1928), 84.

31. See Carlos A. Mayo, *Fuentes para la historia de la frontera: Declaraciones de cautivos* (Mar del Plata: Universidad de Mar del Plata, 1985).

32. See Norma Mabel Buffa and Mabel Cernadas de Bulnes, "Aspectos de la vida en la frontera," in *CNH* 3:297–337.

33. Pratt describes a symbolic family of colonists — formed by the white Creole María, "her British husband Brian, and their young daughter" — that is pursued and brutally murdered by the Indians (*Imperial Eyes,* 185), a reading that leads her to conclude that the poem establishes a Creole and masculine order. In Echeverría's

poem, nonetheless, María has not lost a daughter, but rather her father, mother, and son: "Give me it [the dagger] to kill / The insolent savage / Who tries to outrage my honor; / To in one blow avenge / My *father's*, my *tender son's* / and my *mother's* unjust deaths (Diómelo para matar / Al salvaje que insolente / Ultrajar mi honor intente; / Para, a un tiempo, de mi padre / De mi hijo tierno y mi madre / La injusta muerte vengar) (461–62). Brián says the same: "You know? His hands were washed, / with hellish exultation / in the blood of my son" (¿Sabes?— sus manos lavaron, / con infernal regocijo, / En la sangre de mi hijo) (470). Nor can Brián be read as an English colonist: the poem makes very clear that he is a soldier ("Today is the anniversary / Of my first battle" [Hoy es el aniversario / De mi primera batalla] [472]; Brián's comrades in arms ("soldiers of the unfortunate Brián" [soldados son del desdichado Brián] [474]) find María before her death.

34. "Byron seems to have lent . . . a model for the desperation brought on by the loss of origin and ignorance of the direction in which destiny impels men," write Altamirano and Sarlo (*Ensayos,* 30). The other confusion over Brián's nationality is in reading his name without the written accent and taking it as an English appellative; however, it is always accented in Spanish editions.

35. Manuel Olascoaga, *Estudio topográfico de la Pampa y Río Negro,* cited in *CNH* 3:234.

36. María Lugones, "Motion, Stasis, and Resistance to Interlocked Oppressions," in *Making Worlds: Gender, Metaphor, Materiality,* ed. Susan Hardy Aiken et al. (Tucson: University of Arizona Press, 1998), 49–53.

37. Cited in *CNH* 8:303.

38. Cited in ibid., 8:304.

39. See Bonifacio del Carril, "El malón de Rugendas," in *Esteban Echeverría: La cautiva: Dibujos de Mauricio Rugendas* (Buenos Aires: Emecé, 1966); del Carril, *Artistas extranjeros en la Argentina: Mauricio Rugendas* (Buenos Aires: Academia Nacional de Bellas Artes, 1966); and del Carril, *Los indios en la Argentina* (Buenos Aires: Emecé, 1992).

40. Today the painting hangs in the National Museum of Arts: it was one of the triggers of this investigation. It has been used as the cover of the Biblioteca Ayacucho edition of *Una excursión a los indios ranqueles.* Laura Malosetti Costa has rightly observed that part of the painting's force can be attributed to the fact that it sparks nostalgia rather than fear, since the Indians had practically been exterminated by the time Della Valle painted it. This is her description: "the group composed by the horseman and his prey (reiterated later by the artist in isolation) has a sensual character that distinguishes them from the rest of the composition: the violent contrasts are drawn; the Indian seems to a certain point like a tanned and athletic gallant, whose arm encircles the sleeping, submissive woman. This Indian does not raise his head to vociferate, like the others, his victory, but rather inclines slightly over the stolen woman: his gesture is not aggressive. At the same time, the lance held against her indicates his possession by force, as a visualization of masculine power" (*Rapto de cautivas blancas: Un aspecto erótico de la barbarie en la plástica rioplatense del siglo XIX,* Hipótesis y Discusiones, 4 [Buenos Aires: Facultad de Filosofía y Letras, University of Buenos Aires, 1994], 32).

41. Ibid.

42. Bonnie Frederick, "Reading the Warning: The Reader and the Image of the Captive Woman," *Chasqui*, 18, no. 2 (November 1989): 3–11. On the captives and rape, see the chapter in the present volume on the various rewritings of the Lucía Miranda myth.

43. Ibid., 9.

44. Cristina Iglesia, "La mujer cautiva: Cuerpo, mito y frontera," in *Historia de las mujeres*, ed. George Duby and Michelle Perrot (Madrid: Taurus, 1992), 3:558.

45. On these racial conflicts, see chapter 1 in the present volume.

46. Iglesia, "La mujer cautiva," 3:559.

47. If it is true that there are literary antecedents to Echeverría's representation of the raid, none has managed to polarize the imagination so successfully. See Juan Cruz Varela's poem, "En el regreso de la expedición contra los indios bárbaros, mandado por el Coronel D. Federico Rauch," in *Poesías*, ed. Vicente D. Sierra (Buenos Aires: Talleres Gráficos L. J. Rosso, 1943 [1827]), 231–36.

48. Malosetti Costa, *Rapto*, 9.

49. On the theory of the abject, see Julia Kristeva, *Powers of Horror: An Essay on Abjection*, trans. Leon S. Roudiez (New York: Columbia University Press, 1982); and Victor Burgin, "Geometry and Abjection," in *Psychoanalysis and Cultural Theory*, ed. Donald James (New York: St. Martin's Press, 1991).

5. The Return of the Forbidden

Portions of this chapter were published as "Lucía Miranda: Negación y violencia del origen," *Revista Iberoamericana: Siglo XIX: Fundación y fronteras de la ciudadanía*, vol. 178–79 (January–June 1997): 115–28.

1. Ruy Díaz de Guzmán, *Anales del descubrimiento, población y conquista del Río de la Plata* (Asunción: Ediciones Comuneros, 1980).

2. The importance of the food should not be underestimated; in an earlier essay on the Lucía Miranda legend, Cristina Iglesia notes that hunger is repeatedly mentioned as a motive of the conquistadors in Argentina's foundational texts. See her book, written with Julio Schvartzman, *Cautivas y misioneros: Mitos blancos de la conquista* (Buenos Aires: Catálogos, 1987).

3. In the above-mentioned book, Cristina Iglesia explains that Lucía's execution — like St. Lucia's — belongs to the hagiography of the "era of martyrs," the period of the Diocletian persecutions at the end of the third century. On the night after his martyrdom, St. Sebastian appeared to Saint Lucia and showed her the place where his body lay so that it would be buried beside the apostles. Saint Sebastian was a Roman who, as a member of the Praetorian Guard, hid his true faith to defend those who professed the nascent Christian cult; Sebastian Hurtado defends the honor of Lucía, whose body functions in the myth as a temple of God. Lucía is like the Syracuse virgin who offers the Christian God her chastity as a pledge of fidelity and, in the midst of the brothel, resists with miraculous immobility the assault of those who attempt to violate her (Iglesia and Schvartzman, *Cautivas y misioneros*, 54ff.).

4. Mangoré's name changes slightly: Mangora, Mangaroré. Other versions include Martín del Barco Centenera, *Argentina y conquista del Río de la Plata;* Nicolás del Techo, *Historia provincine paraguariae S.J.;* Thomas Moore, *Mangora, King of Timbusians; or, The Faithful Couple;* Pierre François de Charlevoix, *Histoire de Paraguay;* José Guevara, *Historia del Paraguay, Río de la Plata y Tucumán;* Manuel Lassala, *Lucía Miranda: Tragedia, la Bologna;* Félix de Azara, *Voyages dans l'Amerique Meridionale;* Gregorio Funes, *Ensayo de la Historia Civil de Buenos Aires, Tucumán y Paraguay;* Eduardo Madero, *Historia del Puerto de Buenos Aires;* and Damías Menéndez, *Lucía Miranda.* For excellent comparative analyses of some of these texts, see Iglesia's work and Francine Masiello's *Between Civilization and Barbarism: Women, Nation, and Literary Culture in Modern Argentina* (Lincoln: University of Nebraska Press, 1992).

5. Slavoj Zizek, *The Sublime Object of Ideology* (London: Verso, 1989); Judith Butler, *Bodies That Matter: On the Discursive Limits of "Sex"* (New York: Routledge, 1993).

6. Gayle Rubin's article on the traffic in women is essential. Nonetheless, this practice — commonly performed in all eras to seal relationships between groups — never fully acquires a sense of pact in Argentina. The exchange is made only through violence; this, of course, does not eliminate familial relations with the Other, but complicates the void or the negation of the Other that is necessary for *narcissisme blanche.* See Rubin, "The Traffic in Women: Notes on the 'Political Economy' of Sex," in *Toward an Anthropology of Women,* ed. Rayna R. Reiter (New York: Monthly Review Press, 1975), 157–210.

7. Walter Benjamin, *Illuminations,* trans. John Osborn (London: NLB, 1977), 167, 177–78.

8. Paul de Man, "Pascal's Allegory of Persuasion," in *Allegory and Representation,* ed. Stephen Greenblatt (Baltimore: Johns Hopkins University Press, 1981), 1–23. For a discussion of the use of allegory as it is employed in this analysis, see also David Spurr, *The Rhetoric of Empire: Colonial Discourse in Journalism, Travel Writing, and Imperial Administration* (Durham, N.C.: Duke University Press, 1993).

9. Lynn H. Higgins and Brenda R. Silver, eds., *Rape and Representation* (New York: Columbia University Press, 1991), 3.

10. Ernesto Laclau and Chantal Mouffe, *Hegemony and Socialist Strategy: Towards a Radical Democratic Politics,* trans. Winston Moore and Paul Cammack (London: Verso, 1985).

11. De Lafuente Machain, "Alonso Riquelme de Guzmán," document from the García Viñas de A.G. de I. Collection, No. 975-1 (Buenos Aires, 1942), 81; emphasis is mine unless otherwise indicated.

12. As Francine Masiello has noted, Díaz de Guzmán's narrative in addition contains the elements that gauchesque poetry will take up: raids, fires, murders and kidnappings, the punishment of the captives, and the jealousy of the Indian women. See *Between Civilization and Barbarism.*

13. See Dean Funes's version, cited in *Lucía Miranda: A la luz de los versos de Celestina Funes,* ed. Amadeo P. Soler (Rosario, Argentina: Editorial Amalevi, 1992), 15–22. Subsequent references are to this edition.

14. See the chapter of this book entitled "Frontier Bodies," dedicated to Echeverría's *La Cautiva.*

15. Elisabeth Bronfen, *Over Her Dead Body: Myth, Femininity, and the Aesthetic* (New York: Routledge, 1992), 181.

16. Echeverría's poem *La cautiva* can also be read in terms of Catholic symbolism: in this case the figure of María/the Virgin is invoked as the guarantee of a balanced national economy. The woman of flesh and blood (nature and matter) is represented as inert, an incarnation of the Other. Be she a spiritual or a physical creature, woman exists only for man's use, to subject herself to his desires and manipulations; woman has come to life only as an infusion of the masculine mind. See Walter Ong, *In the Human Grain: Further Explorations of Contemporary Culture* (New York: MacMillan, 1967).

17. Lynda Nead, *The Female Nude: Art, Obscenity, and Sexuality* (London: Routledge, 1992).

18. Ibid., 7.

19. According to Paul Groussac, neither of the characters actually existed. Groussac's information is based upon the cursory report left by the leader of the expedition from Spain, Sebastian Cabot, abridged by "Madero before donating it to this Library where all may consult it" (Madero antes de donarla a esta Biblioteca donde todos pueden consultarla). That document states that "the catastrophe . . . was prepared only by the inexperience of Captain Gregorio Caro, commander of the port (since Nuño de Lara is as imaginary as the chaste Lucía, Siripo, Mangoré, and the other *dramatis personae*), and consummated by his cowardice" (la catástrophe . . . sólo fue preparada por la impericia del capitán Gregorio Caro, comandante del puerto [pues Nuño de Lara es tan imaginario como la casta Lucía, Siripo, Mangora, y demás dramatis personae], y consumada por su cobardía) (originally cited by Jorge M. Furt, in the "Noticia" that begins his edition of *Lucía Miranda: Drama de Ortega* [Buenos Aires: Imprenta de la Universidad, 1926]), 53–54). Amadeo P. Soler attempts to prove the veracity of the events narrated, but in the end must be satisfied with the idea that to have survived so many years the legend must have some factual basis; see *Lucía Miranda: A la luz de los versos de Celestina Funes.*

20. Cristina Iglesia, "La mujer cautiva: Cuerpo, mito y frontera," in *Historia de las mujeres,* ed. Georges Duby and Michelle Perrot (Madrid: Taurus, 1992), 3:557.

21. The foundational project of independence-era Argentina was not characterized by negotiation between diverse racial groups. The absence or scarcity of negotiation in the literary canons suggests a technique that is extremely interesting for understanding the mechanisms of collective memory. As has been seen in preceding chapters, it is a question of the *negation* of fragments of the past or present as parts of a totality. Every hegemonic force imposes an organizing principal, and this one is no exception, but in this case the preexistent order is omitted and the negotiation that would emerge from political interaction among social groups is avoided. A reality is silenced or omitted, excluded from tradition and history. On negotiation and hegemony, see Ernesto Laclau, *Emancipation(s)* (London: Routledge, 1996).

22. I owe the idea of white psychosis to Susana Balán. The term is especially

well developed by André Green in *Narcissisme de Vie, Narcissisme de Mort* (Paris: Les Éditions de Minuit, 1983).

23. Donna J. Guy, *Sex and Danger in Buenos Aires: Prostitution, Family, and Nation in Argentina* (Lincoln: University of Nebraska Press, 1991), 39.

24. See Masiello, *Between Civilization and Barbarism;* also George L. Mosse, *Nationalism and Sexuality: Respectability and Abnormal Sexuality in Modern Europe* (New York: Howard Fertig, 1986). Celestina Funes represents her protagonists as martyrs of the nation and marriage: "Lucía Miranda and Sebastián Hurtado, / You know them, don't you? For their foreheads / Where martyrdom wove / Its most funereal crown of thorns / Shining laurels have / The history of love and Argentina! ... / Today I offer to the present / An immortal example / Of eternal love and fervent virtue" (Lucía Miranda y Sebastián Hurtado, / Los conocéis, ¿verdad? Para su frente / Donde tejió el martirio / Su corona más fúnebre de espina / Tienen laurel luciente / La historia del amor y la Argentina! ... / Ofrezco hoy al presente / Como inmortal ejemplo / De eterno amor y de virtud ferviente) (55).

25. Every culture provides its members with organizing fictions that define their relationships; this social and historical construction of identity is called subjectification, or the process of transformation of individuals into their subjects within a combination of values. Identity is constructed over difference: I am neither that nor the Other, but this. The paradox is that the Other, however marginally represented, is always absolutely necessary for the existence of the One. See Ivy Schweitzer, *The Work of Self-Representation: Lyric Poetry in Colonial New England* (Chapel Hill: University of North Carolina Press, 1991). The myth of Lucía Miranda and its subsequent rewritings is a good example of this paradox. On Argentina's organizing fictions, see Nicolas Shumway, *The Invention of Argentina* (Berkeley: University of California Press, 1991).

26. See Homi K. Bhabha, "A Question of Survival: Nations and Psychic States," in *Psychoanalysis and Cultural Theory: Thresholds,* ed. James Donald (New York: St. Martin's Press, 1991), 92.

27. Bonnie Frederick's thesis on the nineteenth-century proliferation of versions of the myth is that the publications of the era were in search of local heroines (foreign women and the wives of notable men were frequently described), and there were few available in History who were examples of virtue, who were not very recent (so as to avoid commenting on the Rosas regime), and who had already died (so that they could be mythified like the women of the Independence War). See *Wily Modesty: Argentine Women Writers, 1860–1910* (Temple, Az.: ASU Center for Latin American Studies Press, 1998), 87–88.

28. ["Maldonada" derives from *mal,* meaning "bad," and *donar,* "to endow" or "to give." — Trans.]

29. On the necessity of mourning to survive the painful disappearance of captured women, see Mitchell Robert Breitwieser, *American Puritanism and the Defense of Mourning: Religion, Grief, and Ethnology in Mary White Rowlandson's Captivity Narrative* (Madison: University of Wisconsin Press, 1990).

30. In Soler's version, "the captains of the Gaboto fleet utilized the women they brought to conquer the will of our chiefs, obtaining in this way certain concessions and especially food" (los capitanes de la armada de Gaboto se sirvieron de las mujeres que traían para conquistar la voluntad de nuestros jefes obteniendo de ese

modo ciertas concesiones y en especial alimentos) (29). This version affirms that in Puerto Gaboto the legend is popularly interpreted as a Creole or indigenous version of the Cain and Abel story; the axis of the tragedy is not the sacrifice of the married couple, but rather the rivalry between brothers.

31. Masiello, *Between Civilization and Barbarism*, 35.

32. Celestina Funes's *Lucía Miranda* declares Lucía a "sublime martyr of love" and tells readers to "Learn, I beg you, to preserve indissoluble the sublime / Tie of love, chain of gold / So that not even the hearth / Could melt them with its potent fire" (Aprended, os lo ruego, A conservar indisoluble el lazo / Sublime del amor, cadena de oro / Que en ellas ni la hoguera / Pudo fundir con su potente fuego) (Amadeo P. Soler, ed., *Lucía Miranda: A la luz de los versos de Cristina Funes* [89]).

33. Masiello, *Between Civilization and Barbarism*, 28ff.

34. For a feminist analysis of the writing of space, see Allison Blunt and Gillian Rose, eds., *Writing Women and Space: Colonial and Postcolonial Geographies* (New York: Guilford Press, 1994); also helpful are Doris Sommer's *Foundational Fictions: The National Romances of Latin America* (Berkeley: University of California Press, 1991), and Mary Louise Pratt's *Imperial Eyes: Travel Writing and Transculturation* (New York: Routledge, 1992).

35. Anne Laura Stoler, "Carnal Knowledge and Imperial Power," in *The Gender/ Sexuality Reader*, ed. Roger N. Lancaster and Micaela di Leonardo (New York: Routledge, 1997), 15.

36. Examples of former captives in similar situations are found in Marcela Tamagnini's *Cartas de frontera: Los documentos del conflicto inter-étnico* (Río Cuarto: National University of Río Cuarto, 1995); see the following chapter, "Captive Texts."

6. Captive Texts

Thanks to Marcela Tamagnini, "individuals of a silent historical reality" have come out "of anonymity" (vi). Tamagnini made a moving selection of 596 documents written between 1868 and 1880 that were preserved in the archives of the Convento de San Francisco in Río Cuarto. See Tamagnini, ed., *Cartas de frontera: Los documentos del conflicto inter-étnico* (Río Cuarto: Universidad Nacional de Río Cuarto, 1995). Donati's letters generally have only his signature at the bottom; sometimes, however, it is accompanied by "Franciscan in Río Cuarto" or "Prefect of San Luis." The same occurs with the other priests: if their assignments are given here it is only for the reader's benefit, since the priests themselves indicated their positions only occasionally. Baigorria signs sometimes with the title of general, other times as colonel.

[As Rotker's quotations show, Tamagnini's *Cartas de frontera* respects the often eccentric orthography and grammar of the original documents. This English translation, produced for *Captive Women*, standardizes spelling but replicates the original syntax and punctuation as closely as possible. Throughout the chapter, the work will be cited in the text as "Tamagnini." — Trans.]

1. See L. Lévy-Brul, *Primitive Mentality* (New York: Beacon Press, 1966). On the supposed inferiority of other ethnic groups and the heritage of Enlightenment

thought, see Emmanuel Chukwudi Eze, ed., *Race and the Enlightenment* (Cambridge: Blackwell, 1997); Ernst Cassirer, *The Philosophy of the Enlightenment,* trans. Fritz C. A. Koelln and James P. Pettegrove (Princeton, N.J: Princeton University Press, 1951); Peter Gay, *The Enlightenment: An Interpretation,* 2 vols. (New York: Norton, 1969); Pierre Saint-Amand, *The Laws of Hostility: Politics, Violence, and the Enlightenment,* trans. Jennifer Curtiss Gage (Minneapolis: University of Minnesota Press, 1996). More useful for Latin America itself are the following: Arthur Preston Whitaker, *Latin America and the Enlightenment* (Ithaca, N.Y.: Cornell University Press, 1967); Antonello Gerbi, *La disputa del Nuevo Mundo: Historia de una polémica 1750–1900,* trans. Antonio Alatorre, 2d ed., corrected and expanded (Mexico City: Fondo de Cultura Económica, 1982); Tzetvan Todorov, *La conquista de América: El problema del otro,* trans. Flora Botton Burlá, 3d ed. (Mexico City: Siglo XXI, 1991); trans. Richard Howard as *The Conquest of America: The Problem of the Other* (New York: Harper and Row, 1984); Todorov, *Nosotros y los otros: Reflexión sobre la diversidad humana,* trans. Martí Mur Ubasart (Mexico City: Siglo XXI, 1991); José Carlos Chiaramonte, ed., *Pensamiento de la ilustración: Economía y sociedad iberoamericanas en el siglo XVIII* (Caracas: Biblioteca Ayacucho, 1979); David Brading, *The First America: The Spanish Monarchy, Creole Patriots, and the Liberal State, 1492–1867* (Cambridge: Cambridge University Press, 1991); trans. Juan José Utrilla as *Orbe indiano: De la monarquía católica a la república criolla, 1492–1867* (Mexico City: Fondo de Cultura Económica, 1994). Also of interest is Ricaurte Soler, *Idea y cuestión nacional latinoamericanas: De la independencia a la emergencia del imperialismo* (Mexico City: Siglo XXI, 1980); and, for Brazil, Lilia Moritz Schwarcz, *O Espetáculo das Raças: Cientistas, instituções e questão racial no brasil 1870–1930* (São Paulo: Companhia das Letras, 1995), especially the chapter "Uma história de 'diferenças e desigualdades': As doutrinas raciais do século XIX" (43–66).

2. Maurice Halbawchs, *Les cadres sociaux de la memoire* (Paris: Presses Universitaires de France, 1952), 249–50. What is more, the frame of collective memory is determined by the structure of the group more than by the group in itself, and it is for that reason that individual memory supports and is supported by the community as a whole; see Roger Bastide, *The African Religions of Brazil: Toward a Sociology of the Interpenetration of Civilizations,* trans. Helen Sebba (Baltimore: Johns Hopkins University Press, 1978), 247.

3. Slavoj Zizek, *The Sublime Object of Ideology* (London: Verso, 1989), 35–46; the same author edited the useful collection of texts in *Mapping Ideology* (London: Verso, 1994). See also Ernesto Laclau and Chantal Mouffe, *Hegemony and Socialist Strategy: Towards a Radical Democratic Politics,* trans. Winston Moore and Paul Cammack (London: Verso, 1985).

4. Blaise Pascal, *Pensées* (London: Harmondsworth, 1966).

5. Father Meinrado Hux, ed., *Memorias de ex cautivo Santiago Avendaño* (Buenos Aires: Elefante Blanco, 1999).

6. Gayle Rubin, "The Traffic in Women," in *Toward an Antropology of Women,* ed. Rayna R. Reiter (New York: Monthly Review Press, 1975). Paraphrasing Marx's reflections on black slavery, she writes, "What is a domesticated woman? A female of the species. The one explanation is as good as the other. A woman

is a woman. She only becomes a domestic, a wife, a chattel, a Playboy bunny, a prostitute, or a human dictaphone in certain relations" (158).

7. Jacques Derrida, *Dissemination,* trans. Barbara Johnson (Chicago: University of Chicago Press, 1981), 212–13. In the Spanish version, *La diseminación,* trans. José Martín Arancibia (Madrid: Fundamentos, 1975), see p. 318.

8. I know of one other letter written by a captive woman, cited by Libertad Demitrópulos, who in turn cites historian Juan Severino López. The letter was written after a raid that captured more than five hundred women, during the period in which political forces divided the country between the Argentine Confederation and the State of Buenos Aires. The letter says: "Tierra adentro. Paulo Belascuen. Brother: I notify you of the misfortune we have had, Baigorria's Indians have been carried off myself, Micaela, Pepa, Sinforosa, Manuela, Alustiza, Hilaria, and Secundina Pereyra. I beg you, brother, that you get Governor Díaz to have Urquiza ask for us, and that you let my dad know as soon as you can so that he gets Mr. Taboada involved. Paulina Belascuen" (Tierra adentro. Paulo Belascuen. Hermano: Te aviso la desgracia que hemos tenido, nos han llevado los indios de Baigorria a mí, a Micaela, Pepa, Sinforosa, Manuela, Alustiza, Hilaria y Secundina Pereyra. Te suplico, hermano, que te valgas del señor gobernador Díaz para que nos pida a Urquiza, y harás saber a mi tata cuanto antes para que se empeñe con el señor Taboada. Paulina Balascuen).

Demitrópulos adds that the letter must have made "a long and uncertain journey. From Tierra Adentro it went to San Luis, from there to Córdoba, later to Santiago del Estero and from there to Paraná to arrive finally in San José, Urquiza's residence. But Paulina Belascuen was never rescued" ("La mujer cautiva en la literatura argentina," in *Mujeres y cultura en la Argentina del siglo XIX,* ed. Lea Fletcher [Buenos Aires: Feminaria, 1994], 161). See Juan Severino López, *El rescate de cautivas: Un episodio de la guerra y la paz en las fronteras del desierto,* special issue, *Investigaciones y Ensayos* no. 21 (Buenos Aires: Academia Nacional de Historia, 1977).

9. If this letter were not written by the hand of the person who signed it, the analysis would change only slightly; the existence of an intermediary would suggest that the ex-captive's origin was even more humble since she had chosen a scribe whose writing was itself so poor. From what I have read, intermediaries wrote in the name of the interested parties but signed their own names.

10. Pascal, *Pensées,* 274.

11. The term "interpellate" is used in Althusser's sense, to convey that the function of all ideology is to constitute individuals as subjects: to make them live their relation with social structures as if they determined that relation autonomously. See Louis Althusser, *Ideología y aparatos ideológicos de Estado: Freud y Lacan,* trans. A. J. Pla and J. Slazbón (Buenos Aires: Nueva Visión, 1988 [1964, 1970]); Ernesto Laclau, *Politics and Ideology in Marxist Theory: Capitalism, Fascism, Populism* (London: NLB, 1977); translated as *Política e ideología en la teoría marxista* (Madrid: Siglo XXI, 1986); and Laclau, *Emancipation(s)* (London: Verso, 1996); translated as *Emancipación y diferencia* (Buenos Aires: Ariel, 1996). Also relevant for this chapter are Judith Butler, *Bodies That Matter: On the Discursive Limits of "Sex"* (New York: Routledge, 1993); James Donald and Stuart Hall, eds., *Politics and Ideology* (Philadephia: Open University Press, 1986); Richard Terdiman, *Discourse/Counter-*

discourse: The Theory and Practice of Symbolic Resistance in Nineteenth-Century France (Ithaca, N.Y.: Cornell University Press, 1985); Zygmunt Bauman, *Modernity and Ambivalence* (Ithaca, N.Y.: Cornell University Press, 1991); Catherine Belsey, *Critical Practice* (London: Routledge, 1987); Fredric Jameson, *The Political Unconscious: Narrative as a Socially Symbolic Act* (Ithaca, N.Y.: Cornell University Press, 1981).

7. The Story of a Journey with No Return

1. On the writing of *Idle Days in Patagonia*, Mónica Szurmuk notes: "Hudson traveled in 1871 to the valley of the Río Negro with the objective of studying birds for an English magazine. The valley of the Río Negro was at the time the southern frontier, the limit of the incipient state, the place where the idea of Argentina ended and the 'desert' began. Hudson has an accident (he shoots himself in the leg), and this prevents him from carrying out his objective of seeing birds, since he can no longer count on the quietude necessary to observe them carefully. This genealogy (that of the accident that impedes natural life but occasions literature) is repeated in Hudson's biography, referring to the genesis of his writing. The occasion of writing for him (and the narrative that will become the crux of his scholarly biography) is the period of infirmity during his childhood, when he learns to read and write about the pampas since he cannot wander about it. In this case, the fact that he cannot observe birds brings him to find another type of alterity— not that of the bird as a personalized animal but that of the animalized human being, the indigenous. As a 'native expatriate,' Hudson has no community and sees himself juxtaposed with three groups of 'Others' in the valley, English colonists, gauchos, and Indians." Hudson leaves Argentina in 1874 and publishes his book twenty-three years after his frustrated visit to Patagonia. What is more, to show how little the reality of what is observed in travel literature matters, Szurmuk cites the following from Ezequiel Martínez Estrada: "Hudson's power of evocation is so vivid that on occasions it can be affirmed that he *surpasses direct vision* in acuity and luminosity" (El poder de evocación de Hudson es tan vívido, que en ocasiones puede afirmarse que *supera* en nitidez y luminosidad *a la visión directa*) (emphasis added). See Mónica Szurmuk, "Imagining Patagonia 1880–1900," presentation at the conference of the Latin American Studies Association (LASA), Miami, 2000.

2. Father Meinrado Hux, ed., *Memorias de ex cautivo Santiago Avendaño (1834– 1874)* (Buenos Aires: Elefante Blanco, 1999); subsequent references to the work will be given in the text.

3. "The manuscript, like numerous letters that formed part of the Archive of the Chiefdom of Salinas Grandes, was hidden in the sand dunes by the Indians in the desperate flight they were forced by the armies of Colonel Lavalle to make, is in my library and I put it at the disposal of the erudite. It is a near-complete history of the origins of the Llalmache nation, which governed the Piedra until 1833" (El manuscrito, como numerosas cartas que formaban parte del Archivo del Cacicazgo de Salinas Grandes, fue escondido en los médanos por los indios en la fuga desesperada que le impusieron las fuerzas del Coronel Lavalle, existe en mi biblioteca y lo pongo a la disposición de los eruditos. Es una historia casi completa de los orígenes de la nación Llalmache, que gobernaron los Piedra hasta 1833).

So writes Estanislao Zeballos in *Callvucurá-Painé-Relmú,* cited in the prologue to *Memorias del ex cautivo Santiago Avendaño.*

4. The use of maps has been studied extensively; see, for example, Michel de Certeau, *The Practice of Everyday Life,* trans. Stephen Randall (Berkeley: University of California Press, 1984); Brian Harley, "Maps, Knowledge, and Power," in *Writing Worlds: Discourse, Text, and Metaphor in the Representation of Landscape,* ed. Trevor J. Barnes and James S. Duncan (London: Routledge, 1992), 193–230; Bill Ashcroft, Gareth Griffiths, and Helen Tiffin, *The Empire Writes Back: Theory and Practice in Post-colonial Literatures* (New York: Routledge, 1989); Walter Mignolo, *The Darker Side of the Renaissance: Literacy, Territoriality, and Colonization* (Ann Arbor: University of Michigan Press, 1995).

5. A. Guinnard, *Tres años de esclavitud entre los patagones (Relato de mi cautiverio)* (Buenos Aires: Espasa-Calpe Argentina, n.d.); Lucio V. Mansilla, *Una excursión a los indios ranqueles* (Caracas: Biblioteca Ayacucho, 1984); subsequent references to the works will be given in the text.

6. For examples of these invocations of the reader in *Memorias del ex cautivo Santiago Avendaño,* see pp. 137, 161, 230, 342, 345, 355.

7. Manuel Baigorria, *Memorias* (Buenos Aires: Solar/Hachette, 1975).

8. After Rosas's fall, Baigorria returned to serve as a soldier on the side of civilization as a high-ranking officer in the national army. His *Memorias* have documentary value, but to understand the fascination of this complex character it is better to read Avendaño's narrative or the novelized version Estanislao Zeballos wrote years later in *Painé y la dinastía de los zorros* (Painé and the dynasty of the foxes) (Buenos Aires: Biblioteca del Suboficial, 1928).

9. On the manipulation of Manzano's *Autobiografía,* see Sylvia Molloy, *At Face Value: Autobiographical Writing in Spanish America* (Cambridge: Cambridge University Press, 1991). The citations that follow correspond to Meinrado Hux's prologue, unpaginated in the book; all of the information I relate about Avendaño's life and the origin of his memoirs comes from that study.

10. [The Mitrist Revolution took place between September and November 1874. The previous April 12, Nicolás Avellaneda had been elected to succeed Domingo F. Sarmiento as Argentina's president. Supporters of his defeated opponent, Bartolomé Mitre, took arms against the government on September 24. Mitre himself led the rebellion from the southern coast of the province of Buenos Aires, where he had arrived with a force of several thousand largely inexperienced soldiers. The national army, at Sarmiento's command, crushed the insurrection by late November. — Trans.]

11. See *Memorias del ex cautivo Santiago Avendaño,* pp. 70, 76, 78, 142–43, 153, 162–63, 166, 180, and 195, for example.

12. De Certeau, *Practice,* 115.

13. See Carlos Alonso, "Oedipus in the Pampas: Lucio Mansilla's *Una excursión a los indios ranqueles,*" *Revista de Estudios Hispánicos* 24, no. 2 (May 1990): 39–59.

14. The question Julio Ramos — reflecting on *Autobiografía de un esclavo* — proposes about the new subject and his identity before the law and the symbolic system is also valid for the text of Avendaño, in this case a hybrid subject from the frontier who vindicates himself as such *from* the culture of the whites. See "La ley es otra," in *Paradojas de la letra* (Caracas: Excultura, 1996), 58.

15. Guinnard coincides with Avendaño in affirming that lived experience among the Indians has made him a specialist on the subject, in contrast to others who opine without this authority: "I have not tried to imitate, like many others; I have limited myself purely and simply to making a scrupulous narrative of my adventures and of the customs and habits of the Patagonians, the Puelches, the Pampas, and the Mauelches, with whom, due to a concatenation of unfortunate circumstances, I have been forced to live during three and a half years. The knowledge of their language and the long time I lived their sort of existence conditioned me to consider them from their own point of view, and thus the different observations I have been able to make *may be taken in comparison to certain writers whom I abstain from naming* (Yo no he tratado de imitar, como tantos otros; me he limitado pura y simplemente a hacer la narración escrupulosa de mis aventuras y de las costumbres y hábitos de los patagones, los puelches, los pampas y los mauelches, con quienes, por un concatenamiento de desgraciadas circunstancias, he debido vivir forzosamente durante tres años y medio. El conocimiento de su idioma y el largo tiempo que viví su género de existencia, me pusieron en condición de considerarles desde su mismo punto de vista, *y así podrán tomarse como términos de comparación con tales o cuales escritores, que me abstengo de nombrar,* las diversas observaciones que he podido hacer) (9).

16. Guinnard held to the superiority of the whites — or those with a larger proportion of white blood — over the indigenous inhabitants of the frontier: "More than ever one finds among the Pampas a very regular type: the children of Indians and captive women. These Indians stand out for their level of intelligence, which is much superior to that of all the other nomads, with the exception, however, of the Araucanians. They station themselves for many months at a time in the same place. Their tents, like those of the Puelches, are made of leather, but they are more spacious and more regular. A certain order and tidiness reigns among them, which does not, however, prevent them from being covered with parasites" (Más que nunca se encuentra ahora entre los pampas tipos muy regulares: son los hijos de indios y cautivas. Estos indios se hacen notar por un grado de inteligencia muy superior al de todos los otros nómadas, con excepción de los araucanos, sin embargo. Se estacionan muchos meses seguidos en el mismo lugar. Sus tiendas, como las de los puelches, están hechas de cuero, pero son más espaciosas, y más regulares. Reina en ellas cierto orden y aseo; lo cual no impide, empero, que estén cubiertos de parásitos) (60).

Mestizos may be seen as superior while they live among the Indians; their indigenous genes, on the other hand, would become a liability if they lived among whites.

17. Avendaño's widow insisted that her husband had not been "a vulgar man; before, on the contrary, he was an enlightened man, of an illustrious family from the province of Mendoza and who was taken captive in an invasion by savages from the pampa. His parents rescued him" (un hombre vulgar, antes, al contrario, era un hombre ilustrado, de familia esclarecida de la provincia de Mendoza y que en una invasión que hicieron los salvages de la pampa se lo llevaron cautivo. Sus padres los rescataron) (cited in the prologue). The problem with her remark is that it is not true that Avendano's parents rescued him (he fled); and for that reason we cannot be certain of the rest of the information.

18. Gilles Deleuze and Félix Guattari, *A Thousand Plateaus: Capitalism and Schizophrenia,* trans. Brian Massumi (London: Athlone Press, 1988), 351–423; *Mil mesetas: Capitalismo y esquizofrenia,* trans. José Vázquez Pérez with Umbelina Larraceleta (Valencia: Pre-Textos, 1988), 359–431.

19. Michael Paul Rogin applies this line of thought to North American policy toward the indigenous in *Fathers and Children: Andrew Jackson and the Subjugation of the American Indian* (New Brunswick, N.J.: Transaction Publishers, 1991).

20. Homi Bhabha, *The Location of Culture* (London: Routledge, 1994), 124.

21. See Molloy, *At Face Value;* also published as *Acto de presencia: La escritura autobiográfica en Hispanoamérica,* trans. José Esteban Calderón, rev. Sylvia Molloy, Jessica Chalmers, and Ernesto Grosman (Mexico City: Fondo de Cultura Económica, 1996). For the comparison to Sarmiento, see Beatriz Sarlo and Carlos Altamirano, *Ensayos argentinos: De Sarmiento a la vanguardia* (Buenos Aires: Centro Editor de América Latina, 1983).

8. News of a Disappearing World

1. Lucio V. Mansilla, *Una excursión a los indios ranqueles,* prologue Saúl Sosnowski (Caracas: Biblioteca Ayacucho, 1984); all quotations from the text are from this edition; emphasis is added unless otherwise indicated.

2. Pierre Nora, *Realms of Memory: Rethinking the French Past,* vol. 1, trans. Arthur Goldhammer (New York: Columbia University Press, 1996).

3. Mansilla's textual "I" — the model for a generation — extends beyond the immediacy of what is declared by the narrative in itself, in which, for example, the narrator occasionally mocks himself: "I understand that there is someone in this land who says, 'I would like to be Mitre, the spoiled son of fortune and of glory, or the Sacristan of San Juan.' But that someone should say: 'I would like to be Colonel Mansilla,' that I don't understand, because in the end, that kid — *who is he?*" (Yo comprendo que haya en esta tierra quien diga: — Yo quisiera ser Mitre, el hijo mimado de la fortuna y de la gloria, o sacristán de San Juan. Pero que haya quien diga: — Yo quisiera ser el Coronel Mansilla — eso no lo entiendo, porque al fin, ese mozo, *¿quién es?*) (5, emphasis in original).

For a fine examination of the definition of identity and the I/he relation, see Mirta E. Stern, *"Una excursión a los indios ranqueles:* Espacio textual y ficción topográfica," *Filología* 20 (1985): 123.

If the "I" is read as an exposition of the era, the Mansilla who narrates *Una excursión* can be read as a perfect example of the politics of the pose in the last third of the nineteenth century in Argentina. Sylvia Molloy writes: "Managed by the *poseur* himself, exaggeration is a strategy of provocation enacted so as not to be disregarded, to oblige the gaze of the other, to force a reading, to oblige a discourse." Also: "Exhibition, as a cultural form, is the preferred genre of the nineteenth century, and scopofilia its animating passion. Everything appeals to sight and everything is specularized: nationalities are exhibited in the universal expositions, nationalisms are exhibited in the great parades (when not in the wars, themselves conceived as spectacles)" ("La política de la pose," in *Las culturas del fin de siglo en América Latina,* ed. Josefina Ludmer [Rosario: Beatriz Viterbo, 1994], 130).

4. Mariano Rosas was "adopted" by Rosas (although reading *Memorias de ex cautivo Santiago Avendaño* one discovers that the "godfather" was really a jailer) and took a Christian name. Chief Ramón is the son of an Indian and a Christian captive (88).

5. See the first chapter of the present work.

6. On the importance of the role played by newspapers in the formation of "imagined communities" (a national sense of belonging or identity), see Benedict Anderson, *Imagined Communities: Reflections on the Origin and Spread of Nationalism* (London: Verso, 1991).

7. David Viñas, *Indios, ejército y frontera* (Mexico City: Siglo XXI, 1983), 149.

8. The text bears marks of complicity with its readers; as a linguistic performance it also demonstrates complicity with the society of equals to which the author belongs. Mansilla uses what R. Brown and A. Gilman describe as a language of "solidarity": the writing exposes similarities in the culture and attitude of author and reader ("The Pronouns and Power and Solidarity," in *Language and Social Context*, ed. P. P. Giglioli [Harmondsworth, England: Penguin, 1972], chap. 2).

9. For historical antecedents, see Silvia Mirta Beatriz Fernández, "Mansilla y los ranqueles: ¿Por qué Lucio V. Mansilla escribió *Una excursión a los indios ranqueles*?"; Carlos Mayol Laferrére, "El coronel Lucio V. Mansilla y la ocupación del Río Cuarto en 1869: Avance de la Frontera Sud y Sud Este de Córdoba," both in *Congreso Nacional de Historia sobre la Conquista del Desierto* (Buenos Aires: Academia Nacional de la Historia, 1981), 2:361–75 and 83–96. In the same volume, see A. J. Pérez Amuchástegui and Irma E. Montani de Perpignan, "Génesis de la Campaña al Desierto," 171–85. Fernández demonstrates that Mansilla's objective was not "to sign a peace treaty but rather to simply divert the Indians' attention until the moment the occupation took place, as it did between May 19 and 23, 1869" (363).

10. Cristina Iglesia, "Mansilla: Dreams and Vigils," *Journal of Latin American Cultural Studies* 4, no. 2 (1995): 158, 154.

11. Viñas, *Indios,* 51.

12. "It is evident that Sarmiento's *ideolegmas,* formulated in the oppositions city/country, Europe/Argentina, urban man or immigrant/gaucho or Creole, are in question here," says Julio Ramos, while the group to which Mansilla refers, the "we" of the text, has elected Sarmiento president of the country (*Paradojas de la letra* [Caracas: Excultura, 1996], 78). Ramos also analyzes this book as a reading of gauchesque poetry in "Entre otros: *Una excursión a los indios ranqueles* de Lucio V. Mansilla," *Filología* (1986): 85.

13. Noé Jitrik, *Ensayos y estudios de literatura argentina* (Buenos Aires: Galerna, 1970), 108–9.

14. Richard Terdiman explains that intellectuals lived the modern as a sense of rupture with the past, rupture with the traditional family and the structure of small towns, and the experience of new, urban forms of living. See *Present Past: Modernity and the Memory Crisis* (Ithaca, N.Y.: Cornell University Press, 1993), 5. See also Marshall Berman, *All That Is Solid Melts into Air: The Experience of Modernity* (New York: Simon and Schuster, 1982); and Matt K. Matsuda, *The Memory of the Modern* (New York: Oxford University Press, 1996), 12.

15. Carlos Alonso proposes the theory that Mansilla's journey across the pampa is an attempt to resolve the author's Oedipal triangle involving the two great figures

of nineteenth-century Argentina. See "Oedipus in the Pampas: Lucio Mansilla's *Una excursión a los indios ranqueles*," *Revista de Estudios Hispánicos* 24, no. 2 (May 1990): 39–59.

16. See Adolfo Prieto, *La literatura autobiográfica argentina* (Buenos Aires: Jorge Álvarez, 1966) and *El discurso criollista en la formación de la Argentina moderna* (Buenos Aires: Sudamericana, 1988); Sylvia Molloy, "Recuerdo y sujeto en *Mis memorias* de Mansilla," *Nueva Revista de Filología Hispánica* 36, no. 2 (1988): 1207–20 and "Imagen de Mansilla," *La Argentina del ochenta al centenario*, ed. Gustavo Ferrari and Ezequiel Gallo (Buenos Aires: Sudamericana, 1980), 745–59, in addition to the previously cited studies by Stern, Ramos, and Iglesia.

17. Alvaro Fernández Bravo discusses the subject in "Literatura y frontera: Procesos de territorialización en la cultura argentina y chilena del siglo XIX" (Ph.D. diss., Princeton University, 1996). Also of interest is Marina Kaplan's "Gauchos e indios: La frontera y la producción del sujeto en obras argentinas del siglo diecinueve" (Ph.D. diss., Tulane University, 1987).

18. For a comparison between the logic of the State and the logic of the nomadic war machine, see chapters 6 and 7 of the present work. The term is from Gilles Delueze and Félix Guattari, *A Thousand Plateaus: Capitalism and Schizophrenia*, trans. Brian Massumi (London: Athlone Press, 1988); *Mil mesetas: Capitalismo y esquizofrenia*, trans. José Vázquez Pérez with Umbelina Larraceleta (Valencia: Pre-Textos, 1988), 359–431.

19. Jitrik, *Ensayos*, 116–17.

20. Terdiman, *Present Past*, 15.

21. Mirta Stern, *"Una excursión,"* gives various examples, including Mansilla's opportunistic denial of Sarmiento's name in an encounter with Mariano Rosas ("And tell me, brother, what is the president's name?" [Y dígame, hermano, ¿cómo se llama el Presidente?]). Mansilla gives voice to the Indian so that he expresses doubts and critiques official policy. The colonel also collects the discourses of the era — like those of poet and journalist José Hernández — about the Indians and the gauchos. The campaign of his uncle Rosas and the works published by his father, Lucio Mansilla — *Proyecto de seguridad de la frontera y de reforma militar* and *Plan de defensa de las fronteras de Buenos Aires* — weigh heavily on Lucio V. Mansilla.

On writing that depicts the Other as a critique of one's own culture, see Michel de Certeau, "Montaigne's 'Of Cannibals': The Savage 'I,'" in *Heterologies*, trans. Brian Massumi (Minneapolis: University of Minnesota Press, 1986), 67–79.

22. Josefina Ludmer, *El género gauchesco: Un tratado sobre la patria* (Buenos Aires: Sudamericana, 1988), 168. See also Eric Hobsbawm, *Bandits*, rev. ed. (New York: Pantheon, 1981 [1969]); and Hobsbawn, *Primitive Rebels: Studies in Archaic Forms of Social Movement in the 19th and 20th Centuries* (New York: W. W. Norton and Co., 1959).

23. Antipathy between the two groups was so great that the disappearance of one was inevitable. Emilio Daireaux explains the situation in "Las razas indias en la América del Sud," *Revue de Deux Mondes* (1877). Daireaux's essay, which refers to the Pampas tribe, is surprisingly broad-minded for the time: "It is difficult to imagine a different end to this long war than the *definitive extermination of those peoples,* but the savagery of the Pampas tribes is not proven by this. . . . But if the war

justifies to a certain extent the antipathy between the races . . . it would be difficult to explain the generalization of this sentiment now that the neo-American race in the process of formation, despite the slow and continuous introduction of European blood, contains as a fixed basis in almost equal proportion the Indian element and the Spanish element. It would be understood, then, that the antipathies would be erased, by proof above all that no reason of judicial inferiority justifies the scorn that the Europeans still express toward the Indian races" (Es difícil entrever otro fin a esta larga guerra que *la exterminación definitiva de esos pueblos,* pero el salvajismo de las tribus pampas no está por eso probado. . . . Pero si la guerra justifica hasta cierto punto la antipatía de las dos razas . . . sería difícil explicar la generalización de este sentimiento hoy que la raza neo-americana en vías de formación, a pesar de la introducción lenta y contínua de la sangre europea, contiene como bases fijas casi en igual proporción, el elemento indio y el elemento español. Se comprendería, pues, que las antipatías se borrasen, estando probado sobre todo, que ninguna razón de inferioridad jurídica justifica el desprecio que los europeos tienen todavía a las razas indias). Cited by Silvia Leonor Belosky et al., "El pensamiento de los conquistadores del desierto (A propósito del general Lorenzo Vintter)," *Congreso Nacional de Historia sobre la Conquista del Desierto,* 4:289.

For her part, Graciela Montaldo analyzes the representation of the countryside and the gaucho as ways of defining the national culture from the space of the lettered in *De pronto, el campo: Literatura argentina y tradición rural* (Rosario: Beatriz Viterbo Editora, 1993).

24. David William Foster, *The Argentine Generation of 1880: Ideology and Cultural Texts* (Columbia: University of Missouri Press, 1990), 16.

25. Slavoj Zizek, *The Sublime Object of Ideology* (London: Verso, 1989).

26. In 1860 the Chilean Santiago Arcos wrote *Cuestión de los indios: Las fronteras y los indios,* in which he proposed to resolve the Indian problem militarily. Mansilla takes the opposite view and proposes to "convert" his friend.

27. Lucio Mansilla, author and narrator, presents himself as the great translator of "Europe to America, America to Europe, barbarism to civilization and vice-versa" (Iglesia, "Mansilla," 154).

28. Mansilla, "El famoso fusilamiento del caballo," in *Entre-nos: Causeries del jueves* (Buenos Aires: Hachette, 1963), 123–24. The text was originally published between 1889 and 1890.

29. Mansilla initially seeks to negotiate: to assimilate them, to teach them to work like the gauchos, to make them sign service contracts, and so on; but he will later concede to the extermination of the Indians, seeing them as different and inconvenient. On the representation of social space, see Yuri M. Lotman, *Estructura del texto artístico* (Madrid: Istmo, 1982), 271.

30. Gareth Griffiths, "The Myth of Authenticity: Representation, Discourse, and Social Practice," in *De-Scribing Empire: Post-colonialism and Textuality,* ed. Bill Ashcroft, Chris Tiffin, and Alan Lawson (New York: Routledge, 1994), 70.

31. Michel Foucault, *The Archaeology of Knowledge and the Discourse on Language,* trans. A. M. Sheridan Smith (New York: Pantheon Books, 1972).

32. An interesting play of mirrors is produced here: *La Tribuna* is the newspaper in which Mansilla's narrative will be published.

33. The writers are also politicians, soldiers, ministers, ambassadors, lawyers,

professors, presidents: by them, through them, the logic of the State is enunciated (see Deleuze and Guattari, *Thousand Plateaus*).

34. Julio Caillet-Bois, "Nuevos documentos sobre *Una excursión a los indios ranqueles*," *Boletín de la Academia Argentina de Letras* 16, no. 58 (January–March 1947): 116. His theory is corroborated by Fernández, "Mansilla," 364.

35. Fernández, "Mansilla," 363–67.

36. Marcela Tamagnini, ed., *Cartas de frontera: Los documentos del conflicto interétnico* (Río Cuarto: National University of Río Cuarto, 1995), document no. 1161, p. 306.

37. See Prieto, *El discurso criollista;* Marvin Lewis, *Afro-Argentine Discourse: Another Dimension of the Black Diaspora* (Columbia: University of Missouri Press, 1996). On the minstrel and *Martín Fierro,* see George Reid Andrews, *The Afro-Argentines of Buenos Aires: 1800–1900* (Madison: University of Wisconsin Press, 1980), 170.

38. Sander L. Gilman, *Inscribing the Other* (Lincoln: University of Nebraska Press, 1991).

39. Marcela Castro and Silvia Jurovietzky, in "Fronteras, mujeres y caballos" (in *Mujeres y cultura en la Argentina del siglo XIX,* ed. Lea Fletcher [Buenos Aires: Feminaria, 1994]), observe that the space destined for the captive women is so meager that all the paragraphs referring to them scattered throughout the book would scarcely total five pages. The disproportion is absurd in a text that professes to document activity on the other side of the frontier for future political-military actions; this absurd disregard represents graphically the real absurdities of state policy toward the captives.

Castro and Jurovietzky note that Mansilla represents the captives within a framework of generalization and, above all, resignation in such a way that "The coercion that establishes the reality of captivity is erased" (153). This is an excellent analysis of the marks of opening and closing that neutralize women.

40. See the previous chapters.

41. This same logic is used to justify the perpetuation of the practice even as this book is being written, after a decade of brutal ethnic confrontation reflected ceaselessly in the rape of women by the persecutors, as has happened again and again in Bosnia, Rwanda, and Kosovo. The body of the woman is always the space of real battles: in that body the enemy is humiliated, unwanted bastards are forcibly engendered, families are destroyed.

42. The same *causerie* reveals a very different scorn for indigenous practices: "And those bad practices also made the populations pick them [the Indians] up like true heralds of peace and before — I don't say the civil authories, but rather the military authories — knew that a commission had arrived, an infinite number of swaps had already taken place between Indians and Christians, giving them ostrich plumes for firewater, or painted cotton handkerchiefs, horses with the marks of ranchers in Buenos Aires or Mendoza . . . for any trinket, or what was even more irritating, selling an *ownerless* captive, or one with a known mark, for a wool poncho or a pair of boots, that is, for a much lower price than for what I have seen sold, I don't say Caucasians, but black women, in the human flesh markets, authorized by the abominable law of slavery, of Cairo, Constantinople, or Rio de Janeiro" (Y esas malas prácticas hacían también que las poblaciones los acogieran [a los

indios] como a verdaderos nuncios de paz y que antes que, no digo las autoridades civiles, sino las militares, supieran que había llegado una comisión, ya estuvieran hechos, entre indios y cristianos, infinidad de cambalaches, dando ellos sus plumas de avestruz por aguardiente, o pañuelos pintados de algodón, o caballos con marca de estancieros de la provincia de Buenos Aires o de Mendoza... por cualquier porquería, o lo que era más irritante aún, vendiendo a una cautiva *orejana* o con marca conocida, por un poncho de paño, o por un par de botas, es decir, por mucho menos precio de lo que yo había visto vender, no digo circasianas, negras, en los mercados de carne humana, autorizados por la ley abominable de la esclavitud, del Cairo, de Constantinopla, de Río de Janeiro) (*Entre-nos,* 124).

The denunciation of the abomination occurs only when Colonel Mansilla, always a character in his texts, no longer has anything to lose: it takes place only after the Conquista del Desierto.

43. See Jan Jindy Peterman, *Worlding Women: A Feminist International Politics* (London: Routledge, 1996); Andrew Parker et al., eds., *Nationalisms and Sexualities* (New York: Routledge, 1992); and Jacqueline Rose, *Sexuality in the Field of Vision* (London: Verso, 1986).

44. Satya P. Mohanty reflects on the difficulty of apprehending the notion of a world shared with the Other in "Political Criticism and the Challenge of Otherness," in *Literary Theory and the Claims of History: Postmodernism, Objectivity, Multicultural Politics* (Ithaca, N.Y.: Cornell University Press, 1997), 147.

45. Studying the formation of identity, Lacan observes that the "Law of the Father" is not always completely achieved and that in fact an inadequate signifier may be produced: this is the source of the foreclosure (*la foreclusion*) of the signifier. For debate, see Jean-Richard Freymann, Jacques Felician, Juan David Nasio, and Christian Oddoux, in *El silencio en psicoanálisis,* ed. Juan David Nasio (Buenos Aires: Amorrortu, 1988). Freud names the mechanism *Verwerfung,* but it is Lacan who develops the theory. The result of foreclosure is a hole, a void in the Symbolic Order.

BIBLIOGRAPHY

Primary Sources

Alberdi, Juan Bautista. *Obras completas*. Vol. 26. Buenos Aires: Luz del Día, 1948–56.

Aráoz de la Madrid, Gregorio. *Memorias del General Gregorio Aráoz de la Madrid*. 2 vols. Buenos Aires: Eudeba, 1969.

Baigorria, Manuel. *Memorias*. Buenos Aires: Solar/Hachette, 1970.

Barros, Alvaro. *Fronteras y territorios federales de las Pampas del Sur.* Buenos Aires: Hachette, 1957 [1872].

Bayo, Ciro. *La América desconocida*. Buenos Aires: Caro Raggio, 1927.

Borges, Jorge Luis. *Obras completas, 1952–1972*. Buenos Aires: Emecé, 1993.

Borges, Jorge Luis, and Adolfo Bioy Casares. *Poesía gauchesca*. Mexico City: Fondo de Cultura Económica, 1955.

Busaniche, José Luis, ed. *Estampas del pasado: Lecturas de historia argentina*. Buenos Aires: Hachette, 1959.

Copello, Santiago Luis, ed. *Gestiones del Arzobispo Aneiros en favor de los indios hasta la Conquista del Desierto*, 227–28. Buenos Aires: Coni, 1945.

Cunninghame Graham, R. B. *South American Sketches*. Edited by John Walker. Norman: University of Oklahoma Press, 1978.

———. *Temas criollos*. Translated by Alicia Jurado. Edited by John Walker. Buenos Aires: Emecé, 1978.

Daireaux, Godofredo. *El fortín*. Buenos Aires: Agro, 1945.

———. *Tipos y paisajes criollos*. Buenos Aires: Agro, 1945.

Daza, José. *Episodios militares*. Buenos Aires: Librería La Facultad de Juan Roldán, 1912.

Del Carril, Bonifacio. *Artistas extranjeros en la Argentina: Mauricio Rugendas*. Buenos Aires: Academia Nacional de Bellas Artes, 1966.

———. *Esteban Echeverría: La cautiva: Dibujos de Mauricio Rugendas*. Buenos Aires: Emecé, 1966.

———. *Los indios en la Argentina*. Buenos Aires: Emecé, 1992.

Díaz de Guzmán, Ruy. *Anales del descubrimiento, población y conquista del Río de la Plata*, chap. 4. Asunción: Ediciones Comuneros, 1980.

Ebelot, Alfred. *La Pampa*. Buenos Aires: A. V. Editor, 1943.

———. *Recuerdos y relatos de guerra de fronteras*. Buenos Aires: Plus Ultra, 1961.

———. *Relatos de la frontera*. Buenos Aires: Solar/Hachette, 1968.

Echeverría, Esteban. *Obras completas.* Edited by Juan María Gutiérrez. 2d ed. Buenos Aires: Antonio Zamora, 1972.

Guerra, Rosa. *Lucía Miranda.* Buenos Aires: Universidad de Buenos Aires, 1956 [1860].

Guinnard, A. *Tres años de esclavitud entre los patagones (relato de mi cautiverio).* Buenos Aires: Espasa-Calpe, n.d.

Hudson, William Henry. *Tales of the Pampas.* New York: Knopf, 1916.

Mallea, Eduardo. *Historia de una pasión argentina.* 4th ed. Buenos Aires: Espasa-Calpe, 1945.

Mansilla, Lucio V. *Entre-nos: Causeries del jueves.* Buenos Aires: Hachette, 1963.

———. *Una excursión a los indios ranqueles,* edited by Saúl Sosnowski. Caracas: Biblioteca Ayacucho, 1984.

Mansilla de García, Eduarda. *Lucía Miranda.* Vol. 35. Buenos Aires: J. C. Rovira, 1860.

Manso, Juana. *Compendio de la historia de las provincias unidas del Río de la Plata: Desde su descubrimiento hasta el año de 1871.* 5th ed. Buenos Aires: Pablo E. Com, 1872.

Meinrado Hux, Father. *Coliqueo, el indio amigo de los toldos.* La Plata: Publicación del Archivo de la Provincia, 1966.

———, ed. *Una apostólica del Padre Salvaire a Salinas Grandes según su esbozo de diario completado por Meinrado Hux.* Buenos Aires: Ministerio de Cultura y Educación, Ediciones Culturales Argentinas, 1979.

———, ed. *Memorias de ex cautivo Santiago Avendaño (1834–1874).* Buenos Aires: Elefante Blanco, 1999.

Molina Massey, Carlos. *De los tiempos de antes (narraciones gauchescas).* Buenos Aires: Agro, 1946.

Moreno, Francisco P. *Viaje a la Patagonia Austral (1876–1877).* Buenos Aires: Solar/Hachette, 1969.

Ortega, Miguel de. *Lucía de Miranda: Drama.* Buenos Aires: Imprenta de la Universidad, 1926.

Paz, José M. *Memorias de la prisión: Buenos Aires en la época de Rosas.* Buenos Aires: Eudeba, 1960.

Paz Illobre, Silvia. "Algunas consideraciones geoeconómicas y geopolíticas acerca de la Conquista del Desierto: Las ideas de la época." *Congreso Nacional de Historia sobre la Conquista del Desierto,* 1:347:58. Buenos Aires: Academia Nacional de la Historia, 1981.

Relación de los cristianos salvados del cautiverio por la División Izquierda del Ejército Expedicionario contra los bárbaros, al mando del señor Brigadier General D. Juan Manuel de Rosas. Chacabo: Published by the State of Buenos Aires. Facsimile edition: *Juan Manuel de Rosas y la redención de cautivos en su campaña al desierto (1833–34).* Buenos Aires: Academia Nacional de Historia, 1979.

Robertson, J. P., and W. P. Robertson. *Letters on South America.* Vol. 3. London: John Murray, 1843.

Sarmiento, Domingo Faustino. *Conflicto y armonía de razas en América*. Buenos Aires: Cultura Argentina, 1915.

———. *Condición del extranjero en América*. Buenos Aires: Facultad, 1928.

———. *Obras completas*. Vol. 26. Buenos Aires: Luz del Día, 1948–56.

———. *Recuerdos de provincia*. Buenos Aires: Sopena, 1966 [1843].

———. *Facundo: Civilización y barbarie*. Introduction by Noé Jitrik. Notes by Nora Dottori and Silvia Zanetti. Caracas: Biblioteca Ayacucho, 1997.

Soler, Amadeo P., ed. *Lucía Miranda: A la luz de los versos de Celestina Funes*. Rosario: Amalevi, 1992.

Tamagnini, Marcela. *Cartas de frontera: Los documentos del conflicto inter-étnico*. Río Cuarto: Universidad Nacional de Río Cuarto, 1994.

Varela, Juan Cruz. "En el regreso de la expedición contra los indios bárbaros, mandada por el Coronel D. Federico Rauch." In *Poesías,* edited by Vicente D. Sierra, 213–36. Buenos Aires: Rosso, 1943 [1827].

Zeballos, Estanislao. *Callvucurá y la dinastía de los Piedra*. 3d ed. Buenos Aires: J. Peuser, 1890.

———. *Painé y la dinastía de los zorros, I. Relmú, reina de los pinares, II*. Buenos Aires: Biblioteca del Suboficial, 1928.

References on Argentina

Academia Nacional de la Historia. *Historia argentina contemporánea, 1862–1930*. Buenos Aires: Ateneo, 1963.

Agüero, Eduardo de. "El paisaje como adversario en 'La cautiva.'" *Cuadernos de Aldeen* 1, nos. 2–3 (1983): 157–74.

Aira, César. *Ema, la cautiva*. Buenos Aires: Belgrano, 1981.

Almiñaque, Conrado. *El indio pampero en la literatura gauchesca*. Miami: Universal, 1981.

Alonso, Carlos J. "Oedipus in the Pampas: Lucio Mansilla's *Una excursión a los indios ranqueles*." *Revista de Estudios Hispánicos* 24, no. 2 (1990): 29–59.

Amar Sánchez, Ana María. "La gauchesca durante el rosismo: Una disputa por el espacio del enemigo." *Revista de Crítica Literaria Latinoamericana* 18, no. 35 (1992): 7–19.

Andrews, George Reid. *The Afro-Argentines of Buenos Aires: 1800–1900*. Madison: University of Wisconsin Press, 1980.

Arce, José. *Roca 1843–1914*. Buenos Aires: Real Academia de la Historia, 1960.

Area, Lelia, and Cristina Parodi. "Lucio V. Mansilla: El peso de una 'conciencia histórica mortificada.'" *Revista de Crítica Literaria Latinoamericana* 21, no. 41 (1995): 177–92.

Astrada, Carlos. *El mito gaucho*. Buenos Aires: Cruz del Sur, 1964.

Avellaneda, Andrés. "Contra su época: Una lectura de la poesía del ochenta." In *On the Centennial of the Argentine Generation of 1880,* edited by Hugo Rodríguez

Alcalá, 191–213. Latin American Studies Program, 4. Riverside: University of California Press, 1980.

———. *Censura, autoritarismo y cultura: Argentina, 1960–1983.* Buenos Aires: Biblioteca Política Argentina, 1983.

Belenky, Silvia Leonor, et al. "El pensamiento de los conquistadores del desierto (a propósito del general Lorenzo Vintter)." In *Congreso Nacional de Historia sobre la Conquista del Desierto,* 4:269–350. Buenos Aires: Academia Nacional de la Historia, 1981.

Biagnini, Hugo Eduardo. *Cómo fue la generación del 80.* Buenos Aires: Plus Ultra, 1980.

Biedma, José Juan. *Crónicas militares: Antecedentes históricos sobre la campaña contra los indios.* Buenos Aires: Eudeba, 1975.

Bordi de Ragucci, Olga Noemí. "Las bases dadas por Roca a la Campaña del Desierto a juicio de sus opositores porteños." In *Congreso Nacional de Historia sobre la Conquista del Desierto,* 3:41–55. Buenos Aires: Academia Nacional de la Historia, 1981.

Borello, Rodolfo. "Notas a *La cautiva.*" *Logos* 13–14 (1977–78): 69–84.

Borget, Auguste. *En las Pampas y los Andes.* Buenos Aires: Pardo-Emecé, 1960.

Buffa, Norma, and Mabel Cernada. "Aspectos de la vida en la frontera." In *Congreso Nacional de Historia sobre la Conquista del Desierto,* 8:297–314. Buenos Aires: Academia Nacional de la Historia, 1981.

Bunge, C. O. "La enseñanza de la tradición y la leyenda." In *Estudios pedagógicos,* 7–23. Madrid: Espasa-Calpe, 1927.

Caillet-Bois, Julio. "Nuevos documentos sobre *Una excursión a los indios ranqueles.*" *Boletín de la Academia Argentina de Letras* 16, no. 58 (1947): 116.

Campoy, Luis. "Conquista del Desierto y desaparición del gaucho: Una perspectiva historico-sociológica." In *Congreso Nacional de Historia sobre la Conquista del Desierto,* 3:315–22. Buenos Aires: Academia Nacional de la Historia, 1981.

Chávez, Fermín. *La cultura en la época de Rosas: Aportes a la descolonización mental de la Argentina.* Buenos Aires: Theoria, 1973.

Ciccerchia, Ricardo. "Familia: La historia de una idea: Los desórdenes domésticos de la plebe urbana porteña: Buenos Aires 1776–1850." In *Vivir en familia,* edited by Catalina Wainerman, 49–72. Buenos Aires: Unicef/Losada, 1994.

Congreso Nacional de Historia sobre la Conquista del Desierto: Celebrado en la ciudad de Gral. Roca del 6 al 10 de noviembre de 1979. Buenos Aires: Academia Nacional de la Historia, 1981.

Cortázar, Augusto R. *Indios y gauchos en la literatura.* Buenos Aires: Instituto de Amigos del Libro Argentino, 1956.

De Lafuente Machain. "Alonso Riquelme de Guzmán." Document from the García Viñas de A. G. de I. Collection, No. 975-1, p. 81. Buenos Aires, 1942.

Destéfani, Laurio H. "Vida y aspectos sociales en la Conquista del Desierto (1852–1892)." In *Congreso Nacional de Historia sobre la Conquista del Desierto,* 4:269–91. Buenos Aires: Academia Nacional de la Historia, 1981.

Diario del Juicio. Buenos Aires: Perfil, May 27, 1985–January 29, 1986.

Fernández, Silvia Mirta Beatriz. "Mansilla y los ranqueles: ¿Por qué Lucio V. Mansilla escribió 'Una excursión a los indios ranqueles'?" *Congreso Nacional de Historia sobre la Conquista del Desierto*, 2:361–75. Buenos Aires: Academia Nacional de la Historia, 1981.

Fernández-Bravo, Alvaro. "Literatura y frontera: Procesos de territorialización en la cultura argentina y chilena del siglo XIX." Ph.D. diss., Princeton University, 1996.

Ferrari, Gustavo, and Ezequiel Gallo, eds. *La Argentina del ochenta al centenario*. Buenos Aires: Sudamericana, 1980.

Fletcher, Lea. "Studies in Comparative Literature: Patriarchy, Medicine, and Women Writers in Nineteenth-Century Argentina." In *The Body and the Text*, edited by Bruce Clarke and Wendell Aycock, 91–101. Lubbock: Texas Tech University Press, 1990.

———, ed. *Mujeres y cultura en la Argentina del siglo XIX*. Buenos Aires: Feminaria, 1994.

Foster, David William. "Knowledge in Mansilla's *Una excursión a los indios ranqueles*." *Revista Hispánica Moderna* 41, no. 1 (1988): 19–30.

———. *The Argentine Generation of 1880: Ideology and Cultural Texts*. Columbia: University of Missouri Press, 1990.

Frederick, Bonnie. "Reading the Warning: The Reader and the Image of the Captive Woman." *Chasqui* 18, no. 2 (1989): 3–11.

———. *Wily Modesty: Argentine Women Writers, 1860–1910*. Tempe, Ariz.: ASU Center for Latin American Studies, 1998.

Fridman, Silvia. "La situación del indígena a través del periodismo." In *Congreso Nacional de Historia sobre la Conquista del Desierto*, 2:377–87. Buenos Aires: Academia Nacional de la Historia, 1981.

Frontera, Luis. *El país de las mujeres cautivas: Sexualidad y despotismo en la Argentina*. Buenos Aires: Galerna, 1991.

Garavaglia, J. C., and J. Moreno, eds. *Población, familia y migraciones en el espacio rioplatense: Siglos XVIII y XIX*. Buenos Aires: Cantaro, 1993.

Garganigo, John F. "El perfil del negro en la narrativa rioplatense." *Historiografía y Bibliografía Americanistas* 21 (1977): 71–109.

Garrels, Elizabeth. "Sobre indios, afroamericanos y los racismos de Sarmiento." *Revista Iberoamericana, Siglo XIX: Fundación y Fronteras de la Ciudadanía* 178–79 (1997): 99–114.

Garrenton, Juan Antonio. *Partes detallados de la expedición al desierto de Juan Manuel de Rosas en 1833*. Buenos Aires: Eudeba, 1975.

Goldberg, Marta B. "La mujer negra rioplatense (1750–1840)." In *La mitad del país: La mujer en la sociedad Argentina*, edited by Lidia Knecher and Marta Panaia, 67–81. Buenos Aires: Centro Editor de América Latina, 1994.

Goobar, Walter, and Rolando Graña. *ESMA: El Diario del Juicio*. Film. Production of Magdalena Ruiz Guiñazu. Buenos Aires, 1998.

Goodrich, Diana S. "From Barbarism to Civilization: Travels of a Latin American Text." *American Literary History* 4, no. 3 (1992): 443–63.

Guy, Donna J. *Sex and Danger in Buenos Aires: Prostitution, Family, and Nation in Argentina.* Lincoln: University of Nebraska Press, 1991.

Haberly, David T. "Captives and Infidels: The Figure of the Captive in Argentine Literature." *The American Hispanist* 4, no. 29 (1978): 7–16.

Halperín Donghi, Tulio. *Revolución y guerra: Formación de una élite dirigente en la Argentina criolla.* Mexico City: Siglo XXI, 1972.

————. "Una nación para el desierto argentino." In *Proyecto y construcción de una nación (Argentina 1846–1880),* 9–101. Caracas: Biblioteca Ayacucho, 1980.

————. *Guerra y finanzas en los orígenes del estado argentino (1791–1850).* Buenos Aires: Belgrano, 1982.

Iglesia, Cristina. "Indias, mestizas y cautivas: Historia y ficción en las crónicas rioplatenses." In *500 años de patriarcado en el nuevo mundo,* edited by Asunción Lavrin, 45–77. Santo Domingo: CIPAF, 1992.

————. "La mujer cautiva: Cuerpo, mito y frontera." In *Historia de las Mujeres,* edited by Georges Duby and Michelle Perrot, 3:557–70. Madrid: Tauris, 1992.

————. "Mansilla: El éxito del escándalo." Manuscript provided by the author, 1997.

Iglesia, Cristina, and Julio Schvartzman. *Cautivas y misioneros: Mitos blancos de la conquista.* Buenos Aires: Catálogos, 1987.

Jitrik, Noé. *Esteban Echeverría.* Buenos Aires: Centro Editor de América Latina, 1967.

————. *Muerte y resurrección de Facundo.* Buenos Aires: Centro Editor de América Latina, 1967.

————. *El 80 y su mundo.* Buenos Aires: Jorge Álvarez, 1968.

————. *Ensayos y estudios de Literatura Argentina.* Buenos Aires: Galerna, 1970.

————. "El *Facundo:* La gran riqueza de la pobreza." In *Facundo: Civilización y barbarie,* by Domingo Faustino Sarmiento, 9–52. Caracas: Biblioteca Ayacucho, 1977.

Jones, Kristine. "La Cautiva: An Argentine Solution to Labor Shortage in the Pampas." In *Brazil and the Río de la Plata: Challenge and Response: An Anthology of Papers Presented at the Sixth Annual Conference of Icllas,* edited by Luis Clay Méndez and Laurence Bates, 91–94. Charleston, Ill., 1983.

————. "Conflict and Adaptation in the Argentine Pampas, 1750–1880." Ph.D. diss., University of Chicago, 1984.

————. "Nineteenth-Century British Travel Accounts of Argentina." *Ethnohistory* 33, no. 2 (1986).

————. "Indian Creole Negotiations." In *Revolution and Restoration,* edited by J. C. Brown and M. Szuchman. Lincoln: University of Nebraska Press, 1994.

Kaplan, Marina. "Gauchos e indios: La frontera y la producción del sujeto en obras argentinas del siglo diecinueve." Ph.D. diss., Tulane University, 1987.

Knowlton, Edgar C. "The Epigraphs in Esteban Echeverría's 'La cautiva.'" *Hispania* 44, no. 2 (May 1961): 212–17.

———. *Esteban Echeverría.* Bryn Mawr, Pa.: Dorrance, 1986.

Lagmanovich, David. "Tres cautivas: Echeverría, Ascasubi, Hernández." *Chasqui* 8, no. 3 (1979): 24–33.

Lanuza, José Luis. *Genio y figura de Lucio V. Mansilla.* Buenos Aires: Eudeba, 1965.

Leguizamón, Martiniano. "La leyenda de Lucía Miranda." *Revista de la Universidad de Córdoba* 6 (1919): 11.

Lewis, Marvin. *Afro-Argentine Discourse: Another Dimension of the Black Diaspora.* Columbia: University of Missouri Press, 1996.

Lichtblau, Myron L. "El tema de Lucía Miranda en la novela argentina." *Armas y Letras* 2 (1959): 23–31.

López, Juan Severino. *El rescate de las cautivas: Un episodio de la guerra y la paz en las fronteras del desierto.* Separata Investigaciones y Ensayos, 21. Buenos Aires: Academia Nacional de Historia, 1977.

Ludmer, Josefina. "Quién educa." *Filología* 20, no. 1 (1985): 105–16.

———. *El género gauchesco: Un tratado sobre la patria.* Buenos Aires: Sudamericana, 1988.

———, ed. *Las culturas de fin de siglo en América Latina.* Buenos Aires: Beatriz Viterbo, 1994.

Lynch, John. *Argentina Dictator: Juan Manuel de Rosas, 1829–1852.* Oxford: Clarendon Press, 1981.

Malosetti Costa, Laura. *Rapto de cautivas blancas: Un aspecto erótico de la barbarie en la plástica rioplatense del siglo XIX.* Hipótesis y Discusiones, 4. Buenos Aires: Facultad de Filosofía y Letras, UBA, 1994.

Martínez, Tomás Eloy. "En defensa de los diferentes." *La Nación* (Buenos Aires), February 27, 1999.

Martínez Estrada, Ezequiel. *Radiografía de la pampa.* Buenos Aires: Losada, 1953.

———. *Muerte y transfiguración del Martín Fierro.* Mexico City: Fondo de Cultura Económica, 1958.

Masiello, Francine. *Between Civilization and Barbarism: Women, Nation, and Literary Culture in Modern Argentina.* Lincoln: University of Nebraska Press, 1992.

———. *La mujer y el espacio público: El periodismo femenino en la Argentina del siglo XIX.* Buenos Aires: Feminaria, 1994.

Mathieu-Higginbotham, Corina. "El concepto de 'civilización y barbarie' en *Una excursión a los indios ranqueles.*" *Hispanofilia* 30, no. 2 (January 1987): 81–87.

Mayo, Carlos A. "El cautiverio y sus funciones en una sociedad de frontera: El caso de Buenos Aires (1750–1810)." *Revista de Indias* 45, no. 175 (1985).

———. *Fuentes para la historia de la frontera: Declaraciones de cautivos.* Mar del Plata: Universidad de Mar del Plata, 1985.

Mayo, Carlos A., and Amalia Latrubesse. *Terratenientes, soldados y cautivos: La frontera (1737–1815).* Mar del Plata: Universidad Nacional de Mar del Plata, 1986.

Mayol Laferrére, Carlos. "El coronel Lucio V. Mansilla y la ocupación del Río Quinto en 1869: Avance de la frontera sud y sud este de Córdoba." *Congreso Nacional de Historia sobre la Conquista del Desierto,* 2:83–135. Buenos Aires: Academia Nacional de la Historia, 1981.

Meléndez, Concha. "La leyenda de Lucía Miranda en la novela." In *La novela indianista en Hispanoamérica,* in *Obras completas,* 1:169–77. San Juan: Instituto de Cultura Puertorriqueña.

Mercado, Juan Carlos. *Building a Nation: The Case of Echeverría.* Lanham, Md.: University Press of America, 1996.

Mignolo, Walter. "Putting the Americas on the Map: Cartography and the Colonization of Space." *Colonial Latin American Review* 1 (1992): 25–63.

Molloy, Sylvia. "Imagen de Mansilla." In *La Argentina del ochenta al centario,* edited by Gustavo Ferrari and Ezequiel Gallo, 745–59. Buenos Aires: Sudamericana, 1980.

———. "Recuerdo y sujeto en *Mis memorias* de Mansilla." *Nueva Revista de Filología Hispánica* 36, no. 2 (1988): 1207–20.

———. *At Face Value: Autobiographical Writing in Spanish America.* Cambridge: Cambridge University Press, 1991.

Montaldo, Graciela. *De pronto, el campo: Literatura argentina y tradición rural.* Rosario: Beatriz Viterbo, 1993.

———. "Territorios y escalas: Ficciones de frontera." Manuscript provided by the author. Caracas: Universidad Simón Bolívar, 1998. 20 pp.

Montecino, Sonia. "La conquista de las mujeres: Las cautivas, símbolo de lo femenino en América latina." In *500 años de patriarcado en el nuevo mundo,* edited by Asunción Lavrin. Santo Domingo: CIPAF, 1992.

Moscoso, Martha, ed. *Palabras del silencio: Las mujeres latinoamericanas y su historia.* Quito: Abya-Yala/Unicef/Royal Embassy of the Netherlands, 1995.

Myers, Jorge. *Orden y virtud: El discurso republicano en el régimen rosista.* Buenos Aires: Universidad Nacional de Quilmes, 1995.

Nunca Más: Informe de la Comisión Nacional sobre la Desaparición de Personas. Buenos Aires: Eudeba, 1984.

Olascoaga, Laurentino. *Algunas verdades históricas sobre la Conquista del Desierto.* Buenos Aires: Gir y Schaffner, 1939.

Operé, Fernando. *Cautivos.* Buenos Aires: Instituto Movilizador de Fondos Cooperativos, 1998.

———. "Cautivos de los indios, cautivos de la literatura: El caso del Río de la Plata." *Hispamérica* 76/77 (1998): 49–76.

Orgambide, Pedro, and Roberto Yahni, directors. *Enciclopedia de la literatura argentina.* Buenos Aires: Sudamericana, 1970.

Paesa, Pascual. "Milicos y fortines." *Revista de la Junta de Estudios Históricos de Bahía Blanca* 2 (1970): 28.

Papier, Sara. "Breve itinerario femenino a través de la Historia Argentina." *Claridad* 18, no. 340 (Buenos Aires, October 1939): 1:223–24.

París, Marta. *Amantes, cautivas y guerreras*. Buenos Aires: Almagesto, 1996.

Paz Illobre, Silvia. "Algunas consideraciones geoeconómicas y geopolíticas acerca de la Conquista del Desierto: Las ideas de la época." In *Congreso Nacional de Historia sobre la Conquista del Desierto,* 1:347–58. Buenos Aires: Academia Nacional de la Historia, 1981.

Pérez Amuchástegui, A. J., and Irma E. Montani de Perpignan. "Génesis de la Campaña del Desierto." In *Congreso Nacional de Historia sobre la Conquista del Desierto,* 2:171–85. Buenos Aires: Academia Nacional de la Historia, 1981.

Pichel, Vera. *Las cuarteleras: Cuatro mil mujeres en la Conquista del Desierto.* Buenos Aires: Planeta, 1994.

Portas, Julio Aníbal Portas. *Malón contra malón: La solución final del problema del indio en la Argentina.* Buenos Aires: La Flor, 1967.

Prieto, Adolfo. *La literatura autobiográfica argentina.* Buenos Aires: Jorge Álvarez, 1966.

———. *El discurso criollista en la formación de la Argentina moderna.* Buenos Aires: Sudamericana, 1988.

Ramos, Julio. "Entre otros: *Una excursión a los indios ranqueles* de Lucio V. Mansilla." *Filología* 21 (1986): 143–71.

———. *Paradojas de la letra.* Caracas: Excultura, 1996.

Ramayon, Eduardo E. *Las caballadas en la guerra del indio.* Buenos Aires: Eudeba, 1974.

Requeni, Antonio. "Eduarda Mansilla, una escritora del 80." *Mundi* 1, no. 2 (Buenos Aires, May 1987): 68–72.

Rivera, Jorge B. *La primitiva literatura gauchesca.* Buenos Aires: Jorge Álvarez, 1968.

Rock, David. *Argentina 1516–1987: From Spanish Colonization to Alfonsín.* Berkeley: University California Press, 1987.

Rodríguez, Martín. *Diario de la expedición al desierto.* Buenos Aires: Sudesta, 1969.

Rodríguez Molas, Ricardo E. *Historia social del gaucho.* Buenos Aires: Centro Editor de América Latina, 1982.

Rodríguez Pérsico, Adriana. "Modelos de Estado: Figuras utópicas y contrautópicas." *Filología* 23, no. 2 (1988): 89–11.

Rojas, Ricardo. *Historia de la literatura argentina: Ensayo filosófico sobre la evolución de la cultura en el Plata.* Vol. 1. 4th ed. Buenos Aires: G. Kraft, 1957.

Romero, José Luis. *Las ideas políticas en la Argentina.* Mexico: Fondo de Cultura Económica, 1946.

Rosa, Nicolás. *El arte del olvido.* Buenos Aires: Puntosur, 1990.

Rosas, Eugenio. *Color de Rosas.* Buenos Aires: Sudamericana, 1993.

Saldías, Adolfo. *Historia de la Confederación Argentina.* Buenos Aires: Juan Carlos Granda, 1967.

Sarlo, Beatriz. *Borges, un escritor en las orillas.* Buenos Aires: Ariel, 1995.

Sarlo, Beatriz, and Carlos Altamirano. *Ensayos argentinos: De Sarmiento a la vanguardia.* Buenos Aires: Ariel/Espasa-Calpe, 1997 [1987].

Schade, George D. "Los viajeros argentinos del ochenta." *Texto crítico* 28 (1984): 82–103.

Schoo Lastra, Dionisio. *El indio del desierto, 1535–1879.* Buenos Aires: Meridion, 1957.

Shumway, Nicolas. *The Invention of Argentina.* Berkeley: University of California Press, 1991.

Slatta, Richard W. *Gauchos and the Vanishing Frontier.* Lincoln: University of Nebraska Press, 1983.

Silva Gruesz, Kirsten. "Facing the Nation: The Organic Life of 'La cautiva.'" *Revista de Estudios Hispánicos* 20 (1996): 3–24.

Socolow, Susan Migden. "Los cautivos españoles en las sociedades indígenas: El contacto cultural a través de la frontera argentina." Translated by G. Malgesini. *Anuario del IEH* 2 (1987): 99–136.

Soler, Amadeo P. *Los 823 días del Fuerte Sancti Spiritus y la vigencia permanente de Puerto Gaboto.* Rosario: Amalevi, 1981.

Sosa de Newton, Lily. "Eduarda Mansilla de García en el recuerdo." *Feminaria* 3, no. 5 (April 1990): 41.

Sosnowski, Saúl. Prologue to *Una excursión a los indios ranqueles,* by Lucio V. Mansilla, ix–xxvi. Caracas: Bibioteca Ayacucho, 1984.

———. *Represión y reconstrucción de una cultura: El caso argentino.* Buenos Aires: Eudeba, 1988.

Stern, Mirta E. "*Una excursión a los indios ranqueles*: Espacio textual y ficción topográfica." *Filología* 20 (Buenos Aires): 117–38.

Szuchman, Mark. *Order, Family, and Community in Buenos Aires: 1810–1860.* Stanford, Calif.: Stanford University Press, 1988.

Taylor, Diana. *Disappearing Acts: Spectacles of Gender and Nationalism in Argentina's "Dirty War."* Durham, N.C.: Duke University Press, 1997.

Terzaga, Alfred. *Historia de Roca: De soldado federal a presidente de la república.* Buenos Aires: Pena Lillo, 1976.

Tzitsikas, Helene. *Los exiliados argentinos en Montevideo durante la época de Rosas.* Montevideo: La Plaza, 1991.

Urraca, Beatriz Dolores. "The Literary Construction of National Identities in the Western Hemisphere: Argentina and the United States, 1845–1898." Ph.D. diss., University of Michigan, 1993.

Valenti, José J. C. *Cuatro mujeres de la historia americana.* Buenos Aires: Artes Gráficas Alfonso Ruiz, 1951.

Villegas, Conrado. *Expedición al Nahuel Huapí.* Buenos Aires: Sudesta, 1881.

Viñas, David. *Literatura argentina y realidad política: De Sarmiento a Cortázar.* Buenos Aires: Siglo Veinte, 1971.

———. *Literatura argentina y realidad política: Apogeo de la oligarquía.* Buenos Aires: Siglo Veinte, 1975.

———. *Indios, ejército y frontera.* Mexico City: Siglo XXI, 1983.

————, ed. *Historia de la literatura argentina*. Buenos Aires: Centro Editor de América Latina, 1986.

Walther, Juan Carlos. *La Conquista del Desierto*. Buenos Aires: Eudeba, 1970.

Weinberg, Félix. "Sarmiento y el problema de la frontera (1845–1858)." *Congreso Nacional de Historia* (1982): 1:495–509.

Zigón, Ana Teresa. "La conciencia territorial en dos momentos del pensamiento argentino (1837–1880)." In *Congreso Nacional de Historia sobre la Conquista del Desierto*, vol. 3. Buenos Aires: Academia Nacional de la Historia, 1981.

Zorilla de San Martín, Juan. *Tabaré*. Edited and introduced by Antonio Seluja Cecín. Montevideo: Universidad de la República, 1984.

Secondary Sources

Althusser, Louis. *Ideología y aparatos de Estado: Freud y Lacan*. Translated by A. J. Pla and J. Sazbón. Buenos Aires: Nueva Visión, 1988.

Anderson, Benedict. *Imagined Communities: Reflections on the Origin and Spread of Nationalism*. London: Verso, 1983.

Appignanesi, L. *Identity: The Real Me*. ICA Documents, 6. London: Institute of Contemporary Art, 1987.

Arendt, Hannah. *The Origins of Totalitarianism*. New York: Schocken, 1958.

Ashcroft, Bill, with Gareth Griffiths and Helen Tiffin. *The Empire Writes Back: Theory and Practice in Post-colonial Literatures*. New York: Routledge, 1989.

Ashcroft, Bill, with Chris Tiffin and Alan Lawson. *De-scribing Empire: Post-colonialism and Textuality*. New York: Routledge, 1994.

Augé, Marc. *Las formas del olvido*. Translated by Mercedes Tricás Precler and Gemma Andújar. Barcelona: Gedisa, 1998.

Balibar, Etienne, and Immanuel Wallerstein. *Race, Nation, Class: Ambiguous Identities*. Translated by Etienne Balibar and Chris Turner. London: Verso, 1996.

Barthes, Roland. *Mythologies*. Selected and translated by Annette Lavers. New York: Hill and Wang, 1972.

Bastide, Roger. "Problems of the Collective Memory." In *The African Religions of Brazil: Toward a Sociology of the Interpenetration of Civilizations*, 240–59. Translated by Helen Sebba. Baltimore: Johns Hopkins University Press, 1978.

Bauman, Zygmunt. *Modernity and Ambivalence*. Ithaca, N.Y.: Cornell University Press, 1991.

Belsey, Catherine. *Critical Practice*. London: Routledge, 1987.

Benjamin, Walter. *Illuminations*. Edited by Hannah Arendt. Translated by Harry Zohn. New York: Schocken, 1969.

Berger, Peter, and Thomas Luckmann. *The Social Construction of Reality: A Treatise in the Sociology of Knowledge*. New York: Irvington, 1980 [1966].

Berman, Marshall. *All That Is Solid Melts into Air: The Experience of Modernity*. New York: Simon and Schuster, 1982.

Bhabha, Homi K. "The Other Question — the Stereotype and Colonial Discourse." *Screen* 24, no. 6 (November–December 1983): 18–36.

———. *Nation and Narration.* London: Routledge, 1990.

———. "A Question of Survival: Nations and Psychic States." In *Psychoanalysis and Cultural Theory: Thresholds,* edited by James Donald. New York: St. Martin's Press, 1991.

———. *The Location of Culture.* London: Routledge, 1994.

Blunt, Allison, and Gillian Rose, eds. *Writing Women and Space: Colonial and Postcolonial Geographies.* New York: Guilford, 1994.

Boon, James A. *Other Tribes, Other Scribes: Symbolic Anthropology in the Comparative Study of Cultures, Histories, Religions, and Texts.* Cambridge: Cambridge University Press, 1982.

Brading, David. *The First America: The Spanish Monarchy, Creole Patriots, and the Liberal State, 1492–1867.* Cambridge: Cambridge University Press, 1991.

Breitweiser, Mitchell Robert. *American Puritanism and the Defense of Mourning: Religion, Grief, and Ethnology in Mary White Rowlandson's Captivity Narrative.* Madison: University of Wisconsin Press, 1990.

Bronfen, Elisabeth. *Over Her Dead Body: Myth, Femininity, and the Aesthetic.* New York: Routledge, 1992.

Brown, R., and A. Gilman. "The Pronouns and Power and Solidarity." *Language and Social Context.* Edited by P. P. Giglioli. Harmondsworth, England: Penguin, 1972.

Brownmiller, Susan. *Against Our Will: Men, Women, and Rape.* New York: Simon and Schuster, 1975.

Butler, Judith. *Bodies That Matter: On the Discursive Limits of "Sex."* New York: Routledge, 1993.

Campuzano, Luisa. "Blancos y blancas en la conquista de Cuba." Universidad de La Habana/Casa de las Américas. Manuscript provided by the author, 1997.

Carey-Webb, Allen. *Making Subject(s): Literature and the Emergence of National Identity.* New York: Garland, 1998.

Cassirer, Ernst. *The Philosophy of the Enlightenment.* Translated by Fritz C. A. Koelln and James P. Pettegrove. Princeton, N.J.: Princeton University Press, 1951.

Castiglia, Christopher. *Bound and Determined: Captivity, Culture-Crossing, and White Womanhood from Mary White Rowlandson to Patty Hearst.* Chicago: University of Chicago Press, 1996.

Certeau, Michel de. "Montaigne's 'Of Cannibals': The Savage 'I.'" In *Heterologies: Discourse on the Other,* 67–79. Translated by Brian Massumi. Minneapolis: University of Minnesota Press, 1986.

———. *The Practice of Everyday Life.* Translated by Steven Randall. Berkeley: University California Press, 1988.

———. *La toma de la palabra y otros escritos políticos.* Translated by Alejandro Pescador. Mexico City: Universidad Iberoamericana, 1995.

Chaunu, Pierre. *L'heritage: Au risque de la hain.* Paris: Aubier, 1995.

Chatterjee, Partha. *Nationalist Thought and the Colonial World: A Derivative Discourse.* Minneapolis: University of Minnesota Press, 1986.

Cheyfitz, Eric. *The Poetics of Imperialism: Translation and Colonization from "The Tempest" to "Tarzan."* New York: Oxford University Press, 1991.

———. "Savage Law: The Plot against American Indians in *Johnson and Graham's Lessee v. M'Intosh* and *The Pioneers.*" In *Cultures of U.S. Imperialism,* edited by Amy Kaplan and Donald E. Pease, 109–28. Durham, N.C.: Duke University Press, 1993.

Chiaramonte, José Carlos, ed. *Pensamiento de la Ilustración: Economía y sociedad iberoamericanas en el siglo XVIII.* Caracas: Biblioteca Ayacucho, 1979.

Chukwudi Eze, Emmanuel, ed. *Race and the Enlightenment.* Cambridge: Blackwell, 1997.

Clifford, James. "Traveling Cultures." In *Cultural Studies,* edited by L. Grossberg, C. Nelson, and P. Treichler, 96–116. New York: Routledge, 1992.

Cohen, Sande. "Structuralism and the Writing of Intellectual History." *History and Theory* 17, no. 2 (1978): 206.

Collingwood, Robin George. *The Idea of History.* Oxford: Clarendon Press, 1967.

Cowper Powys, John. *The Art of Forgetting the Unpleasant.* London: Village Press, 1974.

Deleuze, Gilles. *Nietzsche and Philosophy.* Translated by Hugh Tomlinson. New York: Columbia University Press, 1983.

Deleuze, Gilles, with Félix Guattari. *A Thousand Plateaus: Capitalism and Schizophrenia.* Translated by Brian Massumi. London: Athlone Press, 1988.

De Man, Paul. "Pascal's Allegory of Persuasion." In *Allegory and Representation,* edited by Stephen Greenblatt, 1–23. Baltimore: Johns Hopkins University Press, 1981.

Derrida, Jacques. *Dissemination.* Translated, introduced, and notes by Barbara Johnson. Chicago: University of Chicago Press, 1981.

Donald, James, and Ali Rattansi, eds. *"Race," Culture, and Difference.* London: Sage, 1992.

Fanon, Frantz. *Black Skin, White Masks.* 1952. New York: Grove Press, 1967.

Feldman, Shoshana, and Dori Laub. *Testimony: Crises of Witnessing in Literature, Psychoanalysis, and History.* London: Routledge, 1992.

Fentress, James, and Chris Wickham. *Social Memory.* Oxford: Basil Blackwell, 1992.

Fernández Retamar, Roberto. *Calibán y otros ensayos: Nuestra América en el mundo.* Havana: Editorial Arte y Literatura, 1979. Published in English as *Caliban and Other Essays.* Translated by Edward Baker. Minneapolis: University of Minnesota Press, 1989.

Foucault, Michel. *The Archaeology of Knowledge and the Discourse on Language.* Translated by A. M. Sheridan Smith. New York: Pantheon, 1972.

———. *Language, Counter-memory, Practice.* Edited by Donald F. Bouchard. Translated by Donald F. Bouchard and Sherry Simon. Ithaca, N.Y.: Cornell University Press, 1977.

————. *History of Sexuality.* Translated by Robert Hurley. 3 vols. New York: Vintage, 1980.

————. "Film and Popular Memory." In *Foucault Live (Interviews 1966–1984).* Translated by Martin Jordin. Edited by Sylvere Kitrunger. New York: Semiotext[e], 1989.

Freud, Sigmund. *Totem and Taboo: Resemblances between the Psychic Lives of Savages and Neurotics.* Translated by A. A. Brill. New York: Vintage, 1946 [1918].

Freund, Julien. *L'Essence du politique.* Paris: Sirrey, 1965.

Gates, Henry Louis, ed. *"Race," Writing, and Difference.* Chicago: University of Chicago Press, 1986.

Gay, Peter. *The Enlightenment: An Interpretation.* Vol. 1–2. New York: Norton, 1969.

Geertz, Clifford. *The Interpretation of Cultures.* New York: Basic Books, 1973.

————. "From the 'Native' Point of View: On the Nature of Anthropological Understanding." *Bulletin of the American Academy of Arts and Sciences* 28, no. 1 (1974).

Gillis, John. "Memory and Identity: The History of a Relationship." In *Commemorations: The Politics of National Identity.* Princeton, N.J.: Princeton University Press, 1994.

Gerbi, Antonello. *La disputa del nuevo mundo: Historia de una polémica 1750–1900.* Translated by Antonio Alatorre. 2d, corrected ed. Mexico City: Fondo de Cultura Económica, 1982.

Gilman, Sander. "Black Bodies, White Bodies: Toward an Iconography of Female Sexuality in Late Nineteenth-Century Art, Medicine, and Literature." *Critical Inquiry* (fall 1985): 204–42.

————. *Disease and Representation: Images of Illness from Madness to AIDS.* Ithaca, N.Y.: Cornell University Press, 1988.

————. *Sexuality: An Illustrated History Representing the Sexual in Medicine and Culture from the Middle Ages to the Age of AIDS.* New York: Wiley, 1989.

————. *Inscribing the Other.* Lincoln: University of Nebraska Press, 1991.

González Stephan, Beatriz. *La historiografía literaria del liberalismo hispanoamericano del siglo XIX.* Havana: Casa de las Américas, 1987.

González Stephan, Beatriz, et al., eds. *Esplendores y miserias del siglo XIX: Cultura y sociedad en América Latina.* Caracas: Monte Avila/Equinoccio-USB, 1995.

Green, André. *Narcissisme de Vie, Narcissisme de Mort.* Paris: Éditions de Minuit, 1983.

Halbawchs, Maurice. *The Collective Memory.* New York: Harper, 1980 [1928].

Harley, Brian. "Maps, Knowledge, and Power." In *Writing Worlds: Discourse, Text, and Metaphor in the Representation of Landscape,* edited by Trevor J. Barnes and James S. Duncan, 193–230. London: Routledge, 1992.

Hartman, Geoffrey. Introduction to *Holocaust Remembrance: The Shapes of Memory,* edited by Geoffrey Hartman. Oxford: Basil Blackwell, 1994.

Hartsock, Nancy C. M. *The Feminist Standpoint Revisited and Other Essays*. New York: Westview Press, 1998.

Higgins, Lynn A., and Brenda R. Silver. *Rape and Representation*. New York: Columbia University Press, 1991.

Hobsbawm, Eric. *Primitive Rebels: Studies in Archaic Forms of Social Movement in the 19th and 20th Centuries*. New York: Norton, 1959.

———. *Bandits*. Rev. ed. New York: Pantheon, 1981 [1969].

———. *Nations and Nationalism since 1780: Programme, Myth, Reality*. Cambridge: Cambridge University Press, 1990.

Hobsbawm, Eric, and Terence Ranger, eds. *The Invention of Tradition*. Cambridge: Cambridge University Press, 1983.

Hutton, Patrick. "Collective Memory and Collective Mentalities: The Halbwachs-Aries Connection." *Historical Reflections/Reflections Historiques* 15, no. 2 (1988): 314.

Huyssen, Andreas. *Twilight Memories: Marking Time in a Culture of Amnesia*. New York: Routledge, 1995.

James, Donald, ed. *Psychoanalysis and Cultural Theory: Thresholds*. New York: St. Martin's, 1991.

James, Donald, and Stuart Hall, eds. *Politics and Ideology*. Philadelphia: Open University Press, 1986.

Jameson, Fredric. *The Political Unconscious: Narrative as a Socially Symbolic Act*. Ithaca, N.Y.: Cornell University Press, 1981.

Jan Mohamed, Abdul. *Manichean Aesthetics: The Politics of Literature in Colonial Africa*. Amherst: University of Massachusetts Press, 1983.

———. "The Economy of Manichean Allegory: The Function of Racial Difference in Colonialist Literature." *Critical Inquiry* 12 (fall 1985): 59–86.

Jardine, Alice. *Gynesis: Configurations of Women and Modernity*. Ithaca, N.Y.: Cornell University Press, 1985.

Kaplan, Amy, and Donald E. Pease, eds. *Cultures of U.S. Imperialism*. Durham, N.C.: Duke University Press, 1993.

Kolodny, Annette. *The Land before Her: Fantasy and Experience of the American Frontiers, 1630–1860*. Chapel Hill: University of North Carolina Press, 1984.

———. "Among the Indians: The Uses of Captivity." Book review, *New York Times*, January 31, 1993, 27.

Kosofsky Sedgwick, Eve. *Tendencies*. Durham, N.C.: Duke University Press, 1993.

Kristeva, Julia. *Powers of Horror*. Translated by Leon S. Roudiez. New York: Columbia University Press, 1982.

Kronik, John W. "Editor's Note." *PMLA* 107 (1992): 425.

Lacan, Jacques. *Escritos 2*. Buenos Aires: Siglo XXI, 1975.

———. *Le Séminaire, livre II, le moi dans la théorie de Freud et dans la téchnique de la psychanalyse*. Paris: Seuil, 1978.

———. *Seminario 3*. Barcelona: Paidós, 1984.

Laclau, Ernesto. *Politics and Ideology in Marxist Theory: Capitalism, Fascism, Populism.* London: NLB, 1977.

———. *Emancipation(s).* London: Verso, 1996.

Laclau, Ernesto, with Chantal Mouffe. *Hegemony and Socialist Strategy: Towards a Radical Democratic Politics.* Translated by Winston Moore and Paul Cammack. London: Verso, 1985.

Laurentis, Teresa. *Alice Doesn't: Feminism, Semiotics, Cinema.* Bloomington: Indiana University Press, 1984.

Le Goff, Jacques. *Histoire et mémoire.* Paris: Gallimard, 1988.

Lévi-Strauss, Claude. *Tristes tropiques.* New York: Atheneum, 1974.

Lévy-Brul, L. *Primitive Mentality.* New York: Beacon Press, 1966.

Leydesdorff, Selma, Luisa Passerini, and Paul Thompson, eds. *Gender and Memory.* International Yearbook of Oral History and Life Stories, 4. New York: Oxford University Press, 1996.

Lotman, Yuri M. *Estructura del texto artístico.* Madrid: Istmo, 1982.

Lugones, María. "Motion, Stasis, and Resistance to Interlocked Oppressions." In *Making Worlds: Gender, Metaphor, Materiality,* edited by Susan Hardy Aiken et al., 49–53. Tucson: University of Arizona Press, 1998.

Lukács, George. *History and Class Consciousness.* Translated by Rodney Livingstone. Cambridge: MIT Press, 1971.

Mannoni, Dominique O. *Prospero and Caliban: The Psychology of Colonization.* New York: Praeger, 1964 [1950].

Matsuda, Matt K. *The Memory of the Modern.* New York: Oxford University Press, 1996.

Mohanty, Satya P. *Literary Theory and the Claims of History: Postmodernism, Objectivity, Multicultural Politics.* Ithaca, N.Y.: Cornell University Press, 1997.

Mosse, George L. *Nationalism and Sexuality: Respectability and Abnormal Sexuality in Modern Europe.* New York: Howard Fertig, 1985.

Muller, John P., and William J. Richardson. *Lacan and Language: A Reader's Guide to "Ecrits."* New York: International University Press, 1982.

Nasio, Juan David, ed. *El silencio en psicoanálisis.* Buenos Aires: Amorrortu, 1988.

Nead, Lynda. *The Female Nude: Art, Obscenity, and Sexuality.* London: Routledge, 1992.

Nietzsche, Friederich. *The Use and Abuse of History.* Translated by Adrian Colins. Indianapolis: Liberal Arts Press and Bobbs-Merril, 1957.

Nora, Pierre, ed. *Realms of Memory: Rethinking the French Past.* 2 vols. Translated by Arthur Goldhammer. New York: Columbia University Press, 1996.

Ong, Walter. *In the Human Grain: Further Explorations of Contemporary Culture.* New York: Macmillan, 1967.

Parker, Andrew, and Eve Kosofsky Sedgwick, eds. *Performativity and Performance.* New York: Routledge, 1995.

Parker, Andrew, et al., eds. *Nationalisms and Sexualities.* New York: Routledge, 1992.

Pascal, Blaise. *Pensées*. London: Harmondsworth, 1966.

Pettman, Jan Jindy. *Worlding Women: A Feminist International Politics*. London: Routledge, 1996.

Pratt, Mary Louise. *Imperial Eyes: Travel Writing and Transculturation*. London: Routledge, 1992.

———. "Las mujeres y el imaginario nacional en el siglo XIX." *Revista de Crítica Literaria Latinoamericana* 19, no. 38 (second semester, 1993): 51–62.

Rama, Angel. *La ciudad letrada*. Hanover, N.H.: El Norte. Published in English as *The Lettered City*. Translated by John Charles Chasteen. Durham, N.C.: Duke University Press, 1996.

Rodó, José Enrique. *Ariel*. San Juan: Editorial del Departamento de Instrucción Pública, 1968.

Rose, Jacqueline. *Sexuality in the Field of Vision*. London: Verso, 1986.

Rubin, Gayle. "The Traffic in Women." In *Toward an Anthropology of Women*, edited by Rayna R. Reiter, 157–210. New York: Monthly Review Press, 1975.

Said, Edward. *Orientalism*. New York: Vintage, 1979.

Saint-Amand, Pierre. *The Laws of Hostility: Politics, Violence, and the Enlightenment*. Introduced by Chantal Mouffe. Translated by Jennifer Curtiss. Minneapolis: University of Minnesota Press, 1996.

Sánchez Albornoz, Nicolás, and José Luis Moreno. *La población de América Latina: Bosquejo histórico*. Buenos Aires: Paidós, 1968.

Schwarcz, Lilia Moritz. *O espetáculo das raças: Cientistas, instituições e questão racial no Brasil 1870–1930*. São Paulo: Companhia Das Letras, 1995.

Schweitzer, Ivy. *The Work of Self-Representation: Lyric Poetry in Colonial New England*. Chapel Hill: University of North Carolina Press, 1991.

Shakespeare, William. *The Tempest*. In *The Riverside Shakespeare*, edited by G. Blakemore Evans et. al. Boston: Houghton Mifflin, 1974. Published in Spanish as *La tempestad*. In *Obras completas de William Shakespeare*. Translated, introduced, and notes by Luis Astrana Marín. Madrid: Aguilar, 1951.

Shields, Rob. *Places on the Margin: Alternative Geographies of Modernity*. London: Routledge, 1991.

Singh, Amritjit, Joseph T. Skerret Jr., and Robert E. Hogan. *Memory and Cultural Politics: New Approaches to American Ethnic Literatures*. Boston: Northeastern University Press, 1996.

Sommer, Doris. *Foundational Fictions: The National Romances of Latin America*. Berkeley: University of California Press, 1991.

Sommer, Doris, et al., eds. *Nationalisms and Sexualities*. New York: Routledge, 1992.

Spurr, David. *The Rhetoric of Empire: Colonial Discourse in Journalism, Travel Writing, and Imperial Administration*. Durham, N.C.: Duke University Press, 1993.

Stallybrass, Peter, and Allon White. *The Politics and Poetics of Transgression*. Ithaca, N.Y.: Cornell University Press, 1986.

Stoler, Anne Laura. "Carnal Knowledge and Imperial Power." In *The Gender Sexuality Reader,* edited by Roger N. Lancaster and Micaela di Leonardo, 13–36. New York: Routledge, 1997.

Taussig, Michael. *Mimesis and Alterity: A Particular History of the Senses.* New York: Routledge, 1993.

Terdiman, Richard. *Discourse/Counter-discourse: The Theory and Practice of Symbolic Resistance in Nineteenth-Century France.* Ithaca, N.Y.: Cornell University Press, 1985.

———. *Present Past: Modernity and the Memory Crisis.* Ithaca, N.Y.: Cornell University Press, 1993.

Todorov, Tzvetan. *The Conquest of America: The Problem of the Other.* Translated by Richard Howard. New York: Harper, 1984. Published in Spanish as *La conquista de América: El problema del otro.* Translated by Flora Botton Burlá. Mexico City: Siglo XXI, 1991.

———. *Nosotros y los otros: Reflexión sobre la diversidad humana.* Translated by Martí Mur Ubasat. Mexico City: Siglo XXI, 1991.

Viswanathan, Gauri. "English Literary Study in British India." In *"Race," Culture, and Difference,* edited by James Donald and Ali Rattansi. London: Sage, 1992.

Weber, David J., and Jane Rausch, eds. *Where Cultures Meet: Frontiers in Latin American History.* Wilmington, Del.: SR Jaguar Books on Latin America, 1994.

Whitaker, Arthur Preston. *Latin America and the Enlightenment.* Ithaca, N.Y.: Cornell University Press, 1967.

———. *The Content of the Form: Narrative, Discourse, and Historical Representation.* Baltimore: Johns Hopkins University Press, 1987.

Yates, Frances A. *The Art of Memory.* Chicago: University of Chicago Press, 1966.

Yerushalmi, Y., et al., eds. *Usos del olvido.* Translated by Irene Agoff. 2d ed. Buenos Aires: Nueva Visión, 1998.

Zelizer, Barbie. *Remembering to Forget: Holocaust Memory Through the Camera's Eye.* Chicago: University of Chicago Press, 1998.

Zizek, Slavoj. *The Sublime Object of Ideology.* London: Verso, 1989.

INDEX

Susana Rotker (1954–2000) was professor of nineteenth-century Latin American literature and director of the Center for Hemispheric Studies at Rutgers, the State University of New Jersey. She wrote *Los transgresores* and *Fundación de una escritura: Las crónicas de José Martí,* which was published in English as *The American Chronicles of José Martí.* She edited *Memoirs of Fray Servando Teresa de Mier;* a critical anthology of Martí's chronicles; and the two-volume collection *Ensayistas de nuestra América: Siglo XIX.* She was awarded the prestigious Casa de las Américas prize.

Jennifer French is assistant professor of Spanish and comparative literature at Williams College. She also translated *The American Chronicles of José Martí,* by Susana Rotker.

Jean Franco is professor emerita of English and comparative literature at Columbia University.